THE GREAT SOUTH BAY

A volume in the Great South Bay series
J. R. Schubel, editor

THE GREAT SOUTH BAY

Edited By

J. R. Schubel
T. M. Bell
H. H. Carter

Marine Sciences Research Center
State University of New York
Stony Brook, New York

State University of New York Press

Published by
State University of New York Press, Albany

©1991 State University of New York

For information, address State University of New York
Press, State University Plaza, Albany, N.Y., 12246

Library of Congress Cataloging-in-Publication Data

The Great South Bay / edited by J.R. Schubel, T.M. Bell, H.H. Carter
    (Marine Sciences Research Center, State University of New York,
    Stony Brook, New York).
        p.   cm.
    Includes bibliographical references and index.
    ISBN 0-7914-0911-2 (CH : acid free)
    1. Oceanography—New York (State)—Great South Bay. 2. Clam
fisheries—New York (State)—Great South Bay. I. Schubel, J.R.
II. Bell, T.M.   III. Carter, H.H.   IV. State University of New
York at Stony Brook. Marine Sciences Research Center.
GC512.N7G74   1991
551.46′ 146—dc20   91-13842
                                                       CIP

10 9 8 7 6 5 4 3 2 1

CONTENTS

PREFACE

Since 1965, with the creation of the Oceanographic Committee of the Nassau-Suffolk Regional Planning Board, efforts have been made to organize coastal research on Long Island in a systematic fashion. One of the outgrowths of this effort was the creation of the Marine Sciences Research Center (MSRC) at the State University of New York at Stony Brook. During the past two decades, a significant amount of research has been undertaken by MSRC and the Long Island Regional Planning Board. This research has improved our understanding of natural processes that characterize Long Island's coastal marine environments in general, and the Great South Bay in particular, and our understanding of how society has affected those processes. The Great South Bay deserves such special attention because of the varied and intensive uses made of it by millions of people—people who have derived and who continue to derive their livelihoods, their recreation, their aesthetic enjoyment and, in part, their food supply from this body of water.

This book summarizes the status of an ongoing quest to better understand this complex system so that future generations will be able to continue to benefit from the many and varied resources Great South Bay offers. This is particularly relevant at a time when human impacts on the Bay system as a result of urbanization and suburbanization have impaired portions of the Bay's water quality and its ecosystem. The book offers the general public a scientific introduction to Great South Bay in easily understandable terms—an introduction that we hope will elicit interest, support and, indeed, demand for more effective management practices.

The book begins with a discussion of the geological history of the Bay and proceeds to a discussion of water movements and water quality, which underlie the health of the system and the Bay's ability to serve as a major spawning, nursery and harvest area for fish and shellfish. A discussion then follows of nutrient enrichment of the Bay, with both positive and negative aspects of this enrichment. Since the major fishery of the Bay is the hard clam, both in terms of recreational as well as commercial fishing, the following three chapters discuss the biology of the clam, the industry that has evolved as a result of its presence and that unique brand of self-reliant American, the bayman.

The concluding three chapters address the policy and public issues that must be understood if rational, effective and beneficial management is to occur. A discussion of the plethora of governmental units, statutes, regulations and administrative procedures is followed by a chapter on the uses, misuses and abuses that take place in and around the Great South Bay. This chapter discusses how the various uses are often in competition for the Bay's resources, and how these demands affect the condition of the Bay.

The final chapter addresses the need for a continuing research agenda to increase our scientific understanding of the Bay and to provide the basis for development of effective management. This chapter suggests key management strategies to conserve and, when necessary, to rehabilitate this valuable resource.

Much of the research, which led to findings and conclusions contained in this book, was supported by the New York Sea Grant Institute through the Great South Bay Study, 1979-1984. Credit for the idea of producing the book and much of the support for the initial development goes to the New York Sea Grant Institute and its former director, Donald F. Squires. The Great South Bay Study was designed primarily to develop the knowledge required for management planning to rehabilitate the hard clam fishery. As a result, many other important uses and resources of the Bay such as finfish and finfisheries are not included. These could be the subject of another book.

1902 scene of Great South Bay.

HAL B. FULLERTON

ACKNOWLEDGEMENTS

The many drafts of this book were typed by Regina Anzalone. Marie Gladwish designed the cover and Mitzi Eisel, Grace E. Horan and Catherine Walker prepared the graphics and layout design for the remainder of the book. We are grateful to William Wise, who read the manuscript and many many valuable suggestions, and to Jeri Schoof, whose creative financial management skills permitted completion of this book after the Great South Bay Study had ended. We thank the Oakley family for the photographs they generously provided.

The New York Sea Grant Institute provided much of the support for the research described in many of the chapters and for preparation of early versions of the manuscripts. We thank former Director, Donald F. Squires, for his support, encouragement and patience.

This publication is Contribution 732 of the Marine Sciences Research Center.

INTRODUCTION

J. R. Schubel

*Marine Sciences Research Center
State University of New York
Stony Brook, NY 11794*

The Great South Bay lies along the south shore of Long Island. It is a classic example of a bar-built estuary: an estuary formed when the postglacial rising sea partially sealed off an indentation in Long Island's coastline with a barrier island which became welded to the mainland. Less than 5000 years old, Great South Bay is a geologically ephemeral feature. It was formed within the past few thousand years by the rising sea and continues to change as sediments are deposited within it and as the barrier island evolves. Its remaining lifetime will be a few thousand years. (See Figure 1.1 for a general map of the Bay.)

The Great South Bay extends about 40 km from South Oyster Bay on the west to Moriches Bay on the east. It varies in width from about 300 m (at Smith Point) to 11 km (south of Bay Shore). The Bay proper has an average depth of only about 2 m and a maximum depth of about 4 m north of Fire Island Pines, approximately midway between Fire Island and the mainland. Deeper areas exist in the channels of Fire Island Inlet. The floor of Great South Bay is blanketed with sand except for a few thin patches of estuarine mud in the deeper basins (Fig. 1.2). The most prominent positive topographic features on the Bay floor are the tidal deltas in Moriches and Fire Island Inlets.

The estuarine habitat of Great South Bay is the result of the dynamic balance among three conditions:

1) the flow of fresh ground water from Long Island,
2) the tidal flow of sea water through its inlets, and
3) the degree of protection afforded the Bay by the barrier island.

All of these conditions change naturally in the course of time, and humans have had their effects. Changes of any, or all, of the factors modify the estuarine characteristics of the Bay, which in turn, alter the composition of the flora and fauna found in the Bay.

Freshwater input to the Great South Bay is small, averaging only about 330 m³/yr. The freshwater input comes primarily from a few streams (Table 1.1). All of the rivers are short, have small drainage basins and the elevations of their headwaters are small. The Carmans River is the longest, 11 miles, and has a maximum elevation of + 18 m. The total number of minor streams flowing into the Bay is about 35, each averaging about 1 mile in length with an average maximum elevation of 36 m.

Great South Bay is unusual among estuaries in that it receives a significant fraction, perhaps as much as 11%, of its total freshwater input from **direct** inflow of ground water through its floor. Most of the stream flow is derived from groundwater flow. The Great South Bay has only one direct connection to the sea — through Fire Island Inlet — but it also has indirect connections through Moriches Bay and Moriches Inlet and through Shinnecock Inlet and Jones Inlet.

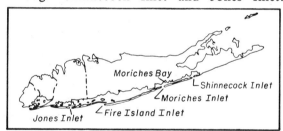

Figure 1.1. Map of Great South Bay.

Hydrographic characteristics of Great South Bay in general are typical of shallow coastal lagoons. The Bay is subject to both tidal and meteorological forcing. Water exchange between the Bay and the ocean is driven primarily by coastal sea level forcing. Tidal forcing is associated with coastal sea level fluctuations of diurnal and semidiurnal periods. The narrow inlets produce strong tidal currents within the inlets but they damp the tidal oscillation, causing tides within the Bay to be small and tidal currents to be weak. The characteristic of this mode of exchange is simultaneous inflow, or outflow, through the ends of the Bay.

The secondary mode of exchange is associated with direct wind forcing at shorter periods. The characteristic of this mode of exchange is a flow through the entire Bay from one end to the other. Meteorological forcing is associated both with wind-induced coastal sea level fluctuations with periods from two to 20 days and with direct wind forcing within the Bay. The low frequency coastal sea level fluctuations are transmitted unattenuated through the inlets. A simple emptying and filling of the Bay through the inlets is the most important response.

Residual currents and drift patterns are influenced by the tide but also are strongly influenced by low frequency meteorologically induced motions.

Salinity levels within the Bay are a result of the dynamic balance of the volume of fresh water sources flowing into the Bay and the volume of the exchange through the inlets. Low frequency motions produce fluctuations in the salinity but may not be important in determining long-term salinity levels.

More than one million people live within the drainage basin of the Great South Bay. They make intensive and often conflicting demands on the estuary: for commercial fishing, for aquaculture, for recreational boating, for swimming and for recreational fishing. It also is used as an avenue for commercial shipping and transportation and as a receiver for society's wastes, both intentionally and unintentionally.

Great South Bay is the receptacle for water from point sources and from non-point sources. Of these, the non-point sources dominate, accounting for up to 100% of the loads of contaminants to surface waters. Non-point sources of nutrients produce eutrophication and increase the levels of fecal bacteria leading to the closure of large segments of the Bay for shell fishing. Undesirable blooms of

phytoplankton occur in the Bay, and the recent "brown tides" may be indicators of a growing problem. These could, perhaps, be controlled in many cases by regulating the inputs of nutrients in run off and ground water.

Great South Bay is noted for its harvest of the hard clam *Mercenaria mercenaria*. The hard clam ranges from Canada to Florida and is especially abundant from Massachusetts to Virginia. It has been introduced on the Pacific coast of the United States, and also in northern England and France. The peak of landings on the Atlantic coast in 1950 was at just under 20 million pounds of meats.

Between 1970 and 1978 the Great South Bay was the nation's most prolific producer of hard clams, accounting for as much as 50% of the nation's total production. In 1979 the landings began to drop, and in 1984 they were only 50% of their peak values. Declines are attributable to a combination of factors: overharvesting, degraded water quality and perhaps to natural fluctuations. The life cycle of the hard clam is only as certain as its weakest link — the early life stages. Clam larvae and seed are very sensitive to environmental quality and are vulnerable to predation. Clams have specific environmental requirements for survival and have

R. GEORGE ROWLAND

Moriches Inlet. Atlantic Ocean is left; Great South Bay right.

Figure 1.2. Great South Bay bottom sand and mud distributions.

◩ MUD DEPOSITS

☐ SAND

Table 1.1 Gauged flow of tributaries of Great South Bay (July 1980).

River	Drainage Area (km²)	Mean	Discharge (m³/sec) Max. Daily	Min. Daily
Carmans	184	.06	3.08	0.03
Swan	23	0.34		
Patchogue	35	0.57	2.35	0.06
Connetquot	62	0.91		
Penatquit Ck.	13	0.11		
Sampawams Ck.	60	0.14		
Santapogue	18	0.08		
Carlls	91	0.62		
Totals	486	3.42		

many natural enemies. The probability of any individual surviving to adulthood is close to zero. The probability of adults dying of old age is small because of predation, environmental stress and harvesting pressure from clammers.

An effective hard clam management program must include a number of actions: limits on the total catch, improved data collection and monitoring of the stock of clams, possible establishment of brood stock sanctuaries and perhaps mariculture. Enforcement will never be perfect, but if management is to work, it must strive to reduce illegal harvesting to a minimum.

It is important to educate and win the confidence of all concerned. Disregard for the laws has been a problem of the industry from the beginning.

Clammers agree that poaching is the most vexing problem, but the clammers, themselves, are the most serious violators. By their own accounts, up to 50% work in uncertified waters, up to 50% work without permits and up to 50% harvest undersized clams.

Primary productivity in the Bay is among the highest for any estuary in the United States and, indeed, in the world. Because of the very shallow depth, the contribution to the total primary production by rooted plants such as eelgrass *Zostera marina* is large. The high productivity is made possible by the large supply of nutrients and the shallow depths which allow nutrients to be resuspended from the bottom and mixed throughout the water column. Even by itself, phytoplankton production is among the highest observed in any marine environment (Table 5.1).

Primary production is at maximum from late spring through summer when food requirements of the Bay's commercially important shellfish are also at a maximum. This is a major reason why the shellfish harvest from the Bay has been so great. Eelgrass production provides a sustained food source throughout the year.

In Great South Bay plant growth is not limited, as it is in most other marine habitats, because of the Bay's abundance of nitrogenous nutrients. Rather, primary production in the Bay is limited by light and water temperature. Nitrogen recycling in Great South Bay waters is most important in terms of producing nitrogen for phytoplankton. The smallest size fraction of plankton (less than 20 μm in diameter) is the most important recycling agent.

The Great South Bay has been subject to large and rapid increases in the pressures of a growing population. Input from non-point sources have increased and water quality has been degraded. Encroachment of society into and over the edges of the shoreline has transformed much of the natural shoreline into a hardened interface through the construction of bulkheads.

Because Great South Bay supports a wide variety of potentially conflicting uses, it is important to monitor water quality. Water quality issues range from aesthetic to those that threaten the Bay's biota. Some measures of water quality include turbidity, floating debris, fecal coliform bacteria, metals, chlorinated hydrocarbons and eutrophication.

Turbidity affects the feeding efficiency of filter feeders such as the hard clam, as well as the growth and distribution of eelgrass. Fecal and total coliform bacteria counts are monitored to determine areas in the Bay where shellfish can be harvested and where public bathing is allowed. Metals negatively affect life forms in the Bay as well as man. Input of chlorinated hydrocarbons to the Bay could result in a long-term accumulation of these chemicals in the food chain. The presence of these chemicals in very small quantities has been shown to be detrimental to the biota and man. Eutrophication due to increased nutrient loading will adversely affect the biota of the Bay. A shift in the availability of nutrients, in turn, alters the species composition of the phytoplankton, which can have disastrous effects on the shellfish and other filter feeding organisms.

Changes in inlet configuration have accounted for the most abrupt and dramatic changes in the Bay's environment and biota. The inlets controlling exchanges of water between the Bay and the ocean are very dynamic. Inlets can be shifted, modified, created and closed. A tremendous amount of sand is moved parallel to the beach on the seaward side of the barrier island. A significant amount is transported into the inlet, which can plug it or cause a migration, and storms can cut new inlets.

Great South Bay is a dynamic ecosystem which has evolved as a result of a complex interplay of social, economic, physical, chemical and biological factors. The Bay plays an important role for Long Island, supporting residential, recreational, commercial and industrial activities. The Bay falls within the boundaries of the Towns of Babylon, Brookhaven and Islip. It is subject to jurisdiction of these three towns, one county, the state and the federal government. As Long Island becomes increasingly developed, water quality issues of Great South Bay promise to become more prominent, requiring Bay management strategies.

Natural margins of the Bay have been "hardened" as a result of residential development. IAN STUPAKOFF

Recreational boat harbors entail extensive modifications to the Bay's shoreline. IAN STUPAKOFF

CHAPTER 2

THE ORIGIN AND DEVELOPMENT OF THE GREAT SOUTH BAY: A GEOLOGICAL PERSPECTIVE

Henry J. Bokuniewicz
J. R. Schubel

Marine Sciences Research Center
State University of New York
Stony Brook, NY 11794

INTRODUCTION

Twenty thousand years ago the site of Great South Bay was dry land on the edge of a vast sheet of glacial ice. During the maximum extent of the last glacial period, called the Wisconsin glaciation, a layer of ice probably 500 m thick covered half of Long Island, all of New England and New York and extended unbroken to the Arctic Circle. So much water was frozen on land in this ice cap that sea level was approximately 120 m below its present position, and the ocean shoreline lay seaward of the edge of the continental shelf, some 150 km south of Long Island. The continental shelf off Long Island was high and dry and covered with conifer and boreal hardwood forests, meadows and freshwater wetlands. Winters were long, wet and harsh; summers short and cool. The Earth's mean annual temperature was 3° or 4°C colder than today.

About 18,000 years ago the climate began to warm and the glaciers began to melt and retreat. The meltwater from the glaciers was returned to the sea. Getting back its own, the sea began to rise. For the first few centuries, its rate of rise was particularly rapid, probably averaging about 0.5 m per century. From about 15,000 years ago to 5000 years ago the sea rose at a rate of about 0.1 m per century and flowed across the exposed continental shelf.

Since the continental shelf off New York has a slope of only about 0.05 degrees, for every meter the sea rose, it pushed the shoreline more than 1500 m landward. During the long period of low-stand of sea level, rivers meandered across the featureless continental shelf depositing a blanket of sand over much of it. As the sea rose, the surf zone led its advance across the shelf. The churning leading edge of the sea reworked this blanket of sand leaving a uniform layer in its wake.

By about 8500 years ago the sea had risen high enough to spill into Long Island Sound and to penetrate far into New York Harbor. Sea level at this time was still almost 27 m below its present level. The shoreline was about 6 km seaward of the present beach where an ancient barrier island and bay had formed. As sea level rose this island was submerged and the bay drowned, but another island and bay reformed about 7500 years ago at a distance of about 2 km seaward of the present shoreline. These were the ancestors of Fire Island and Great South Bay.

As sea level continued to rise, the ocean side of the barrier island was continually eroded and submerged. As the ocean shoreline migrated north, storm waves and tides washed sand over the dunes to rebuild the island on the bay shore. In this way the barrier island and the bay behind it gradually moved northward to its present position. Sea level continues to rise at a rate of about 0.25 cm per year, and presumably the process is continuing.

THE BAY'S GEOLOGICAL SETTING

The Great South Bay is the largest of a series of interconnecting shallow lagoons along Long Island's south shore (Fig. 1.1). The Great South Bay is approximately 40 km long and 9 km wide at its widest point. It covers an area of about 223 km² and has an average depth of only 1.3 m.

Long Island and the floor of Great South Bay mark the upper surface of many layers, or strata, of sands, gravels and clays that were built up over millions of years. If we were to drill a well at the shoreline of Great South Bay, we would begin drilling in the uppermost, youngest surficial layer and penetrate successively deeper and older strata. The well would begin in sands and gravels that were deposited in streams during the most recent retreat of the glaciers. The blanket of glacial sand is about 30 m thick, and at that depth the well would enter a layer of clay 6.1 m thick, called the Gardiners clay, which lies under the outwash sand. At a depth of

about 37 m the well would enter other layers of sand and gravel called the Magothy formation.

The sands of the Magothy formation were deposited in the sea about 75 million years ago. Below the Magothy formation there is another layer of clay called the Raritan clay. The Raritan clay layer is about 34 m thick and, at a depth of about 400 m below sea level, it overlies another stratum of sand and gravel, which makes up the Lloyd formation. Under the Lloyd formation the well would finally strike solid rock buried beneath 530 m of sand, gravel and clay.

If we could follow along this buried rock surface and head north from our drill site at the shoreline of Great South Bay, we would find ourselves not only moving closer and closer to Connecticut, but also closer and closer to the surface. The layers of sand above us would become thinner as we moved north, and all but the stratum of glacial sand would disappear under Long Island Sound. Still clinging to the rock surface, we would break into the open air at the Connecticut shore.

The shore of Great South Bay is mostly sandy beaches interrupted in some areas by fringes of salt marsh. Much of the Bay floor is also sand (Fig. 1.2) — the same sand that was left by the melting glacier and that covers the surface of Long Island, although under the Bay it has been reworked by waves, currents and baymen in search of oysters and clams.

More than three fourths of the Bay floor is covered by sediment, which consists of more than 80% sand. Shallow flats of very fine sand are dominant in the western and southern portions of the Bay. The eastern Bay floor is also predominantly sand. Sandy sediments are found adjacent to the north shore, and extensive sand flats lie along the barrier beach. At Fire Island Inlet, however, coarse gravelly sand is found, and the north shoreline of the Bay is covered with gravel. These are regions in which waves or tidal currents have been strong enough to sweep away finer-grained sediment.

Elsewhere, sediments have very low gravel contents, but in the eastern Bay, for example, there may be substantial amounts of gravel-sized

shell fragments from the Atlantic jackknife clam (*Ensis directus*), duck clam (*Mulinia lateralis*), Atlantic slipper shell (*Crepidula fornicata*), amethyst gem clam (*Gemma gemma*) and hard clam (*Mercenaria mercenaria*).

Five percent of the entire Bay bottom area is covered with sediment that is greater than 80% by weight silt and clay (mud). Areas of high concentration of silt and clay are found near the north shore where currents are sluggish and the water depths are generally greater than 2 m. There are four major muddy areas. One of these patches is found near Bellport and the Carmans River. Another lies south of the Patchogue River. A third is found south of Bayport and Sayville, and small patches lie at the mouth of the Connetquot River and in Great Cove.

The highest silt and clay contents are found in Patchogue Bay where values as high as 95% occur. In the western portion of the Bay, silts, clays and organic detritus are also accumulating within dredged channels where the currents are weak. These layers of mud can be greater than 1 m thick, since devices that are used to sample the sea floor have penetrated that far into some of these deposits without encountering sand. Most of the fine sediment is silt; the clay fraction seldom exceeds 30% and it is typically 15% to 20% of the Bay's muddy sediments.

Most of the fine-grained bottom sediment has been supplied by the streams of Long Island, but some of it is biologically produced within the Bay. Sandy sediments immediately adjacent to the north shore and the extensive sand flats along the barrier beach have less than 1% organic matter. Where finer-grained sediments are accumulating, however, the organic content may be as high as 8%. The organic-rich sediments generally occur in areas with thick eelgrass cover, especially near Smith Point, near the Carmans River, south of the Patchogue River in a region extending westward to Sayville, off the mouth of the Connetquot River and in small dredged channels leading to the barrier beach.

In the eastern Bay the final resting place of mud particles is on the Bay floor as deposits, but in the western Bay and along the south shore the water is generally too shallow for extensive mud deposits to form on the Bay floor. Instead, fine-grained sediment is contained in extensive areas of salt marshes.

Marshland is common along the north shore of Fire Island, around Captree Island near Fire Island Inlet and in many drowned stream valleys east of Patchogue. Most of these marshes are thin blankets, less than a meter thick, made up of mud and plant remains. Their surfaces, however, are extremely productive, and plant remains contribute a great deal of material to the marsh sediment.

The surface of the marsh is biologically zoned. There is a transition from saltwater vegetation, which characterizes the shore of the marsh, to freshwater forms on the high marsh. At the limits of the marshes farthest from the water's edge live plants that can tolerate only occasional wetting at extremely high tides such as cattails and bush *Phragmites*. A little farther seaward and at slightly lower elevations, foxgrass (*Spartina patens*) thrives. These plants do best with regular submersion in salt water every high tide.

On the lowest level of the marsh, which most of the time is underwater, *Spartina patens* gives way to cordgrass (*Spartina alterniflora*), and beyond the marsh fringes, eelgrass is often found in large submerged flats. The zonation of marsh flora gives us a way to study the growth (accretion) of marshes themselves. In several places along the shore of the Bay, layers of sediment containing the remains of *Spartina patens* cover deeper layers that contain only the remains of freshwater plants. In these locations the salt marsh has spread over freshwater marshland.

THE BAY AS AN ESTUARY

Fire Island bears the attack of ocean waves, leaving the Great South Bay with calm waters for both recreational and commercial boating and for an abundance of marine flora and fauna. The Bay is an arm of the sea, however, being connected with the Atlantic Ocean through Fire Island Inlet and, to a lesser extent, through Moriches and Jones Inlets. The exchange of water between the Bay and the ocean is restricted to these narrow inlets. As a result, although the tidal range in the ocean outside of the Bay exceeds 1 m, the tidal range in the Bay is less than 0.3 m.

The volume of water that can push its way through the inlets every tidal cycle is simply not enough to raise a larger tide in the Bay. The constrictions are too small. Nevertheless, on every tidal cycle about four billion gallons of water rushes through Fire Island Inlet alone.

Great South Bay has a salinity less than that of the ocean because fresh water is constantly being supplied to it; almost all of this comes from Long Island's aquifers. Rain that falls on Long Island seeps into the strata of sand and gravel below the surface, and at some depth everywhere under Long Island, these sands are always saturated with water. The depth at which this occurs is called the depth of the water table and it varies from place to place. At the shoreline the water table is exactly at sea level, but northward away from the shore, the elevation of the water table rises about 2 m over every 1000 m.

Layers of outwash sands saturated with rainwater created Long Island's glacial aquifers. All of Long Island's water supply is drawn by pumps from these aquifers. The addition of rain water to the outwash sands created the glacial aquifer. Water also seeps into and through the Gardiners clay, but the clay is very dense and impermeable and water cannot be easily removed from it by wells. As a result, the Gardiners clay is not considered an aquifer, but rather an aquatard. It retards the flow of ground water. The Magothy Aquifer is sandwiched between the Gardiners clay and the Raritan clay, while the deepest of Long Island's aquifers, the Lloyd Aquifer, lies between the Raritan clay and bedrock.

The water in Long Island's aquifers is not stationary; it always moves slowly. Rains continually add water to the aquifers, but the aquifers are never collectively over-filled because their water is gradually taken away by wells or it seeps away into streams or the Bay and ocean. Streams continue to flow even when there is no precipitation because water from the glacial aquifer seeps gradually into stream beds. In order of their mean annual discharge, the largest of these rivers are the Connetquot, the Carlls, the Carmans and the Patchogue rivers (Fig. 1.1). Streams and rivers supply the Bay with about 1 billion liters of water per day. Every day an additional 300 million liters seep into the Bay directly across the Bay floor.

Long Island's leaky aquifers not only supply us with drinking water, but also constantly dilute seawater in the Bay to keep its salinity at an average value of 26 parts per thousand (ppt), about 6 ppt lower than the salinity in the adjacent ocean. The streams of Long Island not only supply fresh water to the Bay but they are also a source of fine-grained sediment particles. In the Bay these particles are carried by the currents, settle to the Bay floor, are swept up again by waves and redistributed until they finally come to rest in the permanent mud patches. Year after year thick layers of mud accumulate in these patches until a substantial thickness is built up. If the rates of accumulation in other estuaries are any indication, an annual mud layer in Great South Bay may be only 1 mm thick, but even such a light dusting requires that over 500,000 tons of sediment be carried to the Bay in a single year. Most of this probably comes down the streams of Long Island, but some may also be carried in by ocean tides and become trapped in the Bay.

Fine-grained sediment is also trapped in the marshes around the shores of the Bay. As water carrying suspended particles flows into the marsh, the marsh grass slows the flow and the suspended particles settle between the plants. Dead plant material is also continually being added to the marsh substrate, so as the sea level rises slightly each year, the surface of the marsh rises too. If the rate of sea level rise is slow enough, the marsh not only can keep pace with the submergence but can expand as well. On the other hand, if the rate of sea level rise is too rapid, sedimentation on the marsh surface will not be able to keep up, and the marsh will be drowned.

CATASTROPHIC CHANGES AND THE FATE OF THE BAY

Not all of the events that shaped Great South Bay occurred at almost imperceptible speeds or in the remote geological past. Important changes can be documented historically. Large alterations of the Bay can happen in a single day. Such changes are largely the work of the Atlantic Ocean.

The south shore of Great South Bay is the north shore of Fire Island, and the shape of this Bay's shore is controlled by events that happen on Fire Island. As discussed elsewhere in this book, the size and shape of the inlets that cut through Fire Island are vital to the Bay's environment. The tides, which keep the Bay supplied with salt water, only occur because oceanic tides can reach around the barrier island and into the Bay through its inlets. At present, however, Great South Bay has only one direct route to the sea — through Fire Island Inlet — but this has not always been the case. Inlets can be born, wander along the shore and die in the space of a human lifetime.

Fire Island Inlet is a venerable senior citizen; it has been around at least 300 years. At one time, however, around the beginning of the 19th century, Fire Island Inlet was probably only one of seven inlets that cut through the barrier island. Those other inlets were each only in existence for about 50 years before the natural wave-driven flow of sand along the Atlantic beaches filled them. In general, the waves from the Atlantic drive sand from east to west along Fire Island. An estimated 230,000 m³ of sand can be moved along the shore every year by oceanic waves. This tremendous volume of sand can overwhelm small inlets and seal them shut unless humans intervene. Strong tidal currents can keep the larger inlets relatively free of sand, but although these inlets resist being closed, they cannot withstand the relentless flow of beach sand and migrate or move slowly under that pressure.

In 1834 the Fire Island Lighthouse stood on shores of the inlet. Since then, however, waves have driven sand slowly from east to west, and the inlet, although it has never closed, has migrated five miles to the west. The inlet's migration was stopped in 1940 by a rock jetty. When the inlet was free to roam, it moved westward at an average rate of about 75 m every year.

Inlets are born in the crashing waves and exceptionally high tides of major storms. During storms Fire Island can be awash in many places as waves drive the sea over the dunes into the Bay, or extremely high Bay tides send Bay water flooding over its barrier island to the sea. These events are called washovers, and only the most severe will persist to create inlets after the storm has subsided. When a washover from the ocean to the Bay occurs, sand is pushed into the Bay forming lobes of sand and shallow water along the Bay's south shore.

A storm in 1963 produced four washovers on eastern Fire Island. A storm in 1953 caused seven or more, while nine washovers were reported after a storm in 1960. Thirteen washovers were found after a storm in 1949, 50 after another in 1962 and 63 after a hurricane in 1944. The hurricane of 1938 washed over the entire beach between Democrat Point and Ocean Beach and many other places as well.

In quieter times the sand that is so violently pushed into Great South Bay through washovers becomes the substrate for shallow, productive fields of eelgrass along the Bay's southern shore. As more sediment is washed over the barrier island and deposited at the south shore of the Bay, the barrier island will be moved northward. As the island's ocean shore is submerged and eroded by a rising sea level, its Bay shore can be extended by the accumulated deposition of many washovers and expanding marshland. At the same time, the increase in sea level will submerge land along the north shore of the Bay.

It has been estimated, for example, that every year the town of Patchogue loses about a half an acre to the Bay. If the rate of sea level rise accelerates, as some scientists believe it will, the rate at which land is submerged may increase as much as fivefold, and it may be impossible for the barrier island to keep pace with the rising sea. The barrier could be drowned by a rapid rise in sea level and, of course, Great South Bay would cease to exist — an ocean beach would be formed along its present north shore.

IAN STUPAKOFF

Phragmites australis bordering Great South Bay beach.

IAN STUPAKOFF

CHAPTER 3

ASPECTS OF CIRCULATION AND EXCHANGE IN GREAT SOUTH BAY

Robert E. Wilson
K-C. Wong*
H.H. Carter
Marine Sciences Research Center
State University of New York
Stony Brook, NY 11794

*Present affiliation:
College of Marine Studies
University of Delaware
Newark, DE 19716

INTRODUCTION

The hydrographic characteristics of Great South Bay are typical of shallow coastal lagoons or bar-built estuaries such as those found along the Gulf Coast of the United States. These estuaries are generally several tens of kilometers long with average depths of only 1 to 5 m. They exchange with the coastal ocean through narrow inlets.

The astronomical tide is the agent most responsible for producing circulation in the Bay. Because the volume of the Bay is small in relation to its surface area, local wind forcing is important in reducing vertical stratification and producing circulation. Large scale weather systems are also important, and sometimes dominant, in controlling the exchange of water between the adjacent ocean and the estuary and among various segments of the estuary.

The Great South Bay is the largest of a series of connected bays on the south shore of Long Island (Fig. 1.1). It is bounded by South Oyster Bay to the west and by Moriches Bay to the east. It is approximately 40 km long and from 2.5 to 8 km wide. The surface area of the Bay is approximately 235 km² and the average mean low water depth is approximately 1.3 m. The bathymetry is characterized by channels and flats (Fig. 3.1).

Fire Island Inlet is the most direct passage for exchange between the Bay and the Atlantic Ocean. Water is also exchanged with the ocean indirectly through Jones and East Rockaway Inlets to the west, through South Oyster Bay and through Moriches Bay and Moriches and Shinnecock Inlets to the east.

Great South Bay receives fresh water from groundwater inflow, stream flow and direct rainfall. The total inflow of ground water across the floor of the Bay was recently estimated to be about 2×10^8 liters per day (L/d) (Bokuniewicz and Zeitlin 1980). This is in good agreement with the results of an earlier study conducted by Pluhowski and Kantrowitz (1964).

A number of small rivers and streams empty into the Bay from Long Island including the Connetquot, Carmans and Patchogue Rivers. The Bay has a drainage basin of 320 km², and the average annual precipitation is approximately 118 cm. Saville (1962) estimated the total freshwater inflow to the Bay, excluding ground water, to be 9.8×10^8 L/d. The total freshwater inflow to the Bay is, therefore, approximately 12×10^8 L/d.

Salinity generally decreases from west to east (Fig. 3.2). Salinity levels within the Bay are determined primarily by the amount of freshwater inflow (and possibly by the intensity of evaporation in summer) and by the intensity of tidal exchange between the Bay and the saltier ocean. We have also found that the meteorologically induced exchange of water between the Bay and the coastal waters at low frequencies (periods longer than the diurnal

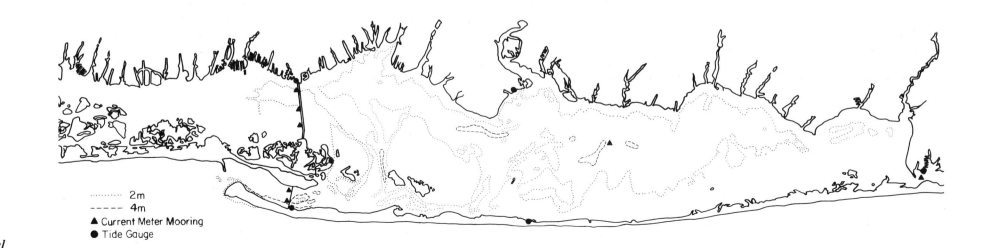

Figure 3.1. Bathymetry of Great South Bay; positions of current meter and coastal tide gauges discussed in text are shown.

.... 2m
- - - - 4m
▲ Current Meter Mooring
● Tide Gauge

and semidiurnal tidal fluctuations, typically two to 20 days) is important in producing fluctuations in salinity.

Factors affecting very long-term salinity changes in the Bay such as inlet configurations have been evaluated by Hollman and Thatcher (1979) and Carter (1985). In a recently completed study, Pritchard and Gomez-Reyes (1986) made use of a numerical model to simulate the effects of dredging Fire Island Inlet on the salinity distribution in the Bay. This study indicated that the removal of 1.9 X 10^6 m^3 of sediment from a shoal area in the critical "throat" of the inlet could produce an increase in the baywide average salinity, ranging from about 0.3 parts per thousand (ppt) to about 1.4 ppt, depending on the amount of the freshwater inflow and the tidal range outside of the Bay (i.e. spring, neap or mean tide range). Dredging within the inlets tends to increase the intensity of tidal exchange. Pritchard and Gomez-Reyes' (1985) study also indicated that the diversion of some 1.14 x 10^8 L/d of fresh water by the Southwest Sewer District Treatment Plant would result in an increase in the average salinity of Great South Bay of nearly 0.4 ppt.

It appears that salinity distribution within the Bay is influenced by the locations of freshwater sources along the north shore of the Bay, which dilute oceanic water of relatively constant salinity entering primarily through Fire Island Inlet and through Moriches Bay and South Oyster Bay. Salt is redistributed within the Bay primarily by mixing processes associated with tidal and low frequency current fluctuations. The transport of salt within the Bay by the residual nontidal currents appears weak.

The remainder this chapter describes some of the most basic characteristics of the Bay's response to the astronomical tides and to low frequency meteorological forcing. The chapter also discusses the mean or residual drift patterns in the Bay because these have implication to hard clam larval movement and disperal. The following section considers specifically

1) the characteristics of sea level fluctuations along the open coast and within the Bay.
2) the characteristics of the tidal currents within the Bay and the residual nontidal currents and particle drifts induced by the tide.
3) the response of the Bay to meteorological forcing.
4) the volume flux between the Bay and coastal waters and between different compartments of the Bay associated with tidal and meteorological forcing.
5) residual drift patterns associated with both tidal and meteorological forcing.
6) salinity fluctuations within the Bay occurring in response to meteorological forcing.

SEA LEVEL

Sea level fluctuations at semidiurnal (12.42 hours), diurnal (24 hours) and longer periods, (two to 20 days) along the open coast are the major agents responsible for exchange of water between the Bay and the shelf, as well as for water move-ments within the Bay. The characteristics of the sea level fluctuations within the Bay provide insight into how it responds to forcing from the shelf.

Records of sea level at stations along the south shore of Long Island and within the Bay show semidiurnal tidal fluctuations with fort-nightly variations in amplitude and long period variations in mean sea level, which are caused by meterological forcing. The tide range along the south shore of Long Island and the tide range on the open coast decrease from west to east. The range is approximately 155 cm at Rockaway Inlet, 137 cm at Long Beach, 125 cm at Fire Island Inlet breakwater, 101 cm at Shinnecock Inlet and about 60 cm at Montauk. The various phases of tide occur progressively earlier from Rockaway Point eastward to Shinnecock Inlet. Between Shinnecock Inlet and Montauk this trend is sharply reversed.

The tide range decreases rapidly with distance inside the narrow inlets. At the Fire Island Inlet breakwater the tide range is approximately 125 cm. At Democrat Point, just inside Fire Island Inlet, the tide range decreases to 79 cm and at the Fire Island Coast Guard Station, located about 3.2 km inside the inlet from Democrat Point, the range is 58 cm.

The tide range within the Great South Bay continues to decrease with distance into the Bay from Fire Island Coast Guard Station, both toward the west and toward the east. The tide range at West Islip is 45 cm and at Smith Point it is about 53 cm. The various tidal phases in the Bay occur progressively later with distance from the inlets. Relative to the Fire Island Inlet breakwater,

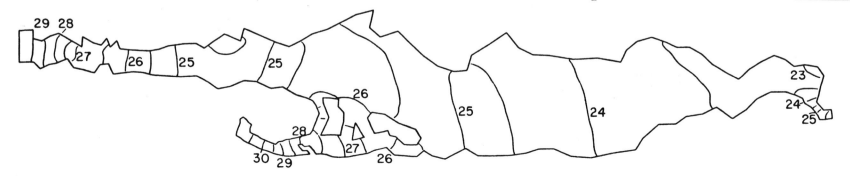

Figure 3.2. Tidal mean salinity distribution in Great South Bay from numerical simulations by Gomez-Reyes (1986); salinity values in ppt. Phase lag of 29° corresponds to a true lag of 1 hour.

the phase lag at Democrat Point is +12 minutes (that is, later) and at Fire Island Coast Guard Station, +27 minutes. West Islip lags Fire Island Coast Guard Station by about 2.5 hours and, possibly because Moriches Inlet has an influence, the lag at Smith Point is somewhat less, approximately two hours.

The long period variations in mean sea level are produced primarily by longshore winds acting on the coastal ocean. The periods of fluctuations are associated with the passage of pressure systems either to the north or south of the Bay at intervals of approximately two to 20 days. The amplitude of these wind-induced fluctuations is substantially lower in summer than in winter; the maximum range encountered in winter was approximately 75 cm. These low frequency coastal sea level fluctuations are relatively undamped as they enter the Bay.

TIDAL CURRENTS AND TIDALLY INDUCED RESIDUAL CURRENTS WITHIN THE BAY

Numerical simulations by Wong (1981) provide some insight into the characteristics of the tidal currents within the Bay and the residual flow patterns induced by the interaction of the tidal currents with the bathymetry. Figures 3.3, 3.4 and 3.5 show the amplitude and relative phase of semidiurnal tidal elevations and the components of tidal current directed along 070°T (along the Bay) and 340°T (across the Bay), respectively. For these simulations the amplitude and relative phase of a mean semidiurnal tide were specified at Seaford, Fire Island Coast Guard Station and Moriches Coast Guard Station (Fig. 1.1).

The easterly component of current generally decreases in amplitude and increases in phase lag proceeding away from the open boundaries. Maximum amplitude is found in Fire Island Inlet;

the strongest spatial gradients in amplitude are also found in the vicinity of Fire Island Inlet. Strong spatial gradients in phase are found near Robert Moses Causeway and in the eastern end of the Bay, where waters coming from different open boundaries meet.

Had these simulations extended through Fire Island Inlet, strong spatial gradients in amplitude and phase would have been demonstrated within the inlet. The cross-bay component of tidal current shows very little spatial variation in amplitude and phase except in a small region in the western part of the Bay near Robert Moses Causeway. Maximum amplitude for this component is found in the channel between Captree Island and the coast. As we shall see later, the spatial variations in amplitude and especially phase are important to the residual drift of water parcels within the Bay.

With these general characteristics of the tidal elevations and the tidal currents in mind, we can go on to look at the characteristics of the residual, or averaged, currents induced by the interaction of

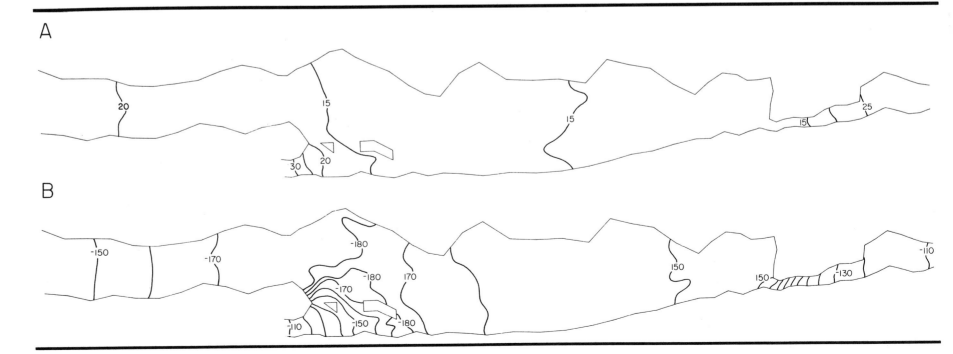

Figure 3.3. Amplitude in cm (a) and relative phase in degrees (b) of semidiurnal tidal elevations from numerical simulations by Wong (1981). Phase lag of 29° corresponds to a true lag of 1 hour.

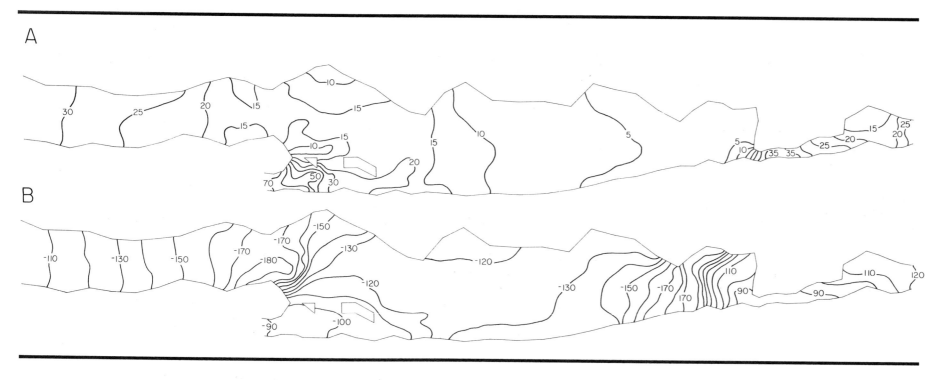

Figure 3.4. Amplitude in cm/s (a) and relative phase in degrees (b) of component of semidiurnal tidal current along 070°T from numerical simulations by Wong (1981). Phase lag of 29° corresponds to a true lag of 1 hour.

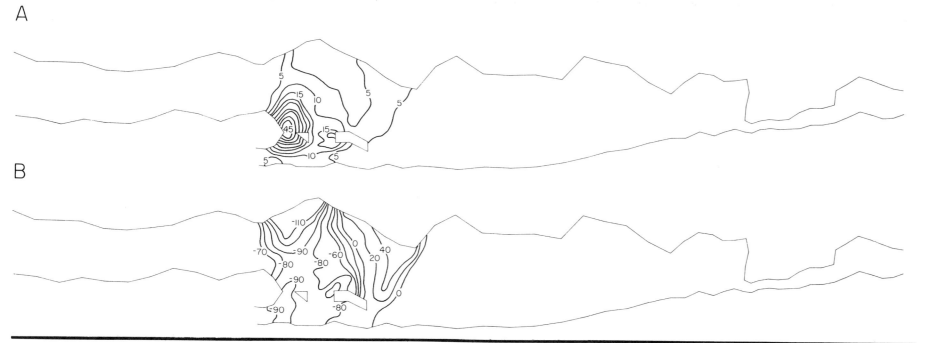

Figure 3.5. Amplitude in cm/s (a) and relative phase in degrees (b) of component of semidiurnal tidal current along 340°T from numerical simulations by Wong (1981). Phase lag of 29° corresponds to a true lag of 1 hour.

the tide with the complex bathymetry of the Bay (Fig. 3.1). We can also look at some of the characteristics of the associated drift of water parcels within the Bay and we will see that the residual drift can be decomposed into two parts: one that is due directly to residual currents at a fixed point and a second that depends on the spatial variations in amplitude and phase of both tidal elevation and tidal currents. Figures 3.6 and 3.7 show numerical simulations for the following:

1) the tidally averaged total transport per unit width at points within the Bay (Fig. 3.6a) representing the average over a tidal cycle of the product of current and surface elevation.

2) the partitioning of the total transport into that due to the averaged currents at a point (Fig. 3.6b) and that due to spatial variations in amplitude and phase of currents and elevation (Fig. 3.6c).

3) the nontidal currents at points within the Bay (Fig. 3.7a) obtained by dividing the transport in Figure 3.6b by the local depth; this is sometimes called the Eulerian current velocity and is that current which is detected by a current meter.

4) the component of the total drift velocity obtained by dividing the transport in Figure 3.6c by the depth (Fig. 3.7b). This is sometimes called the Stokes velocity.

The velocity obtained by dividing the total transport in Figure 3.6a by the depth could be considered the total residual drift velocity which a water parcel might exhibit. This is sometimes called the Lagrangian drift velocity; examples are presented later.

The residual nontidal current velocities in Figure 3.7a are weak in the interior of the Bay, rarely exceeding a few centimeters per second. They are also quite disorganized. The residual drift velocities in Figure 3.7b tend to be stronger and more organized. They are also directed inward at each boundary, which is the direction of propagation of the tidal wave, leading to the conclusion that the total residual drift velocity of a water parcel would tend to be dominated by effects associated with the

characteristics of the tidal wave (spatial variations in amplitude and phase).

In a later section we shall see that the residual drift velocity, which a water parcel exhibits, can depend on the phase of the tidal currents at the time of its release. Of special importance in this system, the residual drift can also be strongly affected by meteorologically induced, low frequency motions within the interior of the Bay.

RESPONSE OF THE BAY TO METEROLOGICAL FORCING

During early winter, sea level along the open coast and within Great South Bay exhibits low frequency fluctuations with a maximum range in excess of 75 cm. During late summer the maximum range typically decreases to approximately 45 cm. Fluctuations along the open coast between Montauk Point and Sandy Hook, New Jersey are highly coherent, or correlated, although there are variations in amplitude and phase.

Low frequency fluctuations at Montauk lag those at Sandy Hook by approximately three hours, and their amplitude is approximately 20% less. This is generally consistent with the findings of Wang (1979). Low frequency fluctuations within the interior of the Bay are highly coherent with those on the open coast. There is, however, a tendency for the magnitude of the coherency to decrease and for the phase lag to increase with increasing distance from Fire Island Inlet which, as pointed out earlier, represents the pathway for most of the direct exchange between the Bay and the open coastal waters.

Insight into the characteristics of low frequency exchange of water between the Bay and the shelf, caused by direct local wind forcing and coastal sea level forcing, can be obtained by examining current records from instruments moored within Fire Island Inlet and within the channel off Smith Point (Fig. 3.1). Records of filtered current (tidally averaged) (Fig. 3.8) show low frequency fluctuations with maximum amplitude of approximately 20 cm/s in both channels during

summer and winter. Wong and Wilson (1985) have studied the relationships among these current fluctuations, fluctuations in alongshore and cross shore wind stress and coastal sea level. They showed that exchange could be separated into two distinct modes, regardless of season.

The first mode accounted for typically 80% of the current variance. It was associated with forcing by coastal sea level fluctuations, which respond to alongshore winds acting on the shelf waters. Winds blowing along the coast towards the east, for example, tend to produce a net transport of water offshore known as Ekman transport (90° to the right of the wind direction in the northern hemisphere) and thereby a drop in coastal sea level. When this happens water flows out of the Bay through two or more inlets simultaneously with a corresponding divergence in the interior.

The second mode typically accounts for 20% or less of the current variance. This mode is associated with direct wind forcing of water in the Bay. The response is characterized by flow through the entire Bay rather than a simultaneous inflow or outflow through either end. A wind stress towards the east produces an inflow through Fire Island Inlet and an outflow through Smith Point channel. This mode is associated with fluctuations in alongshore (which is also along the axis of the Bay) wind stress of relatively short period (approximately three days), which are not as effective in producing coastal sea level fluctuations as are the longer period fluctuations.

In summary, these data sets suggest that the primary mode of exchange is associated with coastal sea level forcing; the characteristic of this mode of exchange is simultaneous inflow or outflow through the ends of the Bay. The secondary mode of exchange is associated with direct wind forcing at shorter periods. The characteristic of this mode of exchange is a flow through the entire Bay from one end to another; it appears to be relatively more important in summer.

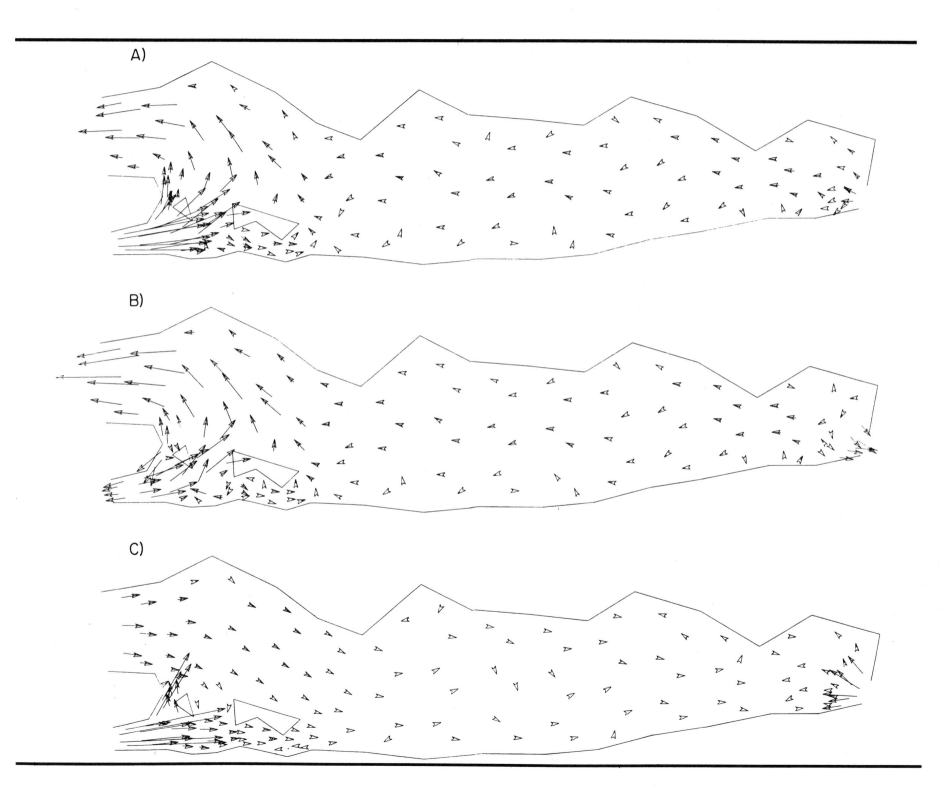

Figure 3.6. Pattern of residual total transport or Lagrangian transport (a), Eulerian transport (b) and Stokes transport (c) from coarse grid numerical simulations by Wong (1981). (See text).

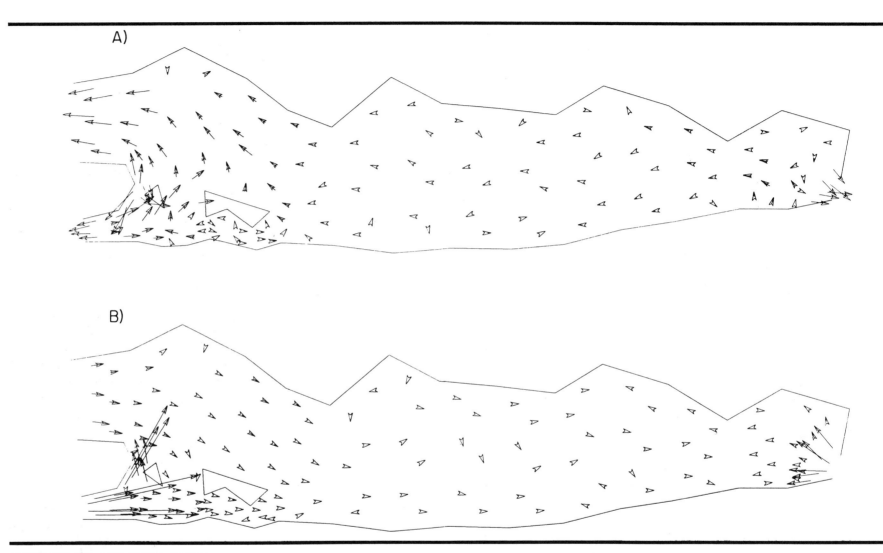

A)

B)

Figure 3.7. Pattern of residual Eulerian velocity (a) and Stokes velocity (b) from coarse grid numerical simulations by Wong (1981). (See text).

VOLUME EXCHANGE BETWEEN THE BAY AND THE SHELF AND BETWEEN DIFFERENT COMPARTMENTS OF THE BAY

Quantitative estimates for the tidal and low frequency volume flux among different segments of the Bay and partitioning among the open boundaries of the total low frequency volume flux to the Bay from the shelf were obtained from numerically simulated currents and sea level elevations. These simulations also allowed us to quantify the volume exchange associated with the two primary modes of low frequency response, which were described in the previous section.

The numerical simulations are described by Wong (1981). The grid used for the simulations (Fig. 3.9) contained 340 nodal points (intersections) and 542 elements (triangles). The smallest nodal spacing was approximately 400 m. The model was run by varying the surface elevation at the three open boundaries over time and by applying a time-varying, but spatially uniform, wind stress to the water surface. Periods for simulation were selected on the basis of availability of boundary sea level information at Seaford, Fire Island Coast Guard Station and Moriches Coast Guard Station and wind records from the meteorological tower at Tiana Beach. The first simulation encompassed the 12-day period from December 13 through December 24, 1979 and the second 28-day period from September 1 through September 28, 1980.

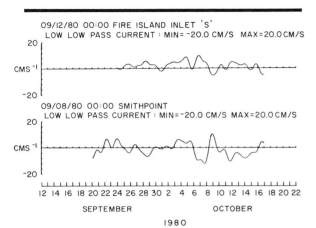

Figure 3.8. *Principal axis residual currents in Fire Island Inlet (top) and off Smith Point (bottom) for periods beginning on September 12, 1980. The range for the abscissae is -20cm/s to 20 cm/s; positive currents are directed towards the east, negative toward the west.*

Model verification is discussed by Wong (1981). The model was first adjusted to reproduce a real data set of currents and then verified by comparison with a data set of currents not used in the adjustment. The winter simulation was relatively short, but the available comparison shows good agreement. The much longer series available for comparison in summer shows that the simulation produced the structure of all of the major features with very good amplitude and phase agreement.

Time series of instantaneous volume flux through a total of seven sections located in Figure 3.9 were computed for winter and summer simulations. The simulations of instantaneous volume flux show that Fire Island Inlet represents the pathway for most of the direct exchange at tidal frequencies; the amplitude of the tidal flux through the inlet is approximately 5×10^3 m³/s. Away from the inlet there is rapid attenuation in the amplitude of tidal fluctuations; the amplitude of the tidal flux through section 5 in eastern Great South Bay, for

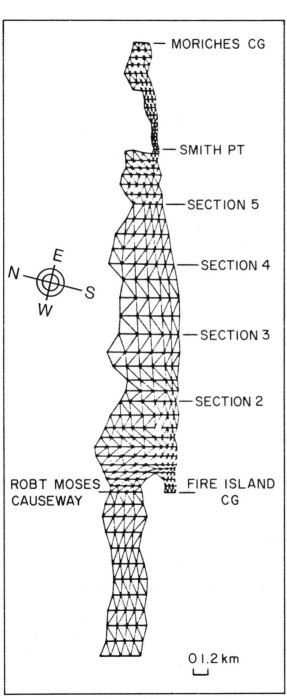

Figure 3.9. *Grid used for numerical simulations of currents and elevations.*

example, is less than 10% of the tidal flux through Fire Island Inlet.

Time series of filtered volume flux for summer at the various sections (Figure 3.10) indicate that the amplitude of the low frequency flux through each of the boundary sections to Great South Bay (Fire Island Inlet, Robert Moses Causeway and Smith Point) is of the order of 5×10^4 m³/s and that there is little attenuation within the interior. Fluctuations in the series for each of the simulations tend to be coherent. A positive flux through each section is directed toward the east, which means that a positive flux represents flow into the Bay at Fire Island Inlet and Robert Moses Causeway and out of the eastern end of the Bay at Smith Point.

The series for filtered volume flux at each of the seven sections were analyzed simultaneously to determine the patterns of subtidal volume exchange which they represented. The results are consistent with the patterns of exchange inferred from the current meter observations described previously. For summer simulations two basic modes of exchange explained more than 80% of the variance in all series and more than 90% of variance for most of the series. The first mode represents the same structure for both winter and summer and corresponds to simultaneous inflow or outflow to the Bay through Fire Island Inlet and Smith Point. Associated with this inflow (or outflow) is a convergence (or divergence) within the central Bay (the sign of the flux reverses between sections 3 and 4) and a divergence (or convergence) between the section at Robert Moses Causeway and section 2.

This mode represents the response to coastal sea level fluctuations produced by alongshore winds. This has already been identified previously as the primary mode of response. The second mode is also the same for winter and summer; it corresponds to unidirectional flow through the entire Bay. It would represent the response to direct wind forcing, which was earlier identified as the secondary mode of response. The second mode explains a significantly greater percentage of the variance in subtidal flux at all sections in summer.

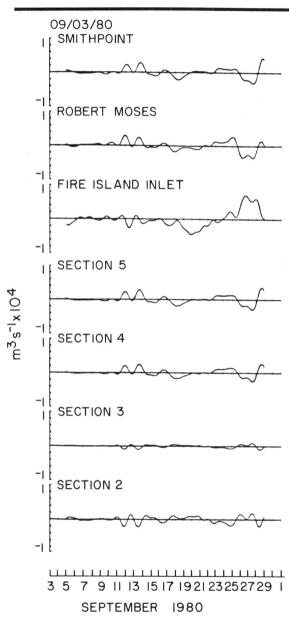

09/03/80

SMITHPOINT

ROBERT MOSES

FIRE ISLAND INLET

SECTION 5

SECTION 4

SECTION 3

SECTION 2

m³s⁻¹×10⁴

3 5 7 9 11 13 15 17 19 21 23 25 27 29 1

SEPTEMBER 1980

Figure 3.10 Residual volume flux through sections located in Figure 3.9 for September 1980. The range for the abscissae is -1.0 x 10⁴ m³/s to 1.0 x 10⁴ m³/s; a positive flux is towards the east.

RESIDUAL DRIFT VELOCITIES AND PARTICLE TRAJECTORIES

In previous sections we have described patterns of residual drift which might be produced by the interaction of the tidal stream with bathymetry. The residual drift can be considered simply as the average displacement over one tidal cycle of a water parcel from its initial position. If this displacement were divided by the tidal period, we would then have an estimate for residual drift velocity.

We have seen that the residual drift velocity of a water parcel has two contributions: one is the averaged current at a fixed point which would, for example, be measured by a current meter; the other is produced by spatial variations in amplitude and phase of the tidal current. We have seen in Figure 3.7b that this latter effect often dominates the residual drift velocity of a water parcel.

In this section we consider some of the patterns of residual drift within the Bay caused by the combined effects of the tide and meteorologically forced coastal sea level fluctuations. Previous discussions were related to residual drift produced by the tide alone. Figure 3.11 shows patterns of residual drift during a period of strong coastal sea level fluctuations in December 1979 (see Fig. 3.10). The drift patterns in Figure 3.11 cover a period of four days beginning at 0000 hours (midnight) December 19. During this period coastal sea level, responding primarily to alongshore winds, was falling during the first two days and rising during the second two days.

Figure 3.11a shows the patterns of residual drift over one semidiurnal tidal cycle beginning on 0000 hours December 19. The remaining patterns in Figure 3.11 are computed over semidiurnal tidal cycles beginning at successive 24.84 hour intervals so that all drift patterns are computed for the same phase of the semidiurnal tide.

Residual drift patterns within the Bay change markedly with time under meteorologically induced coastal sea level fluctuations and differ sub-

stantially from drift patterns due to the tide alone. One simple way to understand the major effects of meteorologically forced coastal sea level fluctuations on residual drift is to consider that they induce a strong and slowly varying averaged current, which is virtually absent under tidal forcing alone.

One further factor affecting the patterns of residual drift is the time of release of a water parcel relative to the phase of the semidiurnal tidal current. To document this effect, four residual drift patterns were computed for water parcel release at successive 0.25 tidal cycles, the first beginning at 0446 on December 18, 1979 (Fig. 3.12a) near the beginning of flood tide at Fire Island Inlet. This was during a period of very weak meteorological forcing.

Figure 3.12c shows the pattern of residual drift over a tidal cycle beginning one half tidal cycle later (near the beginning of ebb at Fire Island Inlet) than that in Figure 3.12a. Figure 3.12 shows that the drift patterns in certain areas of the Bay can change appreciably depending on the time of release relative to the phase of the semidiurnal tide. Especially noticeable is the variation in intensity of residual drift in the vicinity of each open boundary. This effect is most pronounced in the western part of the Bay. Note that a substantial number of parcels initially located near the open boundaries will leave the system if they are released at the beginning of the ebb current; thus, we were unable to assign a mean drift to those particles.

As a final illustration of some of the characteristics of residual drift patterns in the Bay, we calculated trajectories for a total of 10 water parcels for a period of 30 days beginning at 0000 hours, September 1979 (Fig. 3.13). The simulations provide some insight into the magnitude of tidal excursions within different regions of the Bay, and the residual drift patterns for particles released in different areas of the Bay. The particular simulations show that water parcels introduced into northeastern South Oyster Bay and northwestern Great South Bay tend to oscillate along the north shore of the bays while remaining inside the bays.

Parcels introduced into the central and eastern

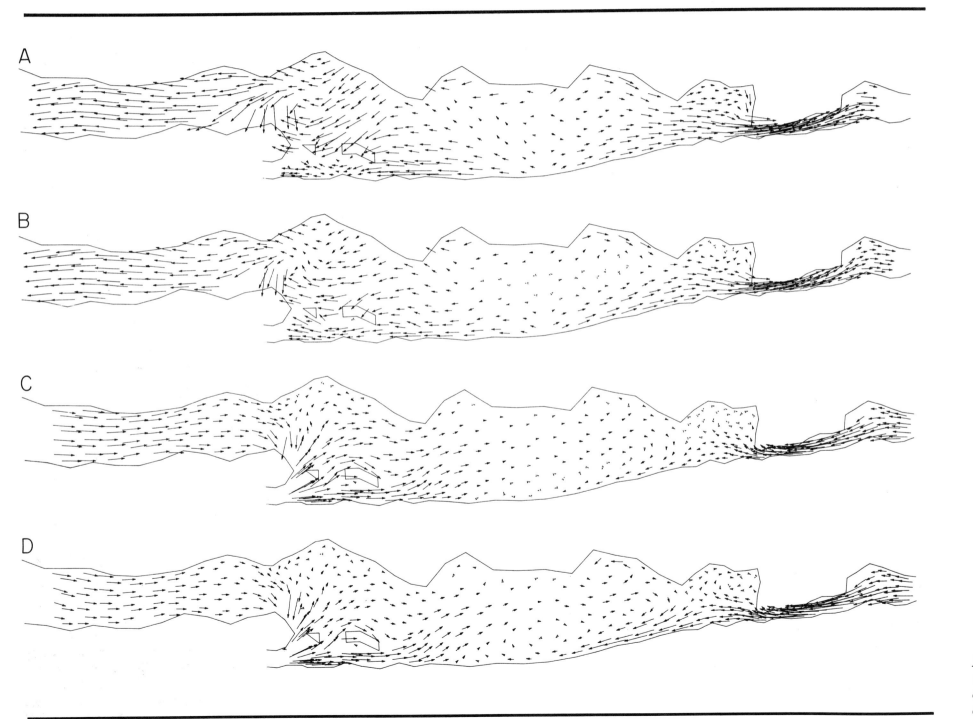

Figure 3.11. Patterns of residual drift for water parcels during periods of falling coastal sea level (a) and (b) and rising coastal sea level (c) and (d). (See text).

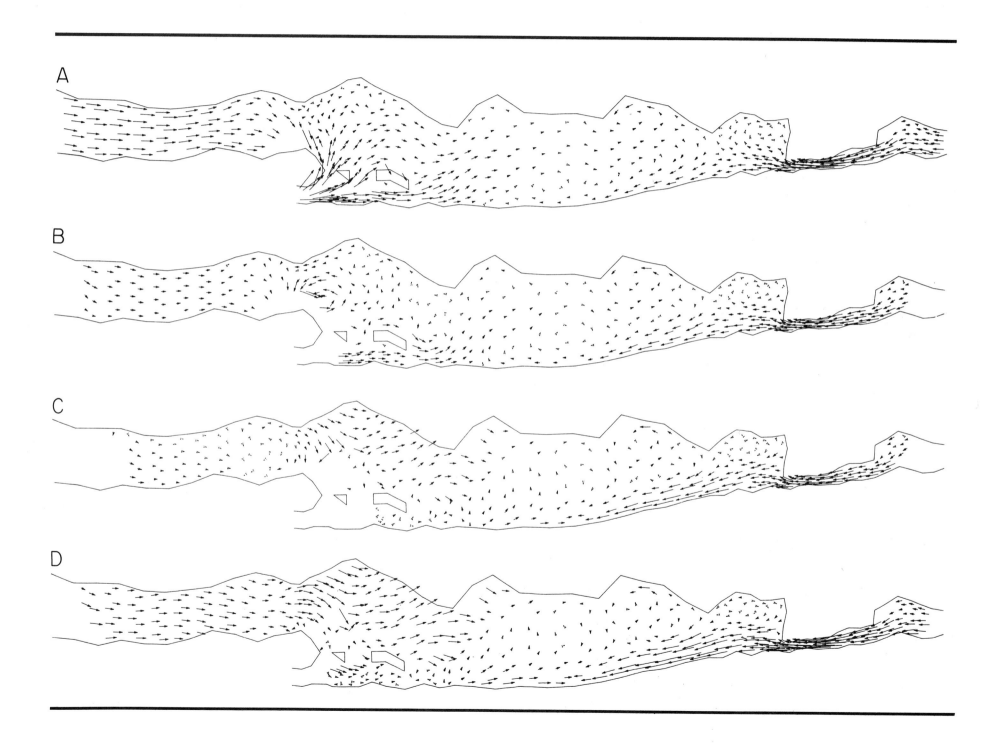

Figure 3.12. Patterns of residual drift for water parcels released at successive 0.25 tidal cycle (a is a slack before flood). (See text).

areas of Great South Bay tended to escape eastward into Moriches Bay, while some of those parcels released into South Oyster Bay tended to escape through Fire Island Inlet. Considering the dependence of residual drift on the time of release relative to the phase of the tide, the patterns in Figure 3.14 should probably not be considered unique.

EFFECTS OF LOW FREQUENCY VOLUME EXCHANGE ON BAY SALINITY

In previous sections we have seen that volume exchange at long periods can produce motions within the Bay which are extremely important to the residual movement of water parcels. Volume exchange at these periods is important to the exchange of dissolved and suspended materials because water entering the Bay has time to mix more completely than that exchanging at tidal periods.

The salinity time series (Fig. 3.14) from a mooring at Smith Point (Fig. 3.1) for the period December 19 to 27, 1979 provides some insight into the effects of low frequency exchange produced by coastal sea level fluctuations on salinity in the eastern Bay. Recall that these sea level fluctuations represented an Ekman response to alongshore winds acting on the shelf waters. On December 19, 1979 a low salinity value of approximately 22 ppt was recorded when an inflow to the Bay began, caused by a rise in coastal sea level.

On December 20, 1979 a high salinity value of 30 ppt was recorded during continued inflow. During the following week, salinity values in the eastern Bay remained approximately 8 ppt above the values on December 19. The time required for salinity to return to its original value appears to be of the order of one to two weeks, comparable to or longer than the time between major synoptic

scale meteorological events, which typically is from two to 10 days.

DISCUSSION AND CONCLUSIONS

Currents in Great South Bay are produced by the astronomical tides, by low frequency wind-induced coastal sea level fluctuations and by direct wind stress action on the Bay. Some of the characteristics of the fluctuations in sea level and currents, as well as associated volume flux, have been inferred from observations and numerical simulations. These simulations also provide some insight into the patterns of residual drift within the Bay and have emphasized that these patterns can be strongly affected by meteorologically induced, low frequency motions within the Bay.

Analyses of time series from observations of wind stress, low frequency sea level and currents

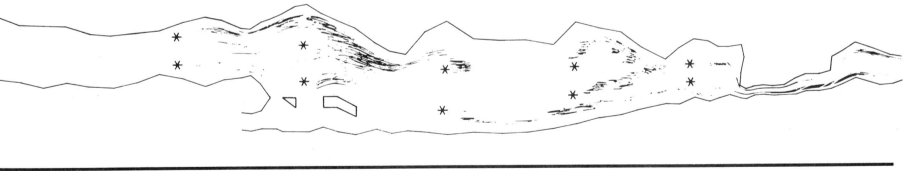

Figure 3.13. Simulated trajectories for ten water parcels (✳) for a period of 30 days released at 0000 hours, September 1, 1980.

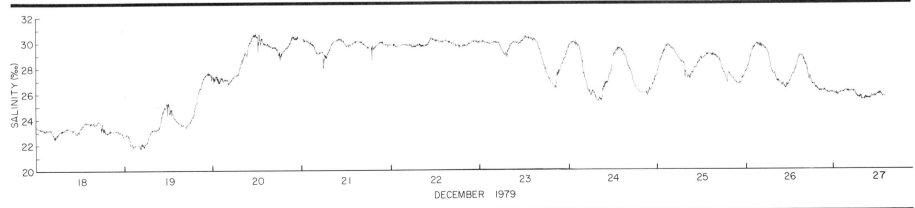

Figure 3.14. Time series of salinity off Smith Point for the period December 18, 1979 through December 27, 1979.

measured during winter and field experiments in summer indicate that during both seasons the same two primary modes of response prevail. The first and primary mode is a response to coastal sea level fluctuations, which in turn, respond to alongshore winds on the shelf. The response is characterized by a simple simultaneous emptying and filling of the Bay through all open boundaries. This mode of response tends to be associated with coastal sea level fluctuations having periods of seven days and longer. At shorter periods, typically on the order of three days, the Bay tends to respond more to direct wind forcing. This second mode of response tends to be associated with a flow through the entire Bay.

Numerical simulations provide quantitative estimates for the volume flux through sections within the Bay. Analysis of the series of low frequency volume flux shows clearly the primary mode representing a response to coastal sea level, with regions of convergence or divergence within the interior of the Bay, and the secondary mode representing a response to direct wind forcing in which there was a unidirectional flow through the entire Bay. The second mode accounted for an appreciably greater percentage of the variance in volume flux in summer than it did during winter.

The importance of volume exchange at low frequencies between sections of the Bay and between the Bay and the shelf is emphasized when comparison is made between the time for internal horizontal mixing within the Bay and the period of the volume exchange. Dye diffusion experiments conducted within the central part of eastern Great South Bay (Carter 1981; Becker 1978) have shown that the time for an introduced substance to diffuse across the Bay is of the order of 10 days. The time scale for internal mixing within the Bay and the period for the primary mode of subtidal volume exchange are, therefore, quite comparable. Water exchanged at low frequencies mixes more completely within the Bay than water exchanged at tidal frequencies, thereby producing an enhanced flushing action.

REFERENCES

Becker, D.S. 1978. Evaluation of a hard clam spawner transplant site using a dye tracer technique. Marine Sciences Research Center Special Report 10, Ref. 77- 6, State University of New York at Stony Brook, NY. 37 pp.

Bokuniewicz, H.J. and M. Zeitlin. 1980. Characteristics of groundwater seepage into Great South Bay. Marine Sciences Research Center Special Report 35, State University of New York at Stony Brook, NY, 32 pp.

Carter, H.H. 1981. A dye diffusion study of Great South Bay. Marine Sciences Research Center Special Report 43, Ref. 81-3, State University of New York at Stony Brook, NY. 20 pp.

Carter, H.H. 1985. Long term salinity changes in Great South Bay. Marine Sciences Research Center Working Paper, State University of New York at Stony Brook, NY, 19 pp.

Hollman, R. and M.L. Thatcher. 1979. Flow augmentation needs study. Great South Bay Salinity. Prepared for Suffolk County, Hauppauge, NY. 94 pp.

Pluhowski, E.J. and I.H. Kantrowitz. 1964. Hydrology of the Babylon-Islip area, Suffolk County, Long Island, NY. U.S. Geological Survey, Water-Supply Paper 1768, 119 pp.

Pritchard, D.W. and E. Gomez-Reyes. 1986. A study of the effects of inlet dimensions on salinity distribution in Great South Bay. Marine Sciences Research Center Special Report 70, Ref. 86-7, State University of New York at Stony Brook, NY. 62 pp.

Saville, T. 1962. Report on factors affecting the population of Great South Bay, Long Island, NY with special reference to algal blooms. Report to Jones Beach Parkway Authority, Babylon, NY. 30 pp.

Wang, D-P. 1979. Low frequency sea level variability on the Middle Atlantic Bight. J. Mar. Res., 37:683-697.

Wong, K-C. 1981. Subtidal volume exchange and the relationship to meteorological forcing in Great South Bay, New York. Ph.D. Thesis, Marine Sciences Research Center, State University of New York at Stony Brook, NY. 230 pp.

Wong, K-C. and R.E. Wilson. 1985. Observations of low-frequency variability in Great South Bay and relations to atmospheric forcing. J. Phys. Oceanogr. 14(12):1893-1900.

Dead eelgrass forms beach wrack.

IAN STUPAKO

WATER QUALITY

William C. Dennison
*University of Maryland
Center for Environmental and
Estuarine Studies
Horn Point Environmental
Laboratories
Cambridge, Maryland 21613*

Lee E. Koppelman
*Center for Regional Policy Studies
State University of New York
Stony Brook, NY 11794*

Robert Nuzzi
*Suffolk County Department
of Health Services
County Center
Riverhead, NY 11901*

INTRODUCTION

The most prominent and persistent water quality issue in Great South Bay has been the Bay's suitability for producing marketable shellfish. The habitat must be suitable for reproduction and growth of shellfish and sufficiently pristine so that shellfish growing areas and shellfish meats conform to appropriate health standards. As the population along the shoreline of Great South Bay increased, public concern for the shellfishery also increased. Originally, that concern was for oysters (*Crassostrea virginica*), and more recently, for hard clams (*Mercenaria mercenaria*).

Because shellfish can accumulate pathogenic microorganisms associated with fecal material of warm-blooded animals, a national monitoring program was developed in an effort to protect the public health (U.S. Dept. of Health and Human

Services 1986). This program, which monitors the coliform group of bacteria as an indicator of fecal contamination and, thus, the possible presence of disease-causing organisms, provides one of the most comprehensive water quality data sets for Great South Bay.

Several other water quality issues, ranging from aesthetic to life-threatening, have arisen concerning Great South Bay. Water quality parameters such as turbidity, odor and the presence of floating debris have been of aesthetic concern. Indications that the biota of the Bay may be affected by cultural eutrophication have led to concern over the Bay's ecology. Contamination of bathing waters by pathogenic microorganisms is a public health concern. Recently, the occurrence of an unprecedented algal bloom, commonly referred to as the "brown tide," has again focused attention on water quality of the Bay and on the factors affecting water quality. This chapter examines water quality issues of Great South Bay, the factors that affect water quality and concerns over its future.

WATER QUALITY ISSUES

TURBIDITY AND SUSPENDED SOLIDS

Aesthetic concerns and, in the case of bathing areas, public safety concerns due to turbidity have arisen at various times. Turbidity of the shallow Bay waters is generally relatively high, because of resuspension of sediments by wind-driven waves. Phytoplankton blooms of varying degrees add to the turbidity. Dredging, boating, shellfishing and runoff from various shoreline and Bay development projects increase turbidity over ambient levels.

Monitoring turbidity is difficult since the major causes of turbidity are variable in time and space, and few data have been collected for Great South Bay. Nonetheless, turbidity is an important water quality indicator. In addition to the aesthetic impacts of turbidity, the feeding efficiency of organisms that ingest suspended food particles (e.g., hard clams, scallops and menhaden) may be reduced in turbid waters (see Chapter 6 for discussion of the effects of suspended particles on

pumping rates of hard clams.

Suspended sediments and planktonic organisms, both of which reduce the depth to which sunlight can penetrate, are important in determining the distribution of rooted vegetation, primarily eelgrass in Great South Bay. The water depth to which eelgrass can grow is directly related to the depth of light penetration (Dennison 1987).

A wide range in concentration of suspended solids (2-167 mg/L) has been noted in Great South Bay, with increased values associated with periods of high winds or runoff (Hardy 1973). During strong winds, suspended solids can increase dramatically in the Bay, exceeding 200 mg/L (Nuzzi, unpublished data). However, monitoring activities during the summer of 1980 by Suffolk County revealed that suspended solids values usually are below 20 mg/L.

FLOATING DEBRIS

Floating mats of eelgrass (*Zostera marina*) and eelgrass washed up on the beaches have stimulated studies on how to remove this rooted plant in western portions of Great South Bay (e.g., Wegman 1967). Eelgrass traditionally was viewed as a nuisance weed, but that perception has moderated with increasing awareness of the important role these plants play in the ecology of nearshore waters.

One consequence of healthy eelgrass beds with their associated fauna is a sloughing of the leaves. This results in floating eelgrass, which can cause beach wrack and fouling of outboard motors. On the other hand, eelgrass beds can reduce turbidity and remove toxic compounds and heavy metals from the water column and sediments (Brinkhuis et al. 1980; Penello and Brinkhuis 1980). They also serve as habitat and a nursery for fish and shellfish.

A map of eelgrass distribution in the Bay is presented in Chapter 5. Increased turbidity and the presence of larger than usual floating eelgrass mats can be attributed to the brown tide, discussed at length later in this chapter.

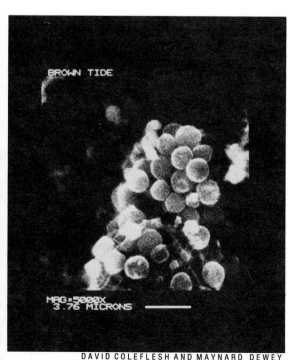

BROWN TIDE

MAG=5000X
3.76 MICRONS

DAVID COLEFLESH AND MAYNARD DEWEY

Scanning electron micrograph of the brown tide organism, Aureococcus anophagefferens.

COLIFORM BACTERIA

Fecal and total coliform bacteria are monitored in the Bay by the New York State Department of Environmental Conservation (NYSDEC) as part of the National Shellfish Sanitation Program to certify areas where shellfish can be harvested. The Suffolk County Department of Health Services also monitors coliform concentrations at bathing beaches to assess the potential public health hazard to swimmers. A historical perspective of coliform data is difficult to obtain because of changes in methodology, sampling intensity and timing and water quality regulations. However, an examination of the historical trends in the areas closed to shellfish harvest provides some insight into the temporal and spatial aspects of coliform contamination of Great South Bay waters.

A 1910 map of "polluted" areas (Fig. 4.1) indicates that contamination of nearshore waters is not a recent problem in the Bay. A composite map of areas that have, at one time or another between 1938 and 1987, been classified by the NYSDEC as uncertified for the taking of shellfish, demonstrates the relationship between closed areas and the proximity to tributary creeks and rivers (Fig. 4.2).

Snow (1982) performed a baywide survey and found coliform bacteria counts to be highest in the tributaries along the north shore of the Bay (Fig. 4.3). In addition, high coliform counts were found in waters near populated areas of Fire Island. Central portions of the Bay had low coliform counts, with higher values in Bellport Bay. Snow found that the lunar tides do not significantly affect coliform values, but that rainfall within two days of sample collection was significantly correlated to the median coliform counts. NYSDEC (1986) conducted a study to determine if the relationship between rainfall and coliform counts could be used as the basis of management strategy to open and close areas based on rainfall; however, a consistent relationship could not be found.

Coliform counts at Great South Bay bathing beaches collected by the Suffolk County Department of Health Services during the bathing season (June 1 to September 15) are highly variable (Fig. 4.4). These data, which are given as most probable number (MPN) per 100 mL, have not been adjusted to include the effects of precipitation, wind or tides, making trends difficult to discern. However, this long-term (1970-1986) data set

provides some insight into the spatial and temporal distribution of coliform bacteria in the Bay.

The log average total coliform values were in excess of 100/100 mL at beaches in the western and eastern reaches of Great South Bay and below 100/100 mL at beaches in central portions of the Bay. Average coliform counts in excess of 200/100 mL were found at three beaches: Venetian Shores Beach between Neguntatogue Creek and the Santapogue River (218/100 mL); Sandspit Beach east of the Patchogue River mouth (312/100 mL); and Mastic-Shirley beach in Bellport Bay just south of the Carmans River (230/100 mL). Possible contributing factors to the high values at these beaches include high population densities nearby and, in the case of the Mastic-Shirley beach, the presence of a river with a large waterfowl population.

The relatively high coliform counts at beaches in Patchogue Bay may be influenced by the sewage treatment plant near the head of the Patchogue River. This is the only area of Great South Bay in which there is any indication that coliform values have increased since 1970 (J. Redman, pers. comm.). The release of sewage effluent with a

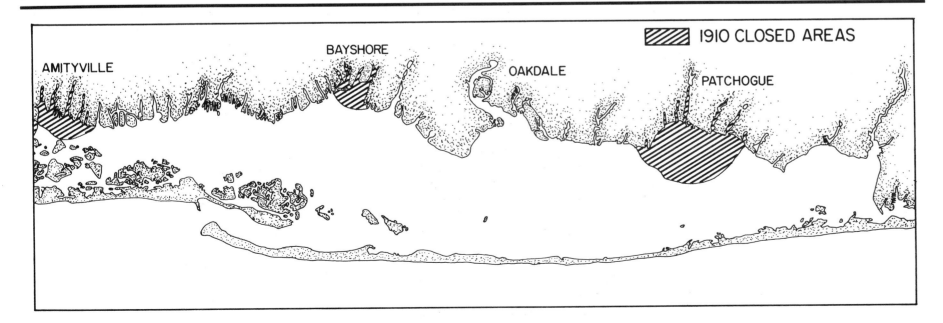

Figure 4.1. Great South Bay "polluted" areas in 1910 (New York Department of Health shellfish investigation).

coliform concentration of 60,000/100 mL could result in coliform values in Patchogue Bay in excess of the maximum allowable for certification of shellfish harvesting (currently set at 70/100 mL, Nuzzi 1986). Recent improvements to this sewage treatment plant have led to reductions in coliform levels, and these reductions may lead to reduced closures in Patchogue Bay (J. Redman, pers. comm.) (Fig. 4.2).

Bay beaches on Fire Island for which sufficient data are available have lower average values (Atlantique, 64/100 mL; Ocean Beach, 80/100 mL; and Seaview, 51/100 mL) than the beaches on the north shore of Great South Bay. The limited watershed within which these bacteria may originate and the rapid exchange of Bay water with ocean water entering Fire Island Inlet (Chapter 3) probably account for the low coliform values in this area.

EUTROPHICATION

Cultural eutrophication—increased nutrient loading from human sources—is an ecological concern in Great South Bay because of its adverse effects on the Bay's biota. Anthropogenic nutrients reach the Bay through surface runoff, groundwater seepage, sewage treatment plants and the atmosphere. Total loading of a major nutrient, nitrogen, to Great South Bay is approximately 6600 pounds per day (Koppelman 1978). Of this total, approximately 82% is from streamflow (including both runoff and groundwater seepage into streams), direct runoff and rainfall; 16% from groundwater seepage directly into the Bay; and only 2% from point sources (treatment plants). Historically, there were large nutrient inputs associated with duck farms, but these have been nearly eliminated. New major nutrient sources are domestic sewage and fertilizer application. Recent investigations in Chesapeake Bay discussed by Fisher et al. (1988) indicate that acid rain may contribute significantly to the nutrient loading of coastal waters.

Studies of nutrient levels in Great South Bay have been sporadic. Comprehensive surveys, however, were undertaken in the 1950s by Ryther (1954) in response to a series of algal blooms (see Chapter 5). In the 1970s, nutrient surveys indicated that increased development along the north shore of the Bay, particularly in western Great South Bay, led to increased nutrient levels (Hair and Buckner 1973).

Suffolk County determined the distribution of the nitrogenous nutrients, ammonium (NH_4) and nitrate (NO_3) in 1977-1978 (Fig. 4.5). At all stations the concentration of NH_4 was higher than NO_3, but levels of both nutrients throughout most of the Bay were not substantially different from concentrations found at the coastal ocean station. Nutrient levels were below 2 μM with the following exceptions: (1) the mouth of the Carlls River (11 μM NH_4 and 6 μM NO_3); (2) Neguntatogue Creek (9 μM NH_4 and 5 μM NO_3); and (3) Carmans Creek (5 μM NH_4 and 3 μM NO_3). Relatively high NH_4 values (2.7 μM) were also found south of Gilgo Island.

Great South Bay is one of the most productive bays in the world (see Chapter 5), due, in part, to the abundance of nutrients. However, while nutrients are indeed necessary for sustaining such high productivity, their form and amount can alter phytoplankton population structure. This alteration of the very base of the food chain can result in profound, and not always welcome, effects on higher trophic levels, including the commercially important shellfish. Such a result was seen during the middle part of this century when blooms of

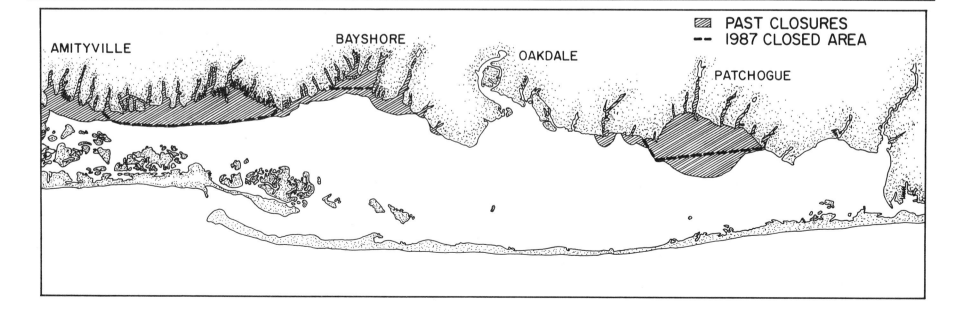

Figure 4.2. Areas of Great South Bay closed to shellfish due to bacterial coliform surveys by New York State Department of Environmental Conservation. Shaded areas have at one time been closed (1938-1987) and dotted lines indicate areas recently closed (1987).

"small form" algae adversely affected the shellfish harvest from the Bay (Chapter 5).

DISSOLVED OXYGEN

Low levels of dissolved oxygen in bottom waters of the Bay have not been a major water quality issue, in contrast to Long Island Sound and many other coastal water bodies. Bacteria consume oxygen as they decompose organic matter, which can result in oxygen depletion, particularly in deeper waters. Because the Bay is shallow, the water column is well mixed and can accommodate the addition of relatively large amounts of organic matter without lowering oxygen content (Foehrenbach 1969). However, the deep waters of tributaries entering the Bay (e.g., Carmans River) can become oxygen deficient because they are shielded from the wind and, therefore, less vigorously mixed (Foehrenbach 1969).

PESTICIDES

Pesticides that can accumulate in various marine organisms with deleterious effects were once used in the mosquito control programs in the marshes of Great South Bay. The use of the pesticide DDT prior to 1966 for this purpose led to high concentrations in the salt marshes of the Bay (Foehrenbach et al. 1967; Woodwell et al. 1967). Pesticides are ingested by adult mosquitos but not the larvae, so the pesticides are generally applied with a monomolecular surface film (oil) that prevents the non-feeding larvae from breathing. The combination of DDT and fuel oil No. 2 for mosquito control undoubtedly led to water quality degradation.

Use of DDT was curtailed in 1966, but the long-lived nature of DDT suggests that there may still be low concentrations remaining in the Bay. Until about 1983 an organophosphate compound (Abate) was used in concert with fuel oil No. 2 for mosquito control. This was replaced with a biological control measure (*Bacillus thuringiensis var. israelensis*) specific to mosquito larvae. The monomolecular surface film now used is a plant-based oil (S. Guirgis, pers. comm.).

FACTORS AFFECTING WATER QUALITY

Water quality of Great South Bay is affected by the kinds and rates of input of contaminants into the Bay and the rates of removal and processing of these contaminants. The introduction of pollutants into the Bay can be divided into point and non-point sources, with non-point sources from laminar flow, streamflow discharge and groundwater seepage predominating.

There are only a few sewage treatment facilities discharging into Great South Bay, and these point sources handle only a small fraction of the total sewage produced within the drainage basin. The pollutants originating from non-point sources are basically the same as those found in point sources: organic chemicals, pathogenic bacteria and viruses, heavy metals and nutrients. However, the patterns of occurrence of the two sources differ in that pollutant loadings from non-point sources show greater variation with time than those from point sources. This makes quantification of non-point source loadings more difficult and control measures more costly.

Stormwater runoff as laminar flow directly into the Bay, as streamflow or ground water introduces various contaminants, depending on the characteristics of the drainage unit. For instance, hydrocarbons and heavy metals often predominate in areas adjacent to roadways or commercial/industrial areas, while microorganisms, nutrients (e.g., fertilizers), pesticides and sediment may predominate in less developed areas. Cesspool and septic systems introduce nutrients, organic chemicals and possibly viruses to the Bay through

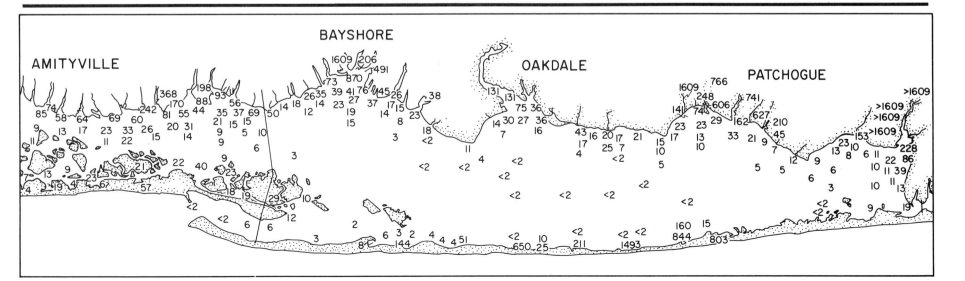

Figure 4.3. Distribution of median values of total coliform counts in Great South Bay between 1973-1980 (from Snow 1982).

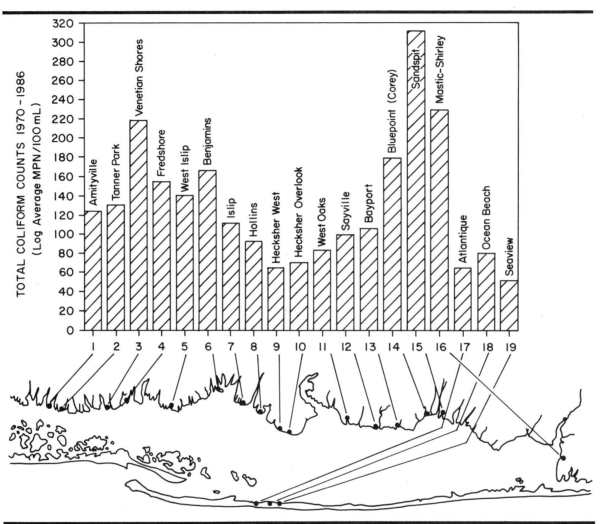

Figure 4.4. Long-term (1970-1986) log averages of total coliform counts of Great South Bay bathing beaches (from Suffolk County Department of Health Services).

ground water (Pluhowski and Kantrowitz 1964). Thus, most water entering the Bay percolates through Long Island's sandy soil and becomes part of the shallow glacial aquifer. The large pollutant loading to the ground water of Long Island is reflected by elevated nitrate values in this aquifer in many areas (Capone and Bautista 1985). However, the relatively long residence time of water in the soil allows for degradation of many organic compounds and reduces the coliform counts before the water enters the Bay.

The fraction of water entering Great South Bay directly as runoff can be extremely important to water quality. Rain storms wash a variety of pollutants into the water, with characteristics not unlike sanitary waste (Sartor et al. 1974). Approximately 90% of the total coliform bacteria loadings to Great South Bay are from stormwater runoff (Koppelman 1978). The volume of direct runoff has increased because of paving and construction of storm sewers (Pluhowski and Spinollo 1978), leading to an increase in the relative importance of direct runoff in determining water quality. In the far western portions of Great South Bay, the Southwest Sewer District Project has reduced the pollutant loading to the Bay by transferring the treated sewage directly to the ocean. A consequence of this diversion is a reduction in the freshwater input to the Bay (WAPORA, Inc. 1981).

The exchange of water between Great South Bay and the ocean (discussed in Chapter 3) is important in flushing pollutants out of the Bay and in controlling salinity levels within the Bay. Thus, the processes affecting this flushing rate are crucial in determining water quality and salinity of the Bay.

It appears that water exchange between Great South Bay and the ocean is dependent on both astronomical and meteorological tides (see Chapter 3). Therefore, meteorological conditions can influence not only the input of pollutants to the Bay in runoff and streamflow, but also the removal of pollutants from the Bay by their effect on exchange with the ocean. This close coupling between weather conditions and water quality of Great South Bay

the ground water.

Other sources of contamination include runoff from construction sites, sand and gravel mining sites, oil storage depots, leaks from pipelines and sewers and discharges from boats. While these may not be as important regionally as the sources described previously, they can cause significant water quality problems locally. For example, discharges from the large number of boats in the Bay are a cause for concern. Most of these boats have direct overboard discharge of their partially treated sewage. This has resulted in a ban of "live-aboards" in many of the villages along the Bay and

in the requirement for houseboats to obtain discharge permits from the Suffolk County Department of Health Services. Powerboats, even during normal use, discharge petroleum compounds into the water. Although the effects of oil on the biota of the Bay are largely unknown, minute quantities of water soluble compounds from fuel oil No. 2 have been shown to be toxic to some species of marine phytoplankton (Nuzzi 1973).

Coliform distributions indicate that stream discharge accounts for a large quantity of pollutants entering the Bay. Ninety-five percent of the water entering streams along Great South Bay comes from illustrates the need to consider these factors together in the design of water quality sampling programs and in the analysis of water quality data.

Inlet configurations which are constantly changing, as illustrated by the many attempts at inlet stabilization (Kassner and Black 1982; Kassner and Black 1983), can produce the most dramatic effects on the water quality and biota of the Bay.

The magnitude of tidal (astronomical) exchange between the Bay and the ocean is significantly affected by inlet configuration. Relatively saline conditions have prevailed since the opening of Moriches Inlet in 1931, while the closing of Moriches Inlet during the brief period from 1951 to 1953 reduced circulation in Great South Bay and contributed to noxious algal blooms (see Chapter 5).

Large changes in the biota of Great South Bay over the past several centuries have been inferred from the pollen preserved in sediment cores taken on Fire Island (Clark 1986). The pollen record suggests that the abundance of salt marshes in the Bay is cyclical. Salt marshes have alternately flourished and been destroyed as a result of changes

in inlet configuration, water levels and local disturbances such as sand deposition.

Simple successional sequences of "pioneer" and "climax" species are not found in this dynamic system where changes in the physical environment regulate the distribution of plants and animals. Historically, salt marshes fringing the barrier islands have been present when many inlets were open, and exchange between Great South Bay and the Atlantic Ocean maintained saline conditions (Clark 1986). These conditions have existed from 1760 to 1835 and again since 1931. There is evidence that freshwater marshes existed in the intervening periods of poor water exchange and low salinity conditions.

Just as water quality influences all of the biota in Great South Bay to varying degrees, reductions in streamflow, declines in water table elevations, and changes in sea level can lead to loss of critical habitats, the salt marshes and freshwater wetlands. Salt water intrusion and reduction in fresh water changes the salinity regime of the wetland habitat, resulting in changes in vegetation and

associated fauna.

Significant lowering of the water table and of potentiometric surfaces has a large effect and has occurred over the past few decades in coastal areas of Long Island (Pluhowski and Spinello 1978). Over 1500 acres of freshwater wetlands have been inventoried within the nine major stream systems of southwestern Suffolk County and southern Nassau county (Beital 1976). Salt marshes made up primarily of cordgrass (*Spartina alterniflora*) and salt hay (*Spartina patens*) occupy large portions of western Great South Bay, for example, Gilgo Island and Cedar Island. These marshes are inundated by salt water twice daily.

Fringing salt marshes, found on the north side of the barrier beach islands and along creeks of the northern shore, also contribute to the total wetland area of Great South Bay. In addition to cordgrass and salt hay, lower portions of the freshwater marsh are often dominated by the non-native reed plant *Phragmites australis*. Higher portions of the fringing marsh are inundated less frequently by salt water, and contain shrubs and forest species.

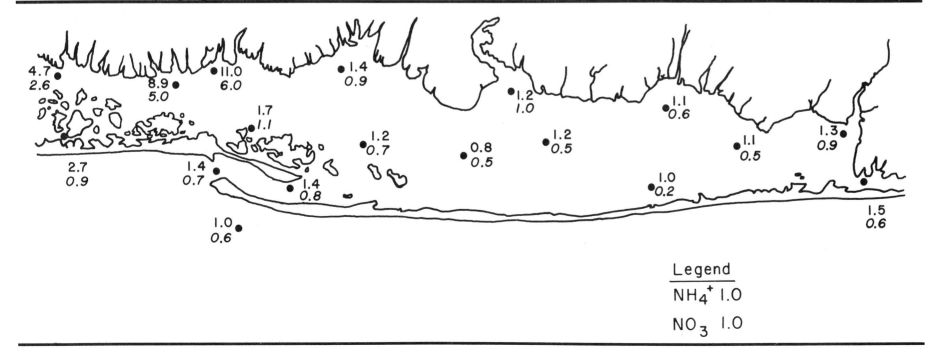

Legend

NH₄⁺ 1.0

NO₃ 1.0

Figure 4.5. Distribution of dissolved inorganic nitrogen concentrations (μM NH₄ and μM NO₃) in Great South Bay determined in 1977-1978 (from Suffolk County Department of Health Services).

The sensitivity of salt marsh and freshwater marsh vegetation to the frequency of inundation has clear implications for any development that affects water table levels. The effects of ditching on marshes has been well documented (e.g., Bourn and Cottam 1950). Ditching effectively lowers the water table in a marsh, creating a drier environment. This leads to changes in the vegetation and associated fauna of the marsh. Invertebrates inhabiting the marsh are particularly affected by drying of the soil, as are the birds and animals that prey on them.

ISSUES OF CONCERN FOR THE FUTURE

An unusual algal bloom in Great South Bay began in 1985 and has continued to a greater or lesser degree to the present (Cosper et al. 1987; Nuzzi, 1988). This bloom, commonly known as the "brown tide," is different from other blooms which have occurred in the Bay in that it was composed of extremely high numbers of a single species (at one point in excess of a billion cells per liter);

Great South Bay salt marsh with mosquito ditching.

R. GEORGE ROWLAND

persisted throughout the entire summer; recurred in successive years; and occurred simultaneously in other geographic areas. Perhaps most importantly, the bloom had deleterious effects on shellfish and eelgrass.

The algal species responsible for the bloom has only recently been identified and named *Aureococcus anophagefferens* (Sieburth et al. 1988). Its name refers to the golden brown color that the organism imparts to the water (aureo), the spherical shape of the cell (coccus), and the decreased feeding response of the shellfish in the presence of the organism (anophagefferens).

During a bloom, the organism multiplies rapidly, but its density remains relatively constant, indicating the presence of significant grazing pressure (Cosper et al. 1987). The feeding rates of scallops and mussels, however, were found to be severely depressed when fed cultures of *Aureococcus* (Bricelj and Kuenstner, 1989) and there are indications that oysters and clams are similarly affected. The brown tide organism was

also found to have a deleterious effect on the growth and survival of scallop larvae (Gallager et al., 1989.)

The 1985 and 1986 bloom episodes began in mid-May, persisted throughout the summer, and extended from Bellport Bay in the east to the area of the Robert Moses Causeway in the west. The westward extent of the bloom is probably influenced by the circulation of ocean waters moving through Jones and Fire Island Inlets (Nuzzi and Waters, 1989). In addition to Great South Bay, simultaneous blooms occurred in Flanders, Peconic and Gardiners Bays on Long Island, Narragansett Bay (Rhode Island) and possibly Barnegat Bay (New Jersey).

Besides decreasing feeding rates of shellfish, the brown tide caused a decrease in the biomass of eelgrass in the Bay by decreasing light penetration through the water column. The maximum depth distribution of eelgrass changed from approximately 3 m (Jones and Schubel 1978) to approximately 1.5 m (Cosper et al. 1987). This reduction in depth of growing areas led to a 56% reduction in the amount of Bay bottom where eelgrass can grow from a potential pre-bloom habitat of 91.1 km² to a potential post-bloom habitat of 50.6 km².

SUMMARY

Long-term trends in the existing data on Great South Bay coliform bacteria counts are difficult to discern, and the effect of changes in sampling intensity and timing needs to be considered. The areas closed for shellfishing have increased from approximately 20 km² in 1964 to approximately 40 km² in 1984, and from 1986 through 1988 have remained at approximately 30 km² (COSMA 1985; C. de Quillfeldt, NYSDEC, pers. comm.). Correlations between increasing urbanization and increasing concentrations of coliform bacteria in other locations are cause for concern for Great South Bay. Continued development of land adjoining the Bay will undoubtedly place into jeopardy areas of the Bay currently suitable for

recreation and shellfishing. Treatment of sewage, which may be an expensive alternative to the existing septic and cesspool systems, may have to be considered to avoid further degradation of the Bay's water quality.

The issue of eutrophication in the Bay will not be solved by the standard methods of sewage treatment. Primary and secondary treatment reduce the solids loading and biological oxygen demand of the sewage, but tertiary treatment is required to remove nitrogen and phosphorus. Novel approaches for nutrient removal such as the use of biological filters (e.g., salt marshes) are difficult to employ without collection systems or primary or secondary sewage treatment facilities and generally require large land areas, which are often not available or are prohibitively expensive.

Concern for the water quality of Great South Bay will likely increase with increased development. The population in the towns adjoining the Bay have significantly increased since World War II, with over 300,000 people living in census tracts adjacent to the Bay in 1984 (COSMA 1985). Most of the sewage derived from these tracts is treated by septic systems and cesspools which recharge into the ground water. Associated with the increase in population density is an increase in use of fertilizer for residential lawns and gardens. A large fraction of the nutrients from these fertilizers ultimately ends up in Great South Bay, further impacting water quality. Accompanying the increase in population is an increase in recreational demands on the Bay. Consequently, water quality issues of Great South Bay promise to become more, rather than less, prominent.

The health and productivity of Great South Bay is vulnerable to a variety of point and non-point sources of contamination. It is also subject to physical modifications, including changes in inlet configuration and runoff patterns that are in part controlled by man. Our ability to impact the water quality and, therefore, the health of the abundant and diverse biota of the Bay provides an impetus for research and effective management. Many of the problems facing the Bay have been well researched, and an understanding of the basic principles dictating water quality has been achieved.

Management options must consider the social, political and economic factors in the resolution of Great South Bay water quality problems. The plethora of jurisdictions identified in Chapter 9, which share an interest and control over Bay management, represent both a benefit and a cause for concern. While there is no want of commissions, agencies, advisory boards and departments in all levels of government, there is often a fragmentation and competition of effort that renders an overall and comprehensive management plan for the entire Great South Bay system an elusive goal.

ACKNOWLEDGEMENTS

We thank S. Guirgis, J. Kassner and J. Redman for providing data used in this chapter.

REFERENCES

Beital, J. 1976. A vegetative survey of the freshwater wetlands of nine major streams in southwestern Suffolk County and southern Nassau County, N.Y. Environ. Defense Fund, New York (draft report).

Bourn, W.S. and C. Cottam. 1950. Some biological effects of ditching tidewater marshes. Res. Rept. 19, U.S. Fish Wildl. Serv. pp 1-17.

Bricelj, V.M. and S. Kuenstner. 1989. Effects of the "brown tide" on the feeding physiology and growth of bay scallops. Pages 493-512 *in* E.M. Cosper, et al., eds. Novel phytoplankton blooms: causes and impacts of recurrent brown tides and other unusual blooms. Springer-Verlag, Berlin.

Brinkhuis, B.H., W.F. Penello and A.C. Churchill. 1980. Cadmium and manganese flux in eelgrass *Zostera marina* II. Metal uptake by leaf and root-rhizome tissues. Mar. Biol. 58:187-196.

Capone, D.G. and M.F. Bautista. 1985. A groundwater source of nitrate in nearshore marine sediments. Nature 313:214-216.

Clark, J.S. 1986. Dynamism in the barrier-beach vegetation of Great South Beach, NY. Ecol. Monogr. 56:97-126.

COSMA. 1985. Suffolk County's hard clam industry: An overview and an analysis of management alternatives. Report of a study by the Coastal Ocean Science and Management Alternatives Program. Marine Sciences Research Center, State University of New York at Stony Brook, NY.

Cosper, E.M., W.C. Dennison, E.J. Carpenter, V.M. Bricelj, J.G. Mitchell, S.H. Kuenstner, D. Colflesh and M. Dewey. 1987. Recurrent and persistent "brown tide" blooms perturb coastal marine ecosystem. Estuaries. 10:284-290.

Dennison, W.C. 1987. Effects of light on seagrass photosynthesis, growth and depth distribution. Aquat. Bot. 27:15-26.

Fisher, D., J. Ceraso, T. Matthew and M. Oppenheimer. 1988. Polluted coastal waters: The role of acid rain. Environ. Defense Fund, New York. 102 pp.

Foehrenbach, J. 1969. Pollution and eutrophication problems of Great South Bay, Long Island, NY. Water Poll. Cont. Fed. 41:1456-1465.

Foehrenbach, J., E. Harris and Q.R. Bennett. 1967. Insecticides in the marine environment. N. Y. Fish Game J. 14:1-89.

Gallager, S.M., V.M. Bricelj, D.K. Stoecker. 1989. Effects of the brown tide alga on growth, feeding physiology and locomotory behavior of scallop larvae *(Argopecten irradians)*. Pages 513-544 *in* E.M. Cosper, et al., eds. Novel phytoplankton

blooms: causes and impacts of recurrent brown tides and other unusual blooms. Springer-Verlag, Berlin.

Lecture Notes on Coastal and Estuarine Studies. Springer-Verlag, NY.

Hair, H.E. and S. Buckner. 1973. An assessment of the water quality characteristics of Great South Bay and contiguous streams. Nassau-Suffolk Regional Planning Board, Hauppauge, NY.

Hardy, C.D. 1973. Chemical oceanography *in* Final report of the oceanographic and biological study for Southwest Sewer District #3, Suffolk County, New York. Vol. 1, Marine Sciences Research Center, State University of New York at Stony Brook, NY.

Jones, C.R. and J.R. Schubel. 1978. Distribution of surficial sediments and eelgrass in New York's south shore bays: An assessment from the literature. Marine Sciences Research Center Special Report 13, State University of New York at Stony Brook, NY.

Kassner, J. and J.A. Black. 1982. Efforts to stabilize a coastal inlet: A case study of Moriches Inlet, New York. Shore and Beach, April 1982, pp 21-29.

Kassner, J. and J.A. Black. 1983. Fire Island Inlet, New York, management of a complex inlet. Shore and Beach, October 1983, pp 3-8.

Koppelman, L.E. 1978. The Long Island comprehensive waste treatment management plan. Vols. I and II. Nassau-Suffolk Regional Planning Board, Hauppauge, NY. 661 pp.

Nuzzi, R. 1973. The effects of water soluble extracts of oil on phytoplankton. Pages 809-813 *in* Proceedings of the 1973 Conference on Prevention and Control of Oil Spills. Am. Pet. Inst.

Nuzzi, R. 1986. A hydrographic study of Patchoque River and Bay—Preliminary findings. Suffolk County Department of Health Services, Unpubl. report.

Nuzzi, R. 1988. New York's brown tide. The Conservationist, N. Y. State Dept. Env. Conserv., Sept.-Oct. pp 30-35.

Nuzzi, R. and R.M. Waters. 1989. The spatial and temporal distribution of "brown tide" in eastern Long Island. Pages 117-138 *in* E.M. Cosper, et al., eds. Novel phytoplankton blooms: causes and impacts of recurrent brown tides and other unusual blooms. Springer-Verlag, Berlin.

Penello, W.F. and B.H. Brinkhuis. 1980. Cadmium and manganese flux in eelgrass *Zostera marina* I. Modelling dynamics of metal release from labelled tissues. Mar. Biol. 58:181-186.

Pluhowski, E.J. and I.H. Kantrowitz. 1964. Hydrology of the Babylon-Islip area, Suffolk County, Long Island, N.Y. U.S. Geol. Survey Water Supply Paper 1768, 119 pp.

Pluhowski, E.J. and A.G. Spinollo. 1978. Impact of sewerage systems on stream base flow and groundwater recharge on Long Island, NY. J. Res. U.S. Geol. Survey 6:263-271.

Ryther, J.H. 1954. The ecology of phytoplankton blooms in Moriches Bay and Great South Bay. Biol. Bull. 106:199-209.

Sartor, J.D., G.B. Boyd and F.J. Agardy. 1974. Water pollution aspects of street surface contaminants. Water Poll. Control Fed. 46:459-467.

Sieburth, J. McN., P.W. Johnson and P. E. Hargraves, 1988. Characterization of *Auerococcus anophagefferens* gen. et sp. nov. (Chrysophyceae): The dominant picoplankter during the summer 1985 bloom in Narragansett Bay. J. Phycol. 24:416-425.

Snow, J.W. 1982. Coliform analysis of Great South Bay. M.S. Thesis, Marine Sciences Research Center, State University of New York at Stony Brook, NY. 47 pp.

U.S. Dept. of Health and Human Services. 1986. National shellfish sanitation program manual of operations, Part I: Sanitation of shellfish growing areas. Interstate Sanitation Commission, Austin, TX.

WAPORA, Inc. 1981. Estuarine impact assessment (shellfish resources) for the Nassau-Suffolk streamflow augmentation alternatives, draft report on existing conditions. U.S. Environ. Prot. Agency, New York. 114 pp.

Wegman L.S. and Company. 1967. Channel and eelgrass study. Report submitted to Nassau County, Dept. of Public Works, Mineola, NY

Woodwell, G.M., C.F. Wurster, Jr. and P.A. Isaacson. 1967. DDT residues in an east coast estuary: A case of biological concentration of a persistent insecticide. Science 156:821.

Population increases and recreational demands have taken their toll on the Bay's water quality.

IAN STUPAKOFF

Typical undeveloped shoreline of Great South Bay.

CHAPTER 5

PRIMARY PRODUCTION AND NITROGENOUS NUTRIENTS IN GREAT SOUTH BAY

Edward J. Carpenter
Boudewijn M. Brinkhuis*
*Marine Sciences Research Center
State University of New York
Stony Brook, NY 11794*

Douglas G. Capone
*University of Maryland
Center for Environmental and
Estuarine Studies
Chesapeake Biological Laboratory
Solomons, MD 20688*

---

*Deceased July 10, 1989

INTRODUCTION

The annual harvest of fish and shellfish from Great South Bay is dependent on the growth of plants in the Bay. Through photosynthesis, plants utilize energy in sunlight to convert inorganic carbon in seawater to organic compounds which can then be used for their growth. This organic carbon in plant material is either consumed directly as food by fish and shellfish, or is eaten by another animal, which is in turn eaten. Thus, plants form the base of the food chain. Photosynthesis by marine plants is virtually the only source of nutrition for animals in the Bay. We may view marine plants as the fuel which drives the Great South Bay shellfish and finfish factory.

MAJOR PLANT GROUPS

The marine plants in the Bay can be divided into two major divisions. Those microscopic algae, which are suspended in the water column, are known as "phytoplankton" (Greek for "wandering plants"). The second group consists of much larger seagrasses and seaweeds, which grow in shallow (less than 3 m) areas of the Bay.

The phytoplankton are a diverse group, with about 200 species present in the Bay throughout the year. They range in diameter from about 1 μm to almost 1 mm. In addition, various species of phytoplankton differ greatly in their behavior, environmental requirements and food value. This latter factor is, of course, of extreme importance to the organisms which consume phytoplankton.

First, let us consider the characteristics of some of the major taxonomic groups of phytoplankton found in the Bay. The diatoms are usually an abundant group and considered a good food for shellfish. Diatom shapes range from those resembling tiny pill boxes to long chains of interconnected cells. Diatoms have a very thin shell consisting of silica, which provides a rigid structure for their cells. They do not have flagellae and, hence, cannot swim to regulate their position. Their photosynthetic pigments are light brown, so when they are abundant, the water may have a golden brown appearance.

Dinoflagellates are the second major phytoplankton group in the Bay. Some of them have an armor consisting of cellulose plates, while others have no armor. Dinoflagellates have two flagellae, which allow them to swim and regulate their position in the water column. Their predominant photosynthetic pigment often has a dark red color so that when they become very abundant, the resultant discoloration of the seawater is sometimes referred to as a "red tide." It is thought that dinoflagellates are a good food source for shellfish, although more research is needed to fully determine their importance.

In the spring some of the small tributaries of the Bay have "blooms," or dense accumulations, of a red tide species *Heterocapsa triquetra*. During July *Gyrodinium aureolum* colors the mouth of some estuaries, such as the Carmans River, a dark brown. A toxic dinoflagellate *Gonyaulax tamarensis* is present in some areas of the south shore Bays, and surveys are currently being conducted (E. Carpenter) to determine whether the abundance of this species is high enough to cause human health problems. This species contains a toxin which can cause shellfish that feed on them to become toxic.

Green microalgae, or chlorophytes, constitute the third major phytoplankton group. Their pigments are a bright lettuce-green. During the 1950s dense blooms of very small green algae were implicated as one of the factors causing the demise of the Long Island oyster industry. Some species of these chlorophytes are not a good food for shellfish, because the shellfish are unable to digest the cell wall of these phytoplankton. We discuss the chlorophytes and their impact on Great South Bay shellfish later in the section entitled "Historical Background."

The remaining phytoplankters in the Bay can, for simplicity, be termed microflagellates. These small, swimming phytoplankton are from a number of diverse taxonomic groups. In general, most microflagellates are good food for shellfish.

Plant life also abounds on the floor of the Bay. Seagrasses and seaweeds (macroalgae) proliferate over the shallower portions of the Bay bottom (less than 3 m) which receive enough light to sustain their growth. Seagrasses are rooted plants which derive required inorganic nutrients from the water column and from sediments. The only seagrass representative in the Bay is the eelgrass *Zostera marina*. Toward the end of the growing season (August to September) its leaves often exceed 1 m in length.

Dense growths of eelgrass stabilize sediments in the Bay, dampen wave action and provide habitats for diverse assemblages of associated plants and animals. In fact, large populations of microscopic and macroscopic algae are found on the blades of eelgrass and supplement the overall contribution of these communities to the productivity of the Bay. Thus, many animals benefit indirectly from seagrasses. For the most part, however, *Zostera* is not used directly as a food resource for the animals in the Bay. The considerable production of eelgrass reaches higher organisms through "detrital food chains." In other words, *Zostera* is decomposed by microorganisms on the bottom, which are in turn consumed by larger organisms.

Benthic macroalgae are yet another important plant form in the Bay. While generally either free floating or attached to the bottom by a holdfast, macroalgae obtain needed nutrients from the overlying waters. Common macroalgae in the Bay include green algae such as sea lettuce (*Ulva lactuca*) and dead man's fingers (*Codium fragile*), and red algae from such genera as *Agardhiella, Gracilaria* and *Polysiphonia*.

IMPORTANCE OF NUTRIENTS

In many ways, the factors which affect growth of marine plants are similar to those which regulate growth of a terrestrial agricultural crop, or even grass in a lawn. Marine plants grow best when they have an ample supply of nutrients just as a lawn grows best when fertilized. In most marine environments, the element nitrogen (N) is usually the nutrient present in concentrations so low as to limit the growth of marine plants. However, factors such as other nutrients, water temperature, sunlight, water transparency and grazing by marine animals can also be of major importance in regulating growth of these plants. Obviously, the growth of phytoplankton, seagrass and seaweeds is controlled in a very complex manner, as all these environmental parameters interact with one another. We shall discuss these interactions, but first let us consider some of the previous research on the Bay and problems that have occurred concerning phytoplankton and eelgrass.

HISTORICAL BACKGROUND

The earliest survey of phytoplankton in the Bay was carried out in 1907 and 1908 because of concern that the diversion of Long Island's freshwater supply might affect the production of oysters (Whipple 1912). The borough of Brooklyn had plans to use Long Island's ground water as its freshwater source, so a survey of the Bay's physical and biological characteristics was made. This survey showed that diatoms were the predominant phytoplankton group, and that there were no major

differences in their distribution and density from one area of the Bay to another. Whipple did note that concentrations of diatoms in the water were severalfold greater on windy days than on calm ones. He hypothesized that wave action on windy days stirred up the water and resuspended diatoms that had settled into deeper water. Of major interest in Whipple's study is the contrast between the dominance of diatoms in 1907 compared with the later increase in microscopic green algae (chlorophytes) in the period between the 1930s and 1950s.

During the 1930s the phytoplankton population in the Bay changed. Instead of being dominated by diatoms, a very small (about 1-2 μm in diameter) species of green (chlorophyte) alga became abundant. These were termed "small forms" because they were so minute and difficult to identify. Later, it was found that small forms consisted of several species of green algae (Ryther 1954). These green algae appeared to have a detrimental effect on the growth, and hence the harvest of shellfish. Note the inverse relationship between the concentration of small forms and the content of oyster meat per bushel off West Sayville between 1933 and 1950 (Fig. 5.1). Clearly, when small forms were present in high concentrations, the oyster harvest as measured by meat content per bushel was low.

The appearance of small forms was apparently related to the introduction of excreta to the Bay from Long Island duck farms. The ducks were usually raised in open pens along the tributaries of eastern Great South Bay and had free access to the tributaries. Their major excretory product, uric acid, was converted to urea by bacteria in seawater. Unlike some of the common diatoms in the Bay, the small forms had enzyme systems which allowed them to utilize the urea as a source of nitrogen. According to Ryther (1954), this gave the small forms a competitive advantage over many of the diatoms. Furthermore, the high concentration of phosphorus relative to nitrogen in the Bay, as well as the ability of small forms to grow over a wide range of salinities, were factors leading to small

form blooms.

The closing of Moriches Inlet on May 15, 1951 reduced the already slow flushing of duck wastes from eastern Great South Bay and western Moriches Bay and led to extremely dense blooms of small forms. The water in Moriches Bay and eastern Great South Bay turned a pea green color in summer when small form concentrations were in the tens of billions of cells per liter.

In September 1953, Moriches Inlet was reopened by hurricane Edna, which led to a reduction in severity of blooms, since wastes in the Bay once again were flushed more readily to the ocean. At the same time, pollution control methods were being implemented on duck farms, and the total number of ducks was decreasing. Today the number of small forms in Great South Bay waters has decreased dramatically, and phytoplankton populations are much more balanced with respect to their species composition. Although there has been a decrease in small form concentrations, it should be noted that they still are present in significant concentrations in summer. During winter they are not abundant.

Phytoplankton in the Bay still are somewhat unusual compared with other coastal waters of our region. First, the diatom *Skeletonema costatum* is the predominant phytoplankton species in virtually all east coast waters; yet it is rarely dominant in great South Bay (Weaver and Hirschfield 1976; Cassin 1978; Lively et al. 1983). Bay phytoplankton populations today are dominated by microflagellates, particularly cryptomonads.

Recently, the Bay has experienced dense blooms of a chrysophyte named *Aureococcus anophagefferens*. This 2-3 μm diameter organism has bloomed in the summers of 1985 through 1988. The cause of the bloom is currently under study by scientists from the Marine Sciences Research Center at the State University of New York at Stony Brook.

The Bay usually has dense blooms of *Phaeocystis pouchetii* during March and April; concentrations frequently are high enough to clog plankton nets and even fish nets. This phytoplankter is known as "Dutchman's 'baccy juice'" by fishermen, because

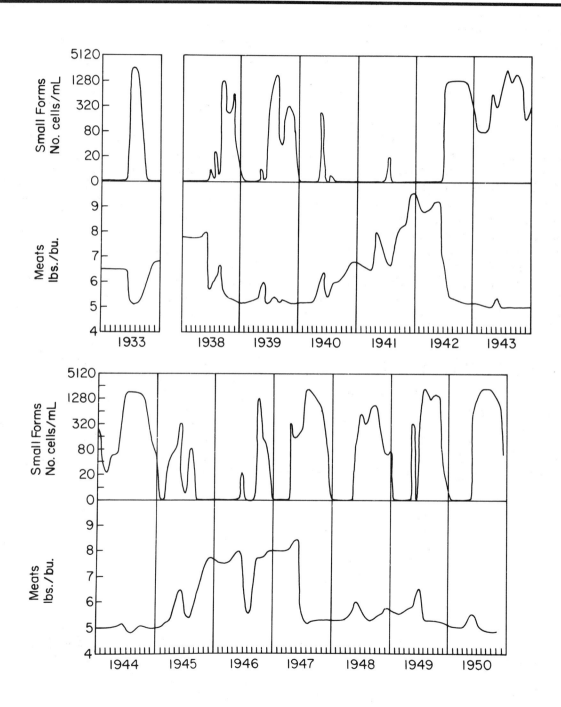

Figure 5.1. Monthly concentration of small forms off west Sayville and volume of meats per bushel of oysters between 1933 and 1950.

it gives seawater a color of tobacco juice.

Like phytoplankton, seagrasses along the south shore have also been the subject of studies in the past, not only because of their prolific growth, but also because of their demise. Most of the eelgrass in the Bay disappeared during the 1930s, along with populations all along the east coast of the United States. This phenomenon is referred to as the "wasting disease" and has not, as yet, been adequately explained. The prevailing theory is that periods of prolonged warm summer and cold winter temperatures between 1930 and 1933 stressed plant vigor. This stress made the populations more susceptible to infection by a fungus that is present at all times in eelgrass tissues. Scientists working in the Chesapeake Bay area have suggested that increased turbidity and pesticide concentrations caused by increased agricultural use of shore lands may have led to the decline. Seagrass populations in the Chesapeake Bay have undergone an additional decline in recent years, but now are making a comeback.

The demise of eelgrass in Great South Bay in the 1930s apparently led to the reduction and disappearance of many animal species in the Bay. The productivity of Bay scallops, shrimps and oysters has been linked to seagrass abundance (Nelson 1924; Marshall 1947). The decline in oyster landings in the late 1930s may well have been partially associated with the eelgrass demise.

The recovery of eelgrass in Great South Bay is not well documented, but by the mid-1960s eelgrass had reached such dense growths in western Great South Bay and South Oyster Bay that it became a problem to people using the Bay. It fouled motorboat propellers, and *Zostera* detritus accumulated along the shoreline. The Town of Hempstead and the Suffolk County Board of Supervisors commissioned studies to investigate the seagrass problem.

Wilson and Brenowitz (1966) reported an average eelgrass biomass in western Great South Bay of 1.9 kg/m², with maxima in excess of 4.5 kg/m². In their reports on South Oyster Bay to the Town of Hempstead, Wegman (1967) and Burkholder and

Doheney (1968) found standing crops in excess of 2.5 kg dry weight/m² at some sites, with a mean standing crop of 0.7 kg/m². They suggested that these abundances were approximately three times greater than for eelgrass beds in parts of Great South Bay. These values represent extremes among the observed densities of eelgrass over its distribution range (McRoy and McMillan 1977).

The densities reached in the Bay in the mid-1960s may have been a maximum. Elder (1976) used computer models to confirm the fact that the biomass of eelgrass in Oyster Bay was threefold greater than in Great South Bay during the period 1969 to 1972. More recent studies have noted less extensive distributions of eelgrass.

Green et al. (1977) found eelgrass over about one third of the bottom in eastern parts of the Bay, with average densities of 0.2 kg/m² within eelgrass beds. This is about half that of the values predicted by Elder (1976). They also noted that the depth limit of distribution was 1.8 m along the southern edge of the Bay, but only 0.5 m along the northern edge. They related this to the higher turbidity and, hence, lower light transmission in waters adjacent to the highly developed south shore of Long Island. Jones and Schubel (1980) noted a similar phenomenon in the western portions of the Bay. Adamson (1982) found that eelgrass abundance in parts of the Bay in 1981 was similar to that reported by Green et al.

(1977) and Jones and Schubel (1980). Thus, it appears that the abundance of eelgrass in Great South Bay had stabilized in recent years. However, recent "brown tides" have reduced light transmission in Bay water, severely restricting the extent of eelgrass beds (see Chapter 4 for discussion on brown tides).

During early stages of eelgrass colonization, the amount of root matter is considerably less than leaf material. As the beds mature, more root material is produced than leaf material (Nienhuis and DeBree 1977). The leaf to root ratio in the Bay is now between 1:1 and 2:1, indicating that the beds are no longer significantly expanding.

Brinkhuis and Churchill (unpublished data) used remote sensing techniques to determine the distribution of eelgrass over the entire Bay (including South Oyster Bay) during the summer of 1981. The distribution of eelgrass during its period of maximum standing crop (late August) is shown in Figure 5.2.

PRIMARY PRODUCTION

Great South Bay is one of the most productive marine habitats in the world. Production is defined by biologists as the amount of carbon fixed by plants in photosynthesis per unit time. This fixed carbon is virtually the only source of food for the

organisms living in the Great South Bay ecosystem. The data can be expressed either as per volume of water or, to make comparisons easier, per area of sea surface. For the Bay we estimate an annual rate of production of 450 g Carbon (C)/m² of sea surface (Table 5.1). If we include production by eelgrass (about 70 g $C \cdot m^{-2} \cdot y^{-1}$) we obtain a total of 520 g $C \cdot m^{-2} \cdot y^{-1}$, one of the greatest rates ever measured in a marine habitat. Benthic macroalgal production is not included in this figure as there are no estimates available for Great South Bay.

The metabolic activity of fish and shellfish approximately doubles with every 10°C (18°F) rise in water temperature. Thus, the summer is their most active growing period. However, there must be an abundant food supply for maximal growth to occur. Since summer is also the period of maximal photosynthesis in the Bay (Fig. 5.3), food for fish and shellfish is in abundance. In contrast, maximum production in Long Island Sound and many other marine environments occurs during a very short period (i.e., two to three weeks) during the early spring bloom in February and March. Much of this fixed carbon cannot be utilized by fish and shellfish because the bloom is of such short duration and the metabolic rate of the animals is low because of the low water temperature. In Great South Bay, high phytoplankton production is sustained at between 2.0 and 3.0 g $C \cdot m^{-2} \cdot d^{-1}$ from

THICK (>250-375 g/m²)
MEDIUM (>125-250 g/m²)
THIN (>0-125 g/m²)

Figure 5.2. Distribution of eelgrass during August in Great South Bay.

Table 5.1. Annual primary production by phytoplankton in selected estuarine and marine ecosystems.[a]

Location and Reference	g C·m²·y⁻¹	Environment
Port Moody Area, British Columbia Stockner & Cliff, 1979	532	Coastal inlet
Pamlico River, North Carolina Kuenzler et al., 1979	500	Flood plain estuary
Puget Sound, Washington Winter et al., 1975	465	Fjord
Great South Bay, New York Lively et al., 1983	450	Barrier island estuary
New York Bight Malone, 1976	370	Continental shelf water
Straight of Georgia, British Columbia Stockner et al., 1979	345	Coastal straight
Beaufort Channel, North Carolina Williams & Murdock, 1966	225	Flood plain estuary
Narragansett Bay, Rhode Island Smayda, 1957	220	Estuarine embayment
Upper New York Harbor Malone, 1977	200	Drowned river mouth estuary
Peconic Bay, New York Bruno et al., 1980	162-213	Estuarine embayment
St. Margaret's Bay, Nova Scotia Platt, 1971	190	Coastal embayment
Georgia Bight Haines & Dunstan, 1975	171	Continental shelf system
Nassau Sound Estuary Turner et al., 1979	90	Salt marsh estuary

[a] Adapted from original table by Lively, J. et al. 1983, with permission of the publisher, Academic Press, Inc.

July through October when water temperatures are high and grazing organisms can best use it.

Eelgrass production is maximal in the spring and summer, reaching rates of up to 1 g C·m⁻²·d⁻¹ within the eelgrass beds (Adamson 1982). Unlike phytoplankton, however, there are few direct grazers on eelgrass. With senescence, eelgrass leaves fall to the bottom and, along with root material, are slowly degraded by microorganisms (Wilson 1983). Macroalgae and phytoplankton trapped by the eelgrass beds also become a food source for

these microorganisms. This detrital food chain provides a sustained source of food for organisms in the Bay during periods of minimum phytoplankton input. By promoting bacterial activities in the sediments, eelgrass detritus also fuels regenerative processes in the bottom sediments with the concomitant recycling and release of inorganic nutrients back into the water (Dietz 1982). The nutritional qualities of phytoplankton and eelgrass complement each other well to provide the Bay with a "well-balanced diet" of plant material.

During the summer most of the phytoplankton production is done by the smallest size fraction, that known as the nanoplankton (Fig. 5.4). These organisms are smaller than 10 μm in diameter and account for over 80% of the total primary production at that time.

Chlorophyll *a* is the dominant photosynthetic pigment in phytoplankton, and marine scientists use it as an index of biomass. As can be seen from Figure 5.5, the concentration of phytoplankton chlorophyll *a* is greatest during summer months, with typical values between 20 and 25 μm of chlorophyll *a* per liter of seawater. However, chlorophyll *a* concentration and the rate of phytoplankton photosynthesis (Fig.5.3) was considerably lower over eelgrass beds sampled along the southern area of the Bay.

We believe that this lower concentration is the result of two factors. First, a portion of the Atlantic Ocean seawater enters through Fire Island Inlet, and all significant sources of freshwater in Great South Bay are along the northern shore of the Bay. Salinity values in these eelgrass beds are greater than those in the central and northern areas of the Bay, thus indicating larger proportions of oceanic water which contain fewer phytoplankton and chlorophyll *a* than is found in the Bay.

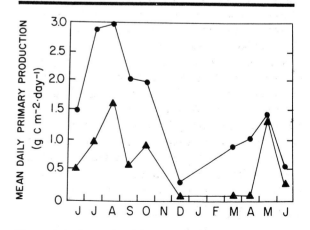

Figure 5.3. Rate of photosynthesis by phytoplankton in open bay water ● and eelgrass beds ▲ .

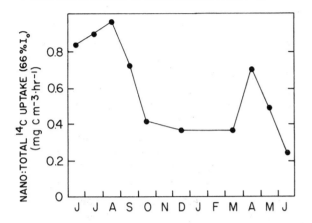

Figure 5.4. *Relative rate of photosynthesis by nanoplankton (less than 10 μm diameter cells) in Great South Bay. I° = light intensity at sea surface.*

Second, dense stands of eelgrass divert some of the water flow carrying the oceanic phytoplankton, and the beds themselves slow the water passing through them. The decreased water velocities permit particles, including phytoplankton, to settle out of the water. However, these dense growths of eelgrass that occur along the south side of the Bay (north side of Fire Island), where the clearer oceanic waters allow sufficient light penetration to support eelgrass growth, complement the lower phytoplankton production.

Basically, we can characterize the plant production in the Bay as being very high relative to other marine habitats, with the bulk of production performed by the smallest phytoplankton during summer. Phytoplankton production provides a readily utilizable food source during periods of maximum animal demands, whereas eelgrass production is utilized more slowly, sustaining the system throughout the year.

THE CYCLING OF NITROGENOUS NUTRIENTS

Primary production (photosynthesis) is high during summer months primarily because there is

an abundant supply of nutrients at that time. As mentioned previously, nitrogen is one essential element that is present in limiting concentration in many marine habitats (Ryther and Dunstan 1971; Nixon 1981). Fortunately, there are adequate concentrations of nitrogenous nutrients in Great South Bay to sustain high primary production for most of the year.

Figure 5.6 shows that available nitrogen never reaches zero, and the lowest value that the combined concentrations of ammonium, nitrate and urea reach is about 3.0 μmol/L (μM) in the Bay in summer. This concentration is high relative to summer values in other coastal marine habitats. In fact, the supply of nitrogenous nutrients is so high that Adamson (1982) and Lively el al. (1983) considered light availability to be the major factor limiting primary production in the Bay.

Some of the light attenuation is from self-shading, in which the dense phytoplankton population near the surface shades or blocks the light from those in deeper water; however, Lively et al. (1983) estimated that through the year 65% to 95% of the total light extinction was caused by suspended sediment particles. These are extremely small particles of sediment and organic

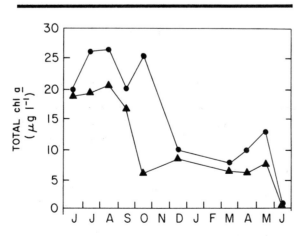

Figure 5.5. *Standing crop of phytoplankton as chlorophyll* a *in Great South Bay, in open bay water* ● *and in eelgrass beds* ▲ *(Lively et al. 1983).*

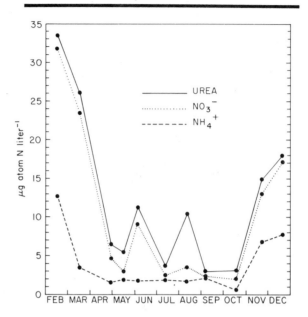

Figure 5.6. *Concentrations of nitrogenous nutrients through the year in central Great South Bay.*

material, which are resuspended from the bottom when winds cause mixing.

The extreme shallowness of the Bay is a major factor maintaining an abundance of nitrogenous nutrients throughout summer. Zooplankton, benthic animals and bacteria are responsible for breaking down organic material and releasing dissolved nitrogenous compounds. These excretory products are immediately available for uptake by phytoplankton because the water column is so shallow and wind easily mixes surface and bottom waters.

Eelgrass also contributes nutrients to the water from the sediments via its roots. Barton (1983) found that ammonium is removed from the sediments by eelgrass roots in summer and released through the leaves to the water. Eelgrass leaves preferentially take up nitrate vs ammonium; therefore, less ammonium is taken up by eelgrass leaves. With senescence of the leaves at the end of summer, large amounts of ammonium are released back to the sediments from the roots. Thus, phytoplankton are provided with an adequate supply of nutrients.

Great South Bay is somewhat unusual in that urea constitutes a major fraction of the nitrogen taken up by phytoplankton. As mentioned previously, ammonium is the nitrogenous nutrient preferred by phytoplankton because it is energetically easiest to assimilate and use for synthesizing amino acids. Urea, on the other hand, must be degraded to ammonium before it can be used in the cell. Over a one-year study, urea nitrogen averaged 52% of the total assimilated, while ammonium accounted for 33% and nitrate accounted for 13%. It should be noted that in most coastal environments urea is a significant nitrogen source for phytoplankton, but usually it does not exceed 25% to 45% of the total nitrogen used.

The apparent preferential uptake of urea by Great South Bay phytoplankton might be explained by its high concentration relative to ammonium: urea concentrations averaged 2.0 μM over the year, a concentration more than twice that of ammonium. The high concentration and high utilization of urea are somewhat puzzling; ammonium rather than urea is the major excretory product of fish, zooplankton and marine benthic organisms. Since there are few duck farms today, this is probably not the source of urea. Also, according to Kaufman et al. (1984), urea turnover times (time for phytoplankton to totally remove the existing urea concentration) were rapid in the summer, averaging 3.7 hours.

There must be a relatively continuous source of urea because a relatively constant concentration exists in the water column through the summer. It is unlikely that ground water sources (e.g., septic tank leaching) are important since the concentrations of urea around the Bay are quite uniform. If ground water were a major contributor, one would expect to find higher concentrations along the north shore of Great South Bay, where freshwater input and potential urea sources are greater. Bacteria in the benthos are a possible source of urea, but only future research will provide us with an answer.

By calculating the phytoplankton nitrogen demand during the year, we may determine the importance of various sources of nitrogen to the phytoplankton. If carbon fixation by phytoplankton is about 1.25 g C·m⁻²·d⁻¹ (Lively et al. 1983), then the nitrogen requirement by phytoplankton is about 0.21 g N·m⁻²·d⁻¹ (phytoplankton require six carbon atoms for every nitrogen atom). This is a demand of about 15 x 10³ μmol N·m⁻²·d⁻¹.

There are a number of sources of nitrogen for phytoplankton, which may be separated into those which provide "new" nitrogen and those yielding "old," or recycled, nitrogen. Stream flow is probably the most significant source of new nitrogen to the Bay (Fig. 5.7). Hair and Buckner (1973) estimated that on an annual basis the Bay receives 6.8 x 10⁸ L/d of stream water with a mean nitrogen concentration (nitrate, nitrite and ammonium) of 15 μM N. This gives a total inorganic nitrogen input to the Bay of 10 x 10⁹ μmol/d.

The surface area of the Bay is 200 million m². Thus, the daily nitrogen input from stream flow is about 50 μmol/m². This is less than 0.3% of the daily nitrogen needs of phytoplankton. While on an immediate basis this appears small, one must remember that stream flow is the major source of "new" nitrogen to the Bay. Without this constant input, nitrogen would become limiting and plant photosynthesis would decrease.

The second major source of new nitrogen is groundwater seepage. This enters the Bay along its north shore in a narrow band, at an estimated rate of 200 million L/d (Bokuniewicz 1980). A typical concentration of nitrate in sediments subject to groundwater seeps is about 10 μM, so this yields an input of 10 μmol·m⁻²·d⁻¹ averaged over the Bay area. Again, this is very low relative to daily needs (about 0.07%), but it may be very important as a source of new nitrogen.

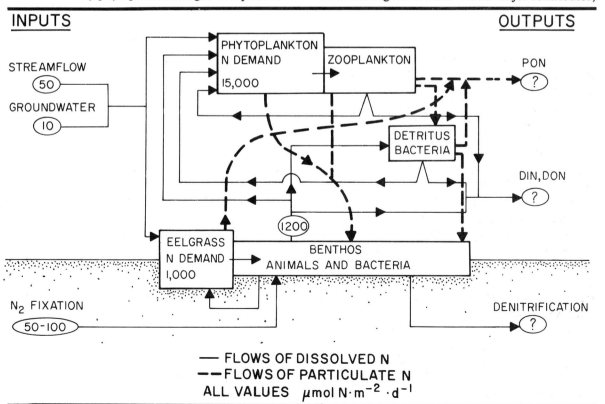

INPUTS   OUTPUTS

STREAMFLOW (50)
GROUNDWATER (10)

PHYTOPLANKTON N DEMAND 15,000   ZOOPLANKTON

DETRITUS BACTERIA

EELGRASS N DEMAND 1,000

(1200)

BENTHOS ANIMALS AND BACTERIA

N₂ FIXATION (50-100)

PON (?)
DIN, DON (?)
DENITRIFICATION (?)

— FLOWS OF DISSOLVED N
-- FLOWS OF PARTICULATE N
ALL VALUES μmol N·m⁻²·d⁻¹

Figure 5.7. Schematic of nitrogen cycle in Great South Bay. PON = Particulate organic nitrogen; DIN = dissolved inorganic nitrogen, and DON = dissolved organic nitrogen.

The bulk of nitrogen used by phytoplankton, therefore, must come from recycled nitrogen. One such source is the benthos. Dietz (1982) measured ammonium release in three sediment types within Great South Bay under calm conditions and observed a mean for the whole Bay of about 1.2×10^3 μmol N·m^{-2}·d^{-1}. Thus, benthic regeneration of ammonium supplies about 7% of the phytoplankton nitrogen demand. This value is a minimum since other nitrogen compounds are also likely to be recycled and released by sediments. Furthermore, Great South Bay is so shallow that a moderate wind mixes it from surface to bottom and brings these nutrients and those trapped near the sediment surface up to where phytoplankton can utilize them.

Dietz (1982) also simulated the effects of clam raking on release of ammonium from the sediments. Her results indicated that there was little impact on baywide rates of nutrient release by raking.

If we sum the contributions from stream flow, ground water and benthos, we obtain a total of about 8% of the daily nitrogenous needs of phytoplankton. The remainder must, therefore, come from recycling of nitrogen by bacteria and zooplankton within the water column. This is an area of active research in the Marine Sciences Research Center.

The nitrogen requirement of eelgrass is also substantial. Given a productivity of 1 g C·m^{-2}·d^{-1} during the summer, eelgrass requires about 70 mg N·m^{-2}·d^{-1}, since the ratio of carbon to nitrogen in fresh eelgrass tissue is about 15:1. Eelgrass, an advanced plant, is able to obtain nitrogen from the sediments via uptake by roots and from the water via its leaves. Furthermore, it likely can recycle some nitrogen from aging leaves to partially offset demands for growth.

It is generally thought that eelgrass obtains most of the new nitrogen it needs for growth by uptake of ammonium through its roots. Unlike the overlying waters, there are generally high amounts of ammonium in the sediments. Ammonium concentrations in eelgrass bed sediments are about tenfold greater than in sediments not colonized by seagrass (Dietz 1982; Barton 1983). During rapid growth in spring and early summer, ammonium in eelgrass sediments decreases dramatically despite the temperature-induced increase in microbial activity that breaks down organic matter into ammonium.

Nonetheless, the productivity of eelgrass is high enough so that if there were no resupply sources of nitrogen in the sediments, the available nitrogen would be depleted in a matter of days. In fact, the microbial degradation of organic detritus (including eelgrass itself) in the sediments provides a steady source of nitrogen. Another source of utilizable nitrogen results from the bacterial conversion of nitrogen gas into ammonia, a process called nitrogen fixation. One of us, (Capone) has found that nitrogen fixing bacteria both in the sediments and directly on the roots and rhizomes of eelgrass can provide from 3% to 28% of the plant's net nitrogen requirement (Capone 1982; Capone 1983; Capone and Budin 1982).

SUMMARY

Great South Bay is one of the world's most productive marine habitats. Primary production by phytoplankton and eelgrass together amounts to about 520 g C·m^{-2}·y^{-1}. High photosynthetic rates by phytoplankton and eelgrass are a major reason for the great commercial harvest of shellfish from the Bay. Phytoplankton production is present at high rates through summer months, and eelgrass provides nourishment for shellfish via the detrital food chain through the year.

Production is high because of an abundance of nutrients and the shallow depth of the Bay, which allows winds to mix the water column between the surface and bottom. Plant growth is not limited by abundance of nitrogenous nutrients as in most other marine habitats, but by availability of light and water temperature.

Sources of new nitrogenous nutrients to the Bay are stream flow, ground water and microbial nitrogen gas fixation. These supply but a small fraction of daily nitrogen needs of phytoplankton and eelgrass. Relatively efficient remineralization of organic nitrogen within the water column provides the remaining fraction of nitrogen required by plants.

REFERENCES

Adamson, B.A. 1982. Seasonal variation of carbon uptake and translocation by eelgrass (*Zostera marina* L.) in Great South Bay, New York. M.S. Thesis. Marine Sciences Research Center, State University of New York at Stony Brook, NY. 95 pp.

Barton, H., III. 1983. Uptake and translocation of nitrogenous nutrients by eelgrass (*Zostera marina*). M.S. Thesis. Marine Sciences Research Center, State University of New York at Stony Brook, NY. 90 pp.

Bokuniewicz, H.J. 1980. Groundwater seepage into Great South Bay, New York. Estuarine Coastal Mar. Sci. 10:437-444.

Brinkhuis, B. and A.C. Churchill. 1981. Marine Sciences Research Center, State University of New York at Stony Brook, NY. (Unpublished).

Burkholder, P.E. and T.E. Doheny. 1968. The biology of the eelgrass. Contribution No. 3, Dept. of Conserv. and Waterways, Town of Hempstead, NY.

Capone, D.G. 1982. Nitrogen fixation (acetylene reduction) by rhizosphere sediments of the eelgrass, *Zostera marina* L. Mar. Ecol. Prog. Ser. 10:67-75.

Capone, D.G. 1983. N$_2$ fixation in seagrass communities. Mar. Technol. Soc. J. 17:32-37.

Capone, D.G. and J.M. Budin. 1982. Nitrogen fixation associated with rinsed roots and rhizomes of the eelgrass, *Zostera marina*. Plant Physiol. 70:1601-1604.

Cassin, J. 1978. Phytoplankton floristics of a Long Island embayment. Bull. Torrey Bot. Club. 105:205-213.

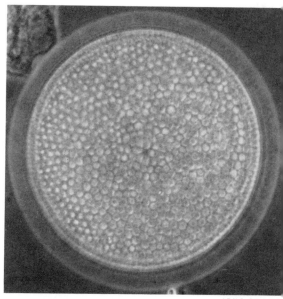

JENG CHANG

Diatoms of the genus Coscinodiscus *(above) and* Thalassiosira decipiens.

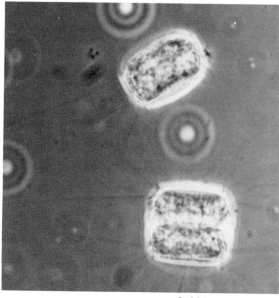

R. GEORGE ROWLAND

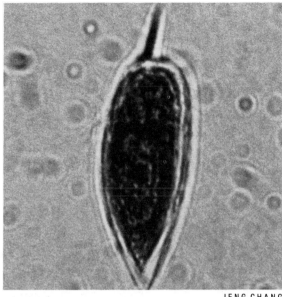

JENG CHANG

Dinoflagellates Prorocentrum triestinum *(above) and* Peridinium trochoideum.

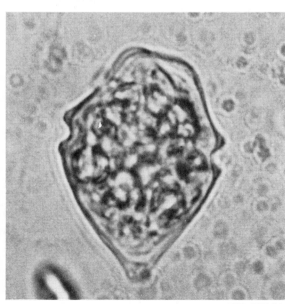

JENG CHANG

Dietz, C.G. 1982. Ammonium fluxes from estuarine sediments: Great South Bay, N.Y. M.S. Thesis. Marine Sciences Research Center, State University of New York at Stony Brook, NY. 128 pp.

Elder, J. 1976. Eelgrass production in Long Island waters. Tetra Tech. Inc., Lafayette, California Prepared for the Nassau Suffolk Regional Planning Board, Hauppauge, NY. 23 pp.

Greene, G.T., A.C.F. Mirchel, W.J. Behrens and D.S. Becker. 1977. Surficial sediments and seagrass of eastern Great South Bay, NY. Marine Sciences Research Center Special Report 12. State University of New York at Stony Brook, NY. 23 pp.

Hair, M.E. and S. Buckner. 1973. An assessment of the water quality characteristics of Great South Bay and contiguous streams. Nassau-Suffolk Regional Planning Board. Hauppauge, NY. 59 pp.

Jones, C.R. and J.R. Schubel. 1980. Distributions of surficial sediment and eelgrass in Great South Bay, New York (from Smith Point, West to Wantaugh State Parkway). Marine Sciences Research Center Special Report 39. State University of New York at Stony Brook, NY. 19 pp.

Kaufman, Z., J. Lively and E.J. Carpenter. 1984. Uptake of nitrogenous nutrients by phytoplankton in a barrier island estuary: Great South Bay, New York. Estuarine Coastal Shelf Sci. 17:483-493.

Lively, J., Z. Kaufman and E.J. Carpenter. 1983. Phytoplankton ecology of a barrier island estuary: Great South Bay, New York. Estuarine Coastal Shelf Sci. 16:51-68.

Marshall, N. 1947. Abundance of bay scallops in the absence of eelgrass. Ecology 28:321-322.

McRoy, C.P. and C. McMillan. 1977. Production ecology and physiology of seagrasses. Pages 53-87 *in* C.P. McRoy and C. Hefferich (eds.) Seagrass ecosystems. Marcel Dekker, New York.

Nelson, T.C. 1924. Food and feeding of the oyster. Pages 197-198 *in* New Jersey Expt. Sta. Rept. 1923.

Nienhuis, H. and B.H.H. DeBree. 1977. Productivity and ecology of eelgrass (*Zostera marina L.*) in the Grevelingen Estuary, Netherlands, before and after closing. Hydrobiolgia 52:55-66.

Nixon, S.W. 1981. Remineralization and nutrient cycling in coastal marine ecosystems. Page 111-138 *in* B.J. Neilson and L.W. Cronin, eds. Estuaries and nutrients. Humana Press, New York.

Ryther, J.H. 1954. The ecology of phytoplankton blooms in Moriches Bay and Great South Bay. Biol. Bull. 106: 199-209.

Ryther, J.H. and W.M. Dunstan. 1971. Nitrogen, phosphorus, and eutrophication in the coastal marine environment. Science 117:1008-1013.

Weaver, S. and H. Hirschfield. 1976. Delineation of two plankton communities from one sampling site (Fire Island Inlet, NY). Mar. Biol. 34:273-283.

Wegman, L.S. and Company. 1967. Channel and eelgrass study. Report submitted to Nassau County Dept. of Public Works, Mineola, NY.

Whipple, G. 1912. Effects of diversion of Suffolk County groundwaters upon the oyster industry in the Great South Bay — Reports, resolutions, authorizations, surveys and designs showing sources and manner of obtaining from Suffolk County, Long Island, No Additional Supply of Water for the City of New York. pp. 455-519 *in* New York City Board of Water Supply: Long Island Sources. New York. Vol. 11, Appendix 12.

Wilson, R.S. and A.H. Brenowitz. 1966. A report on the ecology of Great South Bay and adjacent waters. Adelphi University, Garden City, NY. 57 pp.

Wilson, T.C. Jr. 1983. Sulfate reduction and anaerobic decomposition associated with the seagrass *Zostera marina* L. in Great South Bay, Long Island, New York. M.S. Thesis. Marine Sciences Research Center, State University of New York at Stony Brook, NY. 81 pp.

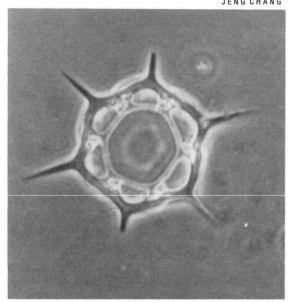

JENG CHANG

Silicoflagellate Distephanus speculum.

One of the remaining duck farms fringing Great South Bay.

R. GEORGE ROWLAND

CHAPTER 6

THE HARD CLAM: ITS BIOLOGY AND THE NATURAL PROCESSES THAT AFFECT ITS SUCCESS

Robert E. Malouf

Marine Sciences Research Center
State University of New York
Stony Brook, NY 11794

TAXONOMY: WHAT IS A HARD CLAM?

The hard clam, or "Northern Quahog" (*Mercenaria mercenaria*), is one of a group of animals known as pelecypod or bivalve molluscs, with gill filaments connected by tissue, two adductor muscles of approximately equal size and a hinge with large "cardinal" teeth (Fig. 6.1). It inhabits estuarine and, less often, inshore coastal waters. It is an active, shallow burrower with short siphons and a relatively large foot. The species ranges from the Gulf of St. Lawrence to Florida (Abbott 1954).

BASIC ANATOMY OF THE HARD CLAM

The most obvious anatomical feature of a hard clam is its shell. The exterior of the shell is generally

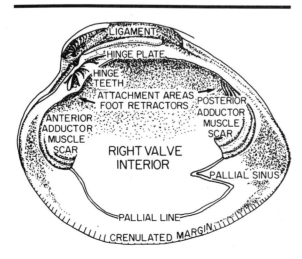

Figure 6.1. Diagram of right valve interior of the hard clam Mercenaria mercenaria.

light brown to white in color, although clams living in dark mud can develop gray or black shells. A few (less than 1%) hard clam shells have irregular red-brown markings (Chanley 1961). The hard clam shell also is characterized by parallel grooves along its ventral margins called crenulations. It is the presence of these crenulations that most clearly distinguishes the shell of a hard clam from that of the virtually inedible "false hard clam," *Pitar morrhuana*.

In profile the shell is shaped like an airfoil, having a more pointed posterior end and a blunter anterior. In the living animal, the more pointed posterior, from which the siphons extend, is positioned upward toward the sediment-water interface.

Like all bivalve molluscs, hard clams have their right and left shells joined dorsally by a ligament that acts in opposition to the adductor muscles to open the shells. Thus, bivalves must exert constant muscular force against the ligament to hold their shells closed. Some burrowing bivalves rely in part on the pressure of the sediment to help hold their shells closed and may tire quickly and gape if they are removed from the sediment. Other bivalves, including hard clams, have the ability to hold their shells closed for days, even when removed from the water. This characteristic allows living clams to be shipped great distances and has played an important role in the development of the hard clam fishery.

The most obvious structures beneath the mantle mass are the two adductor muscles (severed to remove the shell), the large muscular foot extending out the ventral margin of the shells, the retracted siphons and the gills (Fig. 6.2a). Only if the mantle is carefully cut away can the other organs and organ systems be seen (Fig. 6.2b). The large greenish brown mass of the digestive gland ("liver") is sometimes visible through the mantle and can be easily seen if the mantle is cut away. In the center of the digestive gland is the stomach, and in some cases, a long gelatinous rod called the crystalline style, which functions in digestion, can be found nearby in a sac-like structure (Kristensen 1972).

In thickened portions of the mantle tissue,

especially at the base of the foot, is the gonadal (reproductive) tissue. This tissue is particularly evident in spring just prior to the spawning season. At that time, the mantle will appear swollen with milky colored gonadal tissue. Although the sexes are separate in hard clams, there are no anatomical differences between male and female clams. Even during the spawning season, the sexes can be distinguished with certainty only through microscopic examination of gonadal material.

FEEDING AND DIGESTION

Suspension-feeding bivalves rely on the beating of specialized cilia to pump water through their gills. The gill structure is primarily a feeding organ and secondarily an organ of respiration. The gill filaments are heavily ciliated with simple and compound cilia that serve to create a flow of water, as well as to trap and transport particles (Dral 1967; Bayne 1976). Above a threshold particle concentration, excess particles trapped by the gills are rejected in mucous-bound masses called pseudofeces. With the exception of scallops, most bivalves appear to remove particles larger than 5 μm with nearly 100% efficiency (Vahl 1972; Mohlenberg and Riisgard 1978).

Pumping rate is greatly influenced by environmental factors. Common to most physiological processes, it is directly related to temperature up to some maximum temperature tolerance and is also influenced by the types and concentration of suspended particles in the water. In general, pumping rates decline as particle concentration increases; however, different species of bivalves show different degrees of response to increasing particle concentrations. Hard clams, for example, reduce their pumping rates in the presence of increasing particle concentrations (Bricelj 1984).

Because hard clams live buried in the bottom with their siphons nearly flush with the sediment surface, it is inevitable that they will draw in silt particles with their food. It was noted many years ago that silt had a negative influence on the filtration rate of oysters (Loosanoff and Tommers 1948). Only recently, however, has it been shown that the relative concentrations of food and nonfood particles can have as significant an effect as the absolute quantity of food on feeding and growth in bivalves (Widdows et al. 1979). It has also been made clear that the relationship between bivalve growth rate and the concentration of suspended silt in the environment is not a simple one.

It has been shown that many bivalves, including hard clams, have the ability to sort the food particles (phytoplankton) from the nonfood particles (silt) that they filter out of suspension (Kiorbe et al. 1980; Newell and Jordan 1983; Bricelj 1984; Bricelj and Malouf 1984). No bivalve has been shown to be 100% efficient in sorting, but those species that have been studied show some ability to sort and reject silt particles in their pseudofeces. In this way they ingest and process a food-nonfood mixture that contains a higher fraction of food particles than occurs in the natural suspension.

Hard clams are capable of sorting silt from algae. However, they tend to respond to increasing silt loads by reducing their filtration rates, rather than by maintaining relatively high filtration rates and producing large quantities of pseudofeces (Bricelj 1984; Bricelj et al. 1984). Therefore, it appears that hard clams are less well adapted for survival in a turbid environment than many other bivalve species including surf clams, oysters and mussels (Bricelj 1984).

Particles ingested by bivalves pass to the stomach along ciliated tracts through a short esophagus. The interior of the stomach is also ciliated, and ciliated tracts lead particles into the ducts of the digestive gland. Some extracellular digestion occurs in the stomach and digestive gland, but much of the digestion takes place inside the cells of the glands. Larger particles entering the stomach may be shunted directly to the intestine where little or no digestion takes place (Purchon 1971). Apparently some sorting of particles takes place even after the particles have been ingested.

At times when food is very abundant, such as was the case during recent "brown tide" plankton blooms, the digestive system can literally become clogged with particles. When this occurs, some of the food particles may bypass the digestive gland and pass undigested through the intestine. Under these circumstances, food is digested so inefficiently that the animals can starve in the midst of abundant food. Bivalves have been reported to produce two kinds of feces (Van Weel 1961). "Glandular" feces, waste products of the digestive gland, are relatively well digested. "Intestinal" feces are composed of poorly digested material, occasionally even including living phytoplankton.

EXCRETORY SYSTEM

In bivalves, brownish-black paired kidneys are located ventral to the pericardial cavity. The

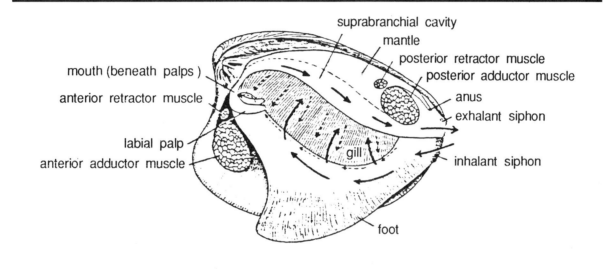

Figure 6.2a. Most obvious structures of the hard clam beneath the mantle mass are the two adductor muscles, muscular foot, gills and retracted siphons (figure 10-97 from Invertebrate zoology, 4th ed., by Robert D. Barnes, copyright © 1980 by Saunders College Publishing, a division of Holt, Rinehart and Winston, Inc., reprinted with permission of the publisher).

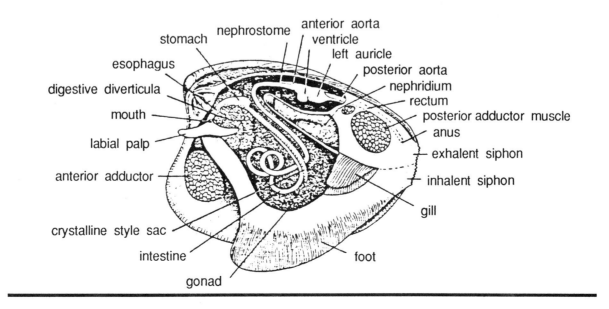

Figure 6.2b. Mantle cut away to show other organs and organ systems (figure 10-97 from Invertebrate zoology, 4th ed. by Robert D. Barnes, copyright 1980 by Saunders College Publishing, a division of Holt, Rinehart and Winston, Inc., reprinted with permission of the publisher).

observation that each kidney is connected to the pericardium by a renopericardial canal led early researchers to conclude that the pericardium had some function in excretion (Galtsoff 1964; Potts 1967), and recent work supports this view (Pirie and George 1979). In the kidney, the urine is modified by resorption and by excretion of granular material.

REPRODUCTION

Bivalves in general, and hard clams in particular, undergo a life cycle that includes a planktonic larval stage and a relatively nonmotile adult stage. The planktonic larval stage, in which the larvae drift in the water for eight to 14 days, provides a means of dispersal. Because these microscopic larvae are subject to extremely high mortality rates, a great many of them must be produced each year to ensure the survival of the species. Bivalves, therefore, invest a significant proportion of their available energy in the annual production of eggs and sperm (gametes).

FECUNDITY

The term "fecundity" refers to the number of viable gametes (usually eggs) produced by an individual animal, an age class or a population. Fecundity can be estimated indirectly by converting weight loss after spawning (weight of gonads) to number of gametes, or directly by repeatedly inducing the animals to spawn and then actually counting the viable gametes released.

Based on work with relatively large animals, Davis and Chanley (1956) estimated that a hard clam produces about 25 million eggs each year. More recent work with hard clams of various sizes from Great South Bay (Bricelj 1979; Bricelj and Malouf 1981) has shown that their fecundity is considerably lower than the earlier estimates indicated:

Clam Size	Eggs Produced Annually Per Individual
Seed (less than 25mm thick)	1.6 million
Little Necks	2.9 million
Cherrystones	5.9 million
Chowders	6.3 million

Bricelj and Malouf (1981) also noted that many of the seed clams could not be induced to spawn at all; the fecundity data (above) does not account for those clams that could not be induced to spawn. They found no significant difference between the fecundities of cherrystones and chowders, although the estimated fecundity values for chowder clams were extremely variable (Fig. 6.3). There was no evidence of reproductive senescence among the older (larger) clams. The eggs released were equally viable among all size classes of clams.

REPRODUCTIVE CYCLES (GAMETOGENESIS)

The annual cycle of egg and sperm production, or gametogenesis, in hard clams has been arbitrarily divided into several stages by a number of authors (e.g. Porter 1964; Keck et al. 1975; Kassner and Malouf 1982). From microscopic examination of thin sections of stained gonadal material it is possible to assign the animal to one of five developmental stages: (1) "indifferent," showing no gamete development; (2) "developing," gametes

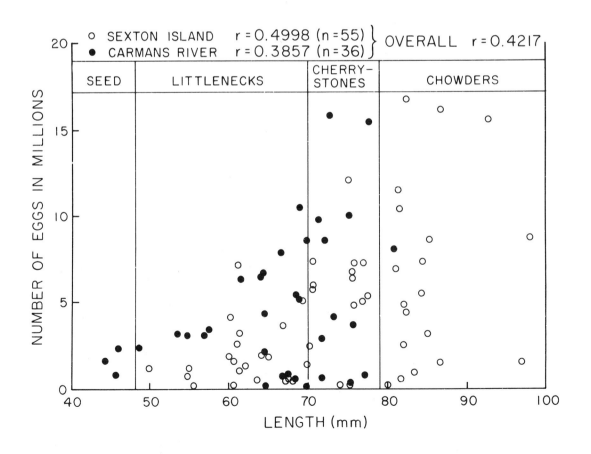

Figure 6.3. The relationship between total annual egg production (fecundity) per female hard clam and shell length in millimeters (r = linear correlation coefficient) (Bricelj and Malouf 1980).

being present but none mature; (3) "mature," gonads being fully ripe with mature gametes; (4) "spawning," showing evidence of loss of mature gametes; and (5) "spent," having very few mature gametes remaining and no indication of new development (Kassner and Malouf 1982).

To permit comparisons among locations or years, a "gonadal index" is sometimes calculated (Kennedy 1977; Kassner and Malouf 1982). Each developmental stage is assigned a numerical value: indifferent = 0.0; developing = 3.0; mature = 4.0; spawning = 2.0; spent = 1.0. This index is essentially a measure of spawning potential. It rises as development proceeds and then declines rapidly once spawning is initiated.

The results of a two-year study of gametogenesis of Great South Bay hard clams is shown in Figure 6.4 (Kassner 1982; Kassner and Malouf 1982). This study showed that the spawning season for Great South Bay hard clams generally peaks in mid-June and terminates in early July. However, there appears to be considerable year-to-year variation in the timing and the intensity of spawning in the Bay.

In 1978 spawning clams were first observed on June 20, but in 1979 spawning began on May 30. The spawning season terminated at about the same time (July 9) in both years. However, it should be noted that in the spring of 1978, Great South Bay water temperatures were approximately 4°C cooler than they were in 1979. It is possible that the earlier spawning in 1979 was related to the warmer temperatures that year. The causes of this variability in hard clams have not been studied.

HARD CLAM LIFE HISTORY

FERTILIZATION

Hard clams, like most bivalves, release eggs and sperm freely into the surrounding water. In laboratory situations male clams, stimulated by a rise in temperature, usually spawn before females. Rising temperatures plus the presence of sperm in the water then stimulate the females to release eggs. Both sperm and eggs have a limited life span once released.

Nonviable sperm may still be highly motile (Ross and Heath 1978) and may still stimulate a female to release eggs. This suggests that the time required for released sperm to encounter a ripe or spawning female could influence the percentage of eggs that become fertilized by that sperm. It further suggests that the distance between males and females could influence success of fertilization and, therefore, the number of larvae produced by a spawning pair of clams.

The possibility that the mean distance between adult clams could influence the effective fecundity of the population has been discussed for many years (e.g. Turner and George 1955); however, no definitive studies have been conducted to evaluate this hypothesis, nor has the longevity of hard clam gametes been determined experimentally.

Estimates of the effective fecundity of clam populations are further complicated by the fact that not all of the eggs released by spawning bivalves have an equal probability of developing into normal larvae, even under the best of conditions. It has been shown that if mussels are not provided with adequate food during gametogenesis, they produce eggs that have insufficient lipid reserves to ensure survival of the larvae (Bayne et al. 1975). It is known that hard clams produce a range of sizes of eggs (Bricelj and Malouf 1981) and that the larger eggs have a higher probability of developing normally than do the smaller ones (Kraeuter et al. 1982).

Fertilization takes place when a single sperm penetrates the egg and the male and female pronuclei fuse. Penetration by the sperm also causes formation of a fertilization membrane which prevents additional sperm from penetrating the egg (Galtsoff 1964). Excess sperm penetration can cause a condition known as "polyspermy," which leads to disintegration of the egg. There is, in fact, an optimum range of egg and sperm concentrations that results in the production of the highest percentage of normal bivalve larvae (Gruffydd and Beaumont 1970). Studies using Great South Bay hard clams demonstrated an optimum ratio of 1:2000 egg per sperm (Bricelj 1979).

LARVAL DEVELOPMENT

After fertilization, the bivalve embryo undergoes a series of cell divisions, which in about 10 hours lead to the development of a transient "trochophore" larva. Within 24 to 48 hours, the trochophore develops into a 75 μm planktonic veliger larva, which is a characteristic stage of development in marine bivalves.

The earliest veliger stage is characterized by a "D" shape of the larval shells. This stage, also called the "straight hinge" stage, lasts one to three days and in hard clams ends when the larvae are about 90-140 μm in shell length. As the larvae grow, they develop a more rounded hinge line ("umbo" or "umbone"), characteristic of the adult clam shape. This larval stage, called the "umboned veliger" stage lasts three to 20 days or until the larvae are 140-220 μm in shell length (Carriker 1961).

When the larvae are six to 20 days old and are 180-230 μm in shell length, they develop a prominent foot and alternate behavior between periods of swimming and crawling. This stage of larval development, called the "pediveliger" stage (Carriker 1956), terminates at metamorphosis, i.e., when the velum is lost. After metamorphosis, hard clam larvae are still dissimilar from adults, lacking siphons and alternating periods of crawling with attachment on or very near the sediment surface. This stage, which lasts until the clams are about 9 mm in shell length, is called the "byssal plantigrade" stage because the clams use long filaments called byssus during their periods of attachment (described by Carriker 1961).

The earliest stages of development in hard clams are the most sensitive to environmental stress. Table 6.1 shows, for example, that hard clam eggs will not fertilize at salinities below about 22 parts per thousand (ppt). However, subsequent larval growth and survival are relatively unaffected by salinities of 20 ppt and lower if the temperature is within the optimum range (about 23 to 28°C). Because larvae can survive and metamorphose in areas where hard clam reproduction cannot otherwise occur (e.g., where salinity is 17.5 ppt), clam populations that

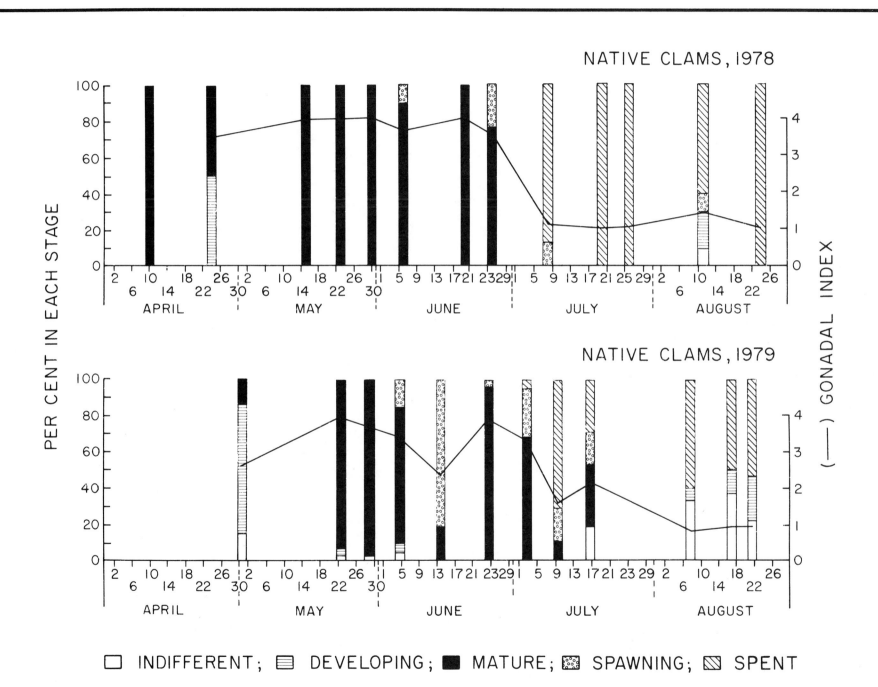

Figure 6.4. Two-year study of gametogenesis of Great South Bay hard clams. (Kassner and Malouf 1983)

are wholly dependent on an influx of larvae from other locations can be created and maintained.

Hard clam larvae have been shown to be relatively resistant to low dissolved oxygen (D.O.) concentrations. They are unaffected by D.O. concentrations as low as 4.2 mg/L and can recover and resume normal development after six days' exposure to a D.O. concentration of only 1.0 mg/L (Morrison 1971). This characteristic allows hard clam larvae to survive transport by currents through areas of low D.O.

For illustrative purposes, an oyster veliger is shown in Figure 6.5. Veligers are protected by a dorsally hinged calcium carbonate (aragonite) bivalve shell. The shells are closed by adductor muscles in essentially the same manner as adult bivalves (Palmer and Carriker 1979). Veligers of the various bivalve species are superficially very similar in appearance. In fact, early veligers of different bivalve species are very difficult to distinguish from one another on the basis of shell morphology (Chanley and Andrews 1971). The unique structure of the shell hinge seems to offer the most promise for developing a reliable scheme for identifying bivalve larvae (Lutz et al. 1982).

Because veligers lack functional gills, the ciliated velum (Fig. 6.5) is important as a site of gas exchange. However, the velum's primary function is as the feeding and swimming organ of the larva. It can be rapidly withdrawn into the larva's shell, an action that causes the larva to sink in the water column.

Bivalve veligers feed primarily on 3-5 μm phytoplankton, particularly flagellates without cell walls. Laboratory studies have demonstrated that there are significant differences in the suitability of various phytoplankton species as food for veligers (see review by Ukeles 1971). It is also known that the food value of an algal species may vary with the age of the veliger or with the conditions under which the algae is grown (Bayne 1976). Because phytoplankton densities in nature tend to be spatially and temporally variable, it is likely that larvae must encounter periods when food is

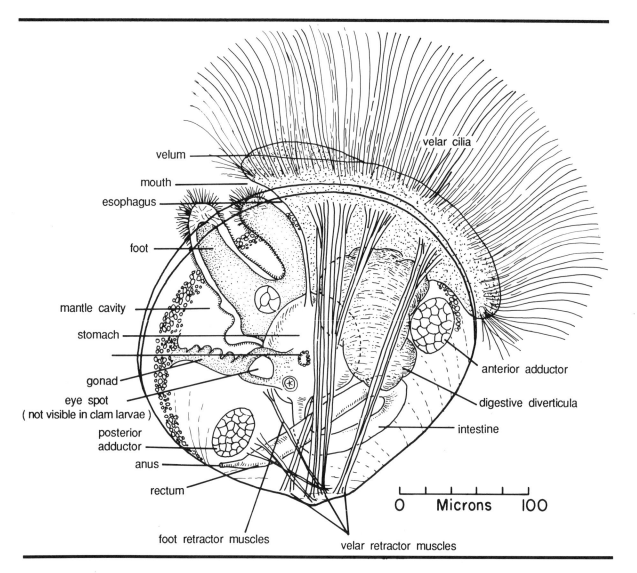

Figure 6.5. Oyster larva (Crassostrea virginica) *showing organ systems and structure typical of bivalve veligers in general.*

qualitatively or quantitatively inadequate.

Veligers are able to survive long periods of starvation; Bayne (1965), for example, showed that mussel veligers could survive up to 26 days without food. Veligers rely on stored lipid reserves when food is scarce (Helm et al. 1973). The rate of food consumption by larvae increases exponentially with shell length, so that large larvae (about 250 μm) consume about 1000 algal cells per hour (Malouf and Breese 1977).

The dark mass of the digestive gland can be seen easily through the veliger's transparent shell. This organ surrounds the stomach and, as in the adult, produces digestive enzymes and functions as the site of intracellular digestion. Droplets of lipid — stored food reserves — are clearly visible in the digestive gland of healthy larvae. In older larvae it is also possible to see the rotating crystalline style.

Table 6.1. Fertilization, larval survival and larval growth for hard clams *(Mercenaria mercenaria)* in various combinations of temperature and salinity.[a]

Percent of Eggs Developing Normally

Salinity (ppt.)	Temperature °C								
	32.5	30.0	27.5	25.0	22.5	20.0	17.5	15.0	12.5
27.0	39	81	93	95	92	95	94	24	0
22.5	1	36	65	79	73	73	52	1	1
20.0	0	0	0	5	0	0	0	0	0
17.5	0	0	0	0	0	0	0	0	0
15.0	0	0	0	0	0	0	0	0	0
12.5	0	0	0	0	0	0	0	0	0

Percent of Larvae Surviving After 10 Days

Salinity (ppt.)	Temperature °C								
	32.5	30.0	27.5	25.0	22.5	20.0	17.5	15.0	12.5
27.0	77	83	81	75	87	75	71	61	56
22.5	48	84	87	83	88	76	70	56	46
20.0	16	72	84	76	77	78	62	50	40
17.5	1	76	74	83	85	69	45	50	49
15.0	0	25	22	57	53	43	58	36	47
12.5	0	1	0	12	0	9	12	19	39

Percent Increase in Length of Larvae After 10 Days

Salinity (ppt.)	Temperature °C								
	32.5	30.0	27.5	25.0	22.5	20.0	17.5	15.0	12.5
27.0	65	98	83	93	83	71	53	30	16
22.5	61	91	85	88	83	68	48	25	12
20.0	54	85	87	82	80	60	39	17	5
17.5	5	63	68	66	59	36	21	5	1
15.0	0	12	17	31	20	9	3	1	0
12.5	0	0	0	2	0	0	0	0	0

[a]Adapted from original table by Davis, H.C. and A. Calabrese, 1964. Combined effects of temperature and salinity on development of eggs and growth of larvae of *M. mercenaria* and *C. virginica*. Fish. Bull. 63(3):643-655.

LARVAL BEHAVIOR AND DISPERSAL

The horizontal swimming ability of bivalve larvae is far too weak to account for their observed widespread dispersal. Laboratory studies have shown, for example, that the maximum horizontal swimming speed of small (75 μm) oyster veligers is 0.6 to 2.0 cm/min (Hidu and Haskin 1978). Horizontal swimming speeds of large (300 μm) oyster larvae were found to be about 5 cm/min. In the highly unlikely event that the larvae maintained this swimming speed continuously, they could travel no more than 72 m/d.

Despite this weak swimming ability, oyster larvae are not flushed out of estuaries or transported passively, but show a net upestuary movement during their larval period (Wood and Hargis 1971). This apparent contradiction (i.e., retention despite very weak swimming ability) has been the subject of considerable study and speculation. Although Moore and Marshall (1967) attempted to explain retention irrespective of larval behavior, vertical migration patterns rather than horizontal swimming appear to offer the most plausible solution to the question, at least for oyster larvae.

That veliger larvae of bivalves move vertically in the water has been known for many years (reviewed by Mileikovsky 1973). Both laboratory and field studies have shown quite clearly that these larvae respond to external stimuli and alter their vertical position in the water column. Carriker (1961) concluded that clam larvae maintain themselves away from the bottom during daylight and descend to the bottom during darkness.

Haskin (1964) reviewed field studies that showed an increased abundance of bivalve larvae on or near the bottom during slack or ebb tide and an increased abundance high in the water column during flood tide. His laboratory studies showed that oyster larvae respond to increasing salinity (flood tide) by increasing their vertical swimming activity. Conversely, their swimming was reduced as salinity declined (ebb tide) and the larvae sank toward the bottom. This behavior, confirmed in later work by Hidu and Haskin (1978), would allow the larvae to utilize residual or net nontidal[1] currents to move upstream. Larvae would be high in the water column, and, therefore, strongly affected by flood tides, but they would be near the bottom where currents are minimal during ebb tides. This mechanism could help retain larvae in an estuary and could account for an upstream net movement.

Under some circumstances these vertical movements by larvae could influence their horizontal dispersal. However, it should be kept in mind that vertical migrations have been more clearly shown for oysters than for clams, and the situation in a shallow, well-mixed estuary such as Great South Bay may be complicated by the lack of clear vertical gradients. It is also important to keep in mind that there is no evidence for horizontal migration among veliger larvae. Although horizontal movement may be influenced by vertical migration, veliger larvae can move horizontally only where the currents carry them.

LARVAL MORTALITY

Most hard clam veliger larvae that are produced each season do not survive to metamorphosis. There are few estimates of larval survival in the field, but logic and some simple mathematics permit an estimate of what the magnitude of larval mortality must be. Consider that an adult female hard clam may produce 5 million larvae each season for 10 years, for a total of 50 million larvae during its lifetime. If two of those larvae survived to become adults, the female would have replaced herself and one male. In other words, given those conditions, the clam could tolerate a mortality from egg to adult of 99.999994%. This simple exercise is not intended to produce a precise estimate of larval mortality, but it does illustrate the probable scale of that mortality.

In his studies of hard clam populations in Little Egg Harbor, New Jersey, Carriker (1961) reported an average larval survival of about 2% from early to late planktonic stage. However, his data show considerable variation, and there are a number of situations where he reported 0% survival. Other studies of hard clams have shown that successful recruitment is episodic and not annual (Greene 1978; Kennish 1978).

In studies of the soft clam (*Mya arenaria*), Brousseau (1978) showed that spawning events producing the largest number of larvae did not necessarily produce the largest number of juvenile clams. Studies of other bivalves have shown that there is not a clear relationship between the number of larvae that set at a location and the number that survive to harvestable size (Muus 1973). It would seem, then, that mortality among bivalve larvae (and juveniles) is both high and variable. The presence of a large number of larvae or newly set clams is no guarantee that a large number of harvestable clams will result.

The causes of larval mortality have not been clearly documented. Much of the mortality is probably due to their dispersal into unfavorable environments. Larvae are also known to be lost to planktivorous predators, including ctenophores (Quayle 1969), anemones and barnacles (Steinberg and Kennedy 1979).

It has also been shown that adult hard clams readily filter out their own larvae from suspension (Kurkowski 1980). The adults do not appear to actually ingest the larvae that they filter out of the water, but rather reject them in pseudofeces. The thin shells of the smallest larvae are broken by this process. The largest larvae are not physically damaged, but they are unable to free themselves from the mucus and eventually die. Only the midsized umboned larvae (e.g., 170 μm) appear to be relatively unaffected by filtration by adults (Kurkowski 1980).

METAMORPHOSIS

Metamorphosis, sometimes called "setting" is a process that occurs over a period of several days. Metamorphosis is considered to be completed when the velum has completely degenerated and the gills are functioning in respiration and feeding.

During the process of metamorphosis, bivalve

---

[1]The current that remains after the tidal component has been removed.

larvae are unable to feed normally. To survive they must rely on lipid reserves, primarily stored in the digestive gland. If the lipid reserves are inadequate, the larvae will not survive metamorphosis (Gallager and Mann 1981). Food availability during larval growth and the nutritional status of the larvae at the time of metamorphosis will have a significant impact on whether or not the larvae will be recruited to the clam population.

HARD CLAM DISTRIBUTION

SETTING

An important feature of setting by hard clams and oysters is that it is spatially nonrandom; that is, larval clams and oysters are stimulated to set at particular sites by a number of factors. This behavior could, to a certain extent, determine the ultimate distribution of adults. Hidu (1969) showed that when one oyster larva set, it increased the probability that another would set nearby. There is some evidence that this "gregarious" setting results from a waterborne pheromone (Veitch and Hidu 1971; Hidu et al. 1978).

Hard clam larvae also have the ability to select a setting site. Under otherwise identical laboratory conditions, hard clams were shown to strongly favor a sand bottom over mud (Keck et al. 1973). This preference was maintained even when the mud and sand were free of organic matter. Keck et al. (1973) also showed that if sediments were treated with unrefined liquids from homogenized adult clams, preference by clams for that sediment increased greatly.

DISPERSAL AFTER SETTING

There is some evidence that the passive movement of postset clams is important in determining the distribution of adults. No definitive studies of postset dispersal of hard clams have been reported. However, Baggerman (1953) reported that young cockles (*Cardium edule*) were transported by currents for at least four weeks after metamorphosis, or until they reached about 2 mm in length. He noted that the cockles tended to accumulate in "quiet places."

Based on observations of distribution patterns of postset hard clams in the field, Carriker (1961) noted that postset clams tend "to move into shaded microhabitats" such as cupped shells and crevices. Carriker also pointed out that it was possible that the observed higher abundances of postset clams in microhabitats could in part be a result of enhanced survival in these protected areas, as well as resulting partly from favored site selection.

GROWTH AND SURVIVAL OF ADULT CLAMS

Surveys of adult clam populations in Great South Bay (WAPORA, Inc. 1981) and in other areas have shown their distribution is nonrandom, or "patchy." Attempts have been made to relate high abundances in certain areas to some environmental variable. A study by Wells (1957) of the clam distribution in Chincoteague Bay, Virginia found that the fewest clams were in mud, more in sand-mud mixtures, still more in sand and the highest densities of all in shell-covered sand. He also noted that clams were excluded from areas where salinities dropped below 20 ppt between January and June. In a study of hard clam distribution in the Providence River, Rhode Island, Saila et al. (1967) related clam abundance to eight environmental variables. Of those variables examined, only sediment particle size and sediment organic content contributed significantly to clam distribution.

From these studies we can conclude that hard clams are gregarious in their distribution and that they show a preference for sand. It should be noted that the distribution of adult clams is profoundly affected by their growth and survival. Dense patches of clams in sandy environments could be the result of enhanced survival in those environments. It is also quite possible that it is some related variable (such as current velocity) in addition to or instead of the direct effects of sediment grain size that leads to higher clam abundance in sand.

Because larger clams have a higher probability of survival than do smaller clams, growth rate and survival are closely linked. In controlled field experiments Pratt and Campbell (1956)

demonstrated that hard clams grow faster in sand than in mud, even when other environmental variables are held constant. In their study they found that growth was not influenced by current speed, D.O. concentration (above 5 mg/L) or Bay salinity between 21 and 32 ppt. They also found a significant negative relationship between clam growth and the abundance of flagellated phytoplankton less than 15 μm in diameter.

In laboratory studies, Bass (1983) showed that juvenile hard clams were capable of filtering and ingesting several species of "small form" flagellates, but that they were not able to digest them. It is interesting to note that Greene (1978) found that the clams in the eastern end of Great South Bay near the mouth of the Carmans River showed exceptionally low growth rates. Carpenter (pers. comm. 1982) found densities of small form flagellates up to 1 billion per liter in the Carmans River area.

HARD CLAM PREDATORS

Young hard clams (less than 10 mm) are subject to predation by a large variety of organisms. Some species that prey on very small clams are generally not thought of as predators. For example, grass shrimp (*Paleomonetes*) were observed carrying off 1-3 mm hard clams being planted by the Town of Brookhaven (Jeffrey Kassner, pers. comm. 1979). Both *Paleomonetes* and the sand shrimp *Crangon* were found in lab studies to be able to crush and consume newly set hard clams up to 0.5 mm in shell length (Gibbons 1984).

Hermit crabs (*Pagurus longicarpus*) can consume up to 240 1 mm hard clams per day under laboratory conditions (Gibbons 1984). These small crabs can crush hard clams up to 3 mm in shell length. Finfish, particularly flounders, also may consume small hard clams (Poole 1964). Several types of rays are known to be voracious hard clam predators on the Eastern Shore of Virginia (Castagna and Kraeuter 1977), and a number of species of ducks and geese have been observed preying on juvenile soft shell clams, *Mya arenaria*

(Schwind 1977). It is possible that they also prey on very small hard clams, although this has not been clearly documented. In intertidal situations, gulls can prey on subadult and adult hard clams. In fact, one study in England showed that herring gulls were the most important hard clam predator on one intertidal mud flat in Southampton (Hibbert 1977).

The dominant predators of 1-10 mm hard clams in Great South Bay are mud crabs (*Neopanope sayi*), calico crabs (*Ovalipes ocellatus*) and oyster drills (*Urosalpinx cinerea*) (MacKenzie 1977, WAPORA, Inc. 1981). Of these three major predator species, the mud crab is the most important because of the combined effects of its high density, great reproductive capacity and high predation rate, using heavy crushing claws that are well adapted to preying on hard clams. Adult mud crabs (15-20 mm wide) can consume 50 to 100 clams per day, can consume hard clams up to 7 mm in length (Gibbons 1984) and occur in isolated patches at densities up to 100/m² in shell or gravel bottoms in Great South Bay (WAPORA, Inc. 1981).

Field experiments in eastern Long Island have shown that mud crabs can easily decimate patches of hard clams (less than 10 mm shell length) in a matter of weeks (Flagg and Malouf 1983). The impact of these predators on natural populations in the Bay is clearly significant (MacKenzie 1977).

In general, mud crabs and calico crabs can consume hard clams that are up to 30% of their carapace width. As hard clams grow larger, fewer predator species are able to attack them. However, there are a number of predators that will attack even the largest hard clams. In Great South Bay, whelks (*Busycon carica*, and *B. canaliculatum*), moon snails (*Polinices duplicatus*) and starfish (*Asterias forbesi*) are the major predators of adult hard clams.

Whelks prey on hard clams by grasping the clam with its muscular foot and then using their own shell to rasp and chip the clam shell until an opening is created. Since this is a time-consuming process, whelks have predation rates of only 0.10 to 0.25 clams per whelk per day (Carriker 1951). A moonsnail grasps the clam with its foot and drills a small hole through the clam's shell using acidic secretions and a rasping radula. This is also a time-consuming process, and moonsnail predation rates are generally 0.02 to 0.10 clams per snail per day (Carriker 1951; Greene 1978). Starfish grasp the clam's shell with the suction of thousands of tube feet on their powerful arms. They exert great force on the clam trying to pull its shell open. Eventually the clam tires and the starfish is able to insert its feeding organs into a slight opening in the clam's shell. Starfish predation rates on hard clams have not been well documented.

Although whelks, moonsnails and probably starfish have predation rates that are significantly lower than those given for crabs preying on small clams, their effect on the clam population can be significant. The overall impact of the loss of a clam that is capable of reproducing is much greater than the loss of an immature "seed" clam.

CONCLUSION

If one could design a clam for the Great South Bay shellfishery, it would be difficult to improve on the hard clam *Mercenaria mercenaria*. Hard clams have an enormous reproductive capacity, are relatively hardy and fast-growing and their resistance to desiccation makes them ideal for shipping and marketing. On the other hand, there is a limit to the abuse that can be tolerated by natural populations of even this resilient species.

Overfishing and environmental degradation have taken their toll on the Bay's hard clams, and the fishery has declined sharply from its peak in 1976. Clearly, as research and experience teach us more about the biology of hard clams, our ability to manage and utilize this species will greatly improve. However, it still remains for us to make the best use of what we know and to assemble management plans that merge the best available biological information with the social and economic realities of shellfishery management.

REFERENCES

Abbott, R.T. 1954. American Seashells. D. Van Nostrand Co., Inc., New York. 541 pp.

Baggerman, B. 1953. Spatfall and transport of *Cardium edule* (L.). Arch. Neerl. Zool. 10:315-342.

Bass, A.E. 1983. Growth of hard clams, *Mercenaria mercenaria*, feeding on picoplankton. M.S. Thesis, Marine Sciences Research Center, State University of New York at Stony Brook, NY. 66 pp.

Bayne, B.L. 1965. Growth and delay of metamorphosis of the larvae of *Mytilus edulis* (L.). Ophelia 2:1-47.

_____. 1976. Marine mussels: Their ecology and physiology. IBP no. 10. Cambridge Univ. Press, Cambridge. 506 pp.

Bayne, B.L., P.A. Gabbott, and J. Widdows. 1975. Some effects of stress in the adult on the eggs and larvae of *Mytilus edulis* L. J. Mar. Biol. Assoc. U.K. 55:675-689.

Bricelj, V.M. 1979. Fecundity and related aspects of hard clam (*Mercenaria mercenaria*) reproduction in Great South Bay, New York. M.S. Thesis, Marine Sciences Research Center, State University of New York at Stony Brook, NY. 98 pp.

_____. 1984. Effects of suspended sediments on the feeding physiology and growth of the hard clam. *Mercenaria mercenaria* L. Ph.D. Thesis, Marine Sciences Research Center, State University of New York at Stony Brook, NY. 157 pp.

Bricelj, V.M. and R.E. Malouf. 1981. Aspects of reproduction of hard clams (*Mercenaria mercenaria*) in Great South Bay, New York. Proc. Nat. Shellfish. Assoc. 70(2):216-229.

_____. 1984. The influence of suspended sediment concentrations on the feeding physiology of the hard clam *Mercenaria mercenaria* (L.). Mar. Biol. 84:155-165.

Bricelj, V.M., R.E. Malouf, and C. de Quillfeldt. 1984. Growth of juvenile *Mercenaria mercenaria* (L.) and the effect of resuspended sediments. Mar. Biol. 84:167-173.

Brousseau, D.J. 1978. Population dynamics of the soft shell clam *Mya arenaria*. Mar. Biol. 50:63-71.

Carriker, M.R. 1951. Observations on the penetration of tightly closing bivalves by *Busycon* and other predators. Ecology 32(1):73-83.

_____. 1956. Biology and propagation of young hard clams, *Mercenaria mercenaria*. J. Elisha Mitchell Sci. Soc. 72:57-60.

_____. 1961. Interrelation of functional morphology, behavior, and autecology in early stages of the bivalve *Mercenaria mercenaria*. J. Elisha Mitchell Sci. Soc. 77(2):168-241.

Castagna, M. and J.N. Kraeuter. 1977. *Mercenaria* culture using stone aggregate for predator protection. Proc. Nat. Shellfish. Assoc. 67:1-6.

Chanley, P.E. 1961. Inheritance of shell markings and growth in the hard clam, *Venus mercenaria*. Proc. Nat. Shellfish. Assoc. 50:163-169.

Chanley, P.E. and J.D. Andrews. 1971. Aids for the identification of bivalve larvae of Virginia. Malacologia 11(1): 45-119.

Davis, H.C. and A. Calabrese. 1964. Combined effects of temperature and salinity on development of eggs and growth of larvae of *M. mercenaria* and *C. virginica*. Fish. Bull. 63(3):643-655.

avis, H.C. and P.E. Chanley. 1956. Spawning and g production of oysters and clams. Biol. Bull. 0(2):117-128.

ral, A.D.G. 1967. The movements of the latero-ontal cilia and the mechanism of particle retention the mussel (*Mytilus edulis* L.). Neth. J. Sea Res. 3):391-422.

agg, P.J. and R.E. Malouf. 1983. Experimental antings of juvenile hard clams, *Mercenaria ercenaria*, in the waters of Long Island, New ork. J. Shellfish. Res. 3(1):19-27.

allager, S.M. and R. Mann. 1981. Use of lipid ecific staining techniques for assaying condition cultured bivalve larvae. J. Shellfish. Res. 1):69-74.

altsoff, P.S. 1964. The American Oyster rassostrea virginica* Gmelin. U.S. Dept. Interior, r. Comm. Fish., Fish. Bull. 64, iii + 480 pp.

bbons, M.C. 1984. Aspects of predation by crabs *opanope sayi, Ovalipes ocellatus,* and *Pagurus ngicarpus* on juvenile hard clams *Mercenaria ercenaria*. Ph.D. Thesis, Marine Sciences search Center, State University of New York at ony Brook, NY. 96 pp.

eene, G.T. 1978. Population structure, growth, d mortality of hard clams at selected locations Great South Bay, New York. M.S. Thesis, arine Sciences Research Center, State University New York, Stony Brook, NY. 199 pp.

uffydd, L.D. and A.R. Beaumont. 1970. etermination of optimum concentration of eggs d spermatozoa for the production of normal rvae in *Pecten maximus* (Mollusca, mellibranchia). Helgo. wiss. Meeresunters 486-497.

Haskin, H.H. 1964. The distribution of oyster larvae. Proc. Symp. Exptl. Mar. Ecol. Occasional Publication No. 2, Graduate School of Oceanography, University of Rhode Island. pp. 76-80.

Helm, M.M., D.L. Holland, and R.R. Stephenson. 1973. The effect of supplementary algal feeding of a hatchery breeding stock of *Ostrea edulis* L. on larval vigour. J. Mar. Biol. Assoc. U.K. 53:673-684.

Hibbert, C.J. 1977. Growth and survivorship in a tidal-flat population of the bivalve *Mercenaria mercenaria* from Southampton Water. Mar. Biol. 44(1):71-76.

Hidu, H. 1969. Gregarious setting in the American oyster *Crassostrea virginica* (Gmelin). Chesapeake Sci. 10(2):85-92.

Hidu, H. and H. Haskin. 1978. Swimming speeds of oyster larvae *Crassostrea virginica* in different salinities and temperatures. Estuaries 1(4):252-255.

Hidu, H., W.G. Valleau, and F.P. Veitch. 1978. Gregarious setting in European and American oyster — response to surface chemistry vs. waterborne pheromones. Proc. Nat. Shellfish Assoc. 68:11-16.

Kassner, J. 1982. The gametogenic cycle of the hard clam, *Mercenaria mercenaria*, from different locations in the Great South Bay, New York. M.S. Thesis. Marine Sciences Research Center, State University of New York at Stony Brook, NY. 72 pp.

Kassner, J. and R.E. Malouf. 1982. An evaluation of "spawner transplants" as a management tool in Long Island's hard clam fishery. J. Shellfish. Res. 2(2):165-172.

Keck, R.T., D. Maurer, and H. Lind. 1975. A comparative study of the hard clam gonad development cycle. Biol. Bull. 148:243-258.

Keck, R.T., D. Maurer, and R.E. Malouf. 1973. Factors influencing the setting behavior of larval hard clams, *Mercenaria mercenaria*. Proc. Nat. Shellfish Assoc. 64:59-67.

Kennedy, V.S. 1977. Reproduction in *Mytilus edulis auteanua* and *Aulacomya maoriana* (Mollusca: Bivalvia) from Taylors Mistake, New Zealand. N.Z.J. Mar. Freshwater Res. 11(2):253-267.

Kennish, M.J. 1978. Effects of thermal discharge on mortality of *Mercenaria mercenaria* in Barnegat Bay, New Jersey. Environ. Geol. 2(4):233-254.

Kiorbe, T., F. Mohlenberg, and O. Nohr. 1980. Feeding, particle selection and carbon absorption in *Mytilus edulis* in different mixtures of algae and resuspended bottom material. Ophelia 19(2):193-205.

Kraeuter, J.N., M. Castagna, and R. Van Dessel. 1982. Egg size and larval survival of *Mercenaria mercenaria* (L.) and *Argopecten irradians* (Lammarck). J. Exp. Mar. Biol. Ecol. 56:3-8.

Kristensen, J.H. 1972. Structure and function of crystalline styles of bivalves. Ophelia 10:91-108.

Kurkowski, K.P. 1980. Effects of filtration by adult *Mercenaria mercenaria* upon its larvae. M.S. Thesis, Marine Sciences Research Center, State University of New York at Stony Brook, NY. 73 pp.

Lossanoff, V.L. and F.D. Tommers. 1948. Effect of suspended silt and other susbstances on rate of feeding of oysters. Science 107:69-70.

Lutz, R., J. Goodsell, M. Castagna, S. Chapman, C. Newell, H. Hidu, R. Mann, D. Jablonski, V. Kennedy, S. Siddall, R. Goldberg, H. Beattie, C. Falmagne, A. Chestnut, and A. Partridge. 1982. Preliminary observations on the usefulness of hinge structures for identification of bivalve larvae. J. Shellfish. Res. 2(1):65-70.

MacKenzie, C.L. 1977. Predation on hard clam (*Mercenaria mercenaria*) populations. Trans. Am. Fish. Soc. 106(6):530-537.

Malouf, R.E. and W.P. Breese. 1977. Food consumption and growth of larvae of the Pacific oyster, *Crassostrea gigas* (Thunberg), in a constant flow rearing system. Proc. Nat. Shellfish. Assoc. 67:7-16.

Mileikovsky, S.A. 1973. Speed of active movement of pelagic larvae of marine bottom invertebrates and their ability to regulate their vertical position. Mar. Biol. 23:11-17.

Mohlenberg, F. and H.V. Riisgard. 1978. Efficiency of particle retention in 13 species of suspension feeding bivalves. Ophelia 17:239-246.

Moore, J.K. and N. Marshall. 1967. The retention of lamellibranch larvae in the Niantic estuary. Veliger 10(1):10-12.

Morrison, G. 1971. Dissolved oxygen requirements for embryonic and larval development of the hardshell clam, *Mercenaria mercenaria*. J. Fish. Res. Board Can. 28(3):379-381.

Muus, K. 1973. Settling, growth, and mortality of young bivalves in the Oresund. Ophelia 12:79-116.

Newell, R.I.E. and S.J. Jordan. 1983. Preferential ingestion of organic material by the American oyster *Crassostrea virginica*. Mar. Ecol. Prog. Ser. 13:47-53.

Palmer, R.E. and M.R. Carriker. 1979. Effects of culture conditions on the morphology of the shell of the oyster *Crassostrea virginica*. Proc. Nat. Shellfish. Assoc. 69:58-72.

Pirie, B.J.S. and S.G. George. 1979. Ultrafiltration of the heart and excretory system of *Mytilus edulis* (L.). J. Mar. Biol. Assoc. U.K. 59:819-829.

Poole, J.C. 1964. Feeding habits of the summer flounder in Great South Bay. N.Y. Fish Game J. 11(1):28-34.

Porter, H.J. 1964. Seasonal gonadal changes in adult clams, *Mercenaria mercenaria* (L.), in North Carolina. Proc. Natl. Shellfish. Assoc. 55:35-52.

Potts, W.T.W. 1967. Excretion in the molluscs. Biol. Rev. 42:1-41.

Pratt, D.M. and D.A. Campbell. 1956. Environmental factors affecting the growth of *Mercenaria*. Limnol. Oceanogr. 1:2-17.

Purchon, R.D. 1971. Digestion in filter feeding bivalves — a new concept. Proc. Malacol. Soc. Lond. 39:253-262.

Quayle, D.B. 1969. Pacific oyster culture in British Columbia. Fish. Res. Board Can. Bull. 169. 192 pp.

Ross, C.D. and E. Heath. 1978. Viability of American oyster, *Crassostrea virginica* spermatozoa exposed to stress. Estuaries 1(4):245-251.

Saila, S.B., J.M. Flowers, and M.T. Cannario. 1967. Factors affecting the relative abundance of *Mercenaria mercenaria* in the Providence River, Rhode Island. Proc. Nat. Shellfish. Assoc. 57:83-89.

Schwind, P. 1977. Practical Shellfish Farming. International Marine Publishing Co., Camden, ME. 91 pp.

Steinberg, P.D. and V.S. Kennedy. 1979. Predation upon *Crassostrea virginica* (Gmelin) larvae by two invertebrate species common to Chesapeake Bay oyster bars. Veliger 22(1):78-84.

Turner, H.J. and C.J. George. 1955. Some aspects of the behavior of the Quahog, *Venus mercenaria*, during the early stages. 8th Rpt. Invest. Shellf. Mass. Dep. Nat. Resour. Div. Mar. Fish., Commonwealth Mass. pp. 5-14.

Ukeles, R. 1971. Nutritional requirements in shellfish culture. Pages 43-64 *in* K. Price and P. Mourer, eds. Artificial propagation of commercially valuable shellfish. University of Delaware Press, Newark, DE.

Van Weel, P.B. 1961. The comparative physiology of digestion in molluscs. Am. Zool. 1:245-252.

Veitch, F.P. and H. Hidu. 1971. Gregarious setting in American oysters, *Crassostrea virginica* (Gmelin), I. Properties of a partially purified "setting factor." Chesapeake Sci. 12(3):173-178.

WAPORA, Inc. 1981. Estuarine impact assessment (Shellfish Resources) for the Nassau-Suffolk streamflow augmentation alternatives, draft report on existing conditions. U.S. Environ. Prot. Agency. New York. 114 pp.

Wells, H.W. 1957. Abundance of hard clams, *Mercenaria mercenaria* in relation to environmental factors. Ecology 38(1):123-128.

Widdows, J., P. Fieth and C.M. Worrall. 1979. Relationships between seston, available food, and feeding activity in the common mussel *Mytilus edulis*. Mar. Biol. 50:195-207.

Wood, L. and W.J. Hargis. 1971. Transport of bivalve larvae in a tidal estuary. Pages 29-44 *in* D.J. Crisp, ed. Fourth European marine biology symposium. Cambridge University Press, London.

THE HARD CLAM FISHERY PAST AND PRESENT

J.L. McHugh

Marine Sciences Research Center
State University of New York
Stony Brook, NY 11794

INTRODUCTION

When Europeans first came to the shores of North America they found that the Indians used shells as money. Wampum was made by Indian tribes living along the coast from New England to Virginia. White wampum was usually made from whelk shells (*Busycon*) and was worth much less than black wampum, which came from the small purple section of the hard clam, or quahog *Mercenaria mercenaria* (Abbott 1972). In fact, the scientific name is supposed to have arisen from the use of the shell as money (Belding 1912). The shells were made into beads, usually one-third inch in diameter and one-eighth inch long, and drilled through the center so that they could be strung. The hard clam was also, next to oysters, the most popular seafood among Indians and Europeans.

The Indians first used wampum as ornaments and, in the form of long, wide belts, to record treaties, declarations and important transactions between Indian nations. Wampum was dyed various colors and shades so that very intricate designs and patterns could be woven into the belts. Soon after the coming of the white man, wampum was used as currency by Indians and whites. A six-foot strand was worth about five shillings, about $1.25 at that time. In the early 1700s, it could even be used on the Brooklyn ferry for passage.

Two enterprising Scotsmen set up a wampum factory in northern New Jersey, which flourished for several years. But wampum was finally outlawed as a form of currency when the market became flooded with counterfeits in the early 1800s (Abbott 1972).

DISTRIBUTION IN THE UNITED STATES

According to Verrill (1873) *Venus (Mercenaria) mercenaria*, the hard clam or quahog, is very abundant from Cape Cod to Florida. North of Cape Cod it is comparatively rare and local, and on the coast of Maine and in the Bay of Fundy it occurs only in small, sheltered bays where the water is shallow and warm. In the southern part of the Gulf of Saint Lawrence, where water is warmer and shallower than on the Maine coast, it occurs in some abundance. Ingersoll (1887) said much the same thing and pointed out that it was especially abundant around Long Island, New York and in New Jersey. Farther south, especially from North Carolina and the southern states, not many were harvested.

Ganong (1890) pointed out that north of Cape Cod, hard clams are identical with those to the south but are entirely cut off from them, relying upon shallow water in sheltered areas for the temperature to rise high enough to spawn. In certain areas of Maine, Indian shell heaps contain large quantities of quahog shells at places where they are now extinct or scarce and small. They obviously spawn only when water temperature is high enough, so that their abundance is highly variable, and this has been confirmed by Dow (1972, 1973).

Although *Venus (Mercenaria) mercenaria* ranges from the Gulf of St. Lawrence to Florida, it is most common in Massachusetts, Rhode Island, New York, New Jersey, and Virginia (Loosanoff 1946). Tiller et al. (1952) gave considerable detail about the hard clam fishery from Maine to Florida, and stated that at that time New York, New Jersey, Rhode Island, and Massachusetts, in that order, produced 85% of the total catch.

Chestnut (1953) was apparently the first to recognize that a closely-related species *Mercenaria campechiensis* is taken in Core Sound, North Carolina, and Merrill and Ropes (1967) extended the range northward to Point Pleasant, North Carolina. This clam, the southern quahog, is now known to be distributed north to New Jersey in

offshore waters. Northern and southern quahogs are closely related and can easily be hybridized. The hybrids have the fast growth of the southern species and the keeping qualities of the northern species, so potentially could compete with *Mercenaria mercenaria*.

INTRODUCTIONS ON THE PACIFIC COAST

Hanna (1966) has summarized introductions of *Venus (Mercenaria) mercenaria* from the Atlantic coast to the Pacific coast of North America. This species was planted in Humboldt Bay, California, and survival has been good. Hard clams were planted in Drake's Estero and Tomales Bay, where they survived and Morro Bay and San Francisco Bay, where they apparently did not. Salchak and Haas (1971) reported that although there are no records of introductions into Colorado Lagoon in southern California, its presence was first recognized in 1967, and they have become well established.

INTRODUCTIONS INTO EUROPE

The most complete account of the history of introductions into Europe to date was given by Heppell (1961). A major commercial fishery began in Southampton Water in 1965, and some have been exported back to the United States as landings have dropped here. Gibson and Duggan (1970, 1973) found that hard clams could be grown in Ireland, but water temperatures were too low for reproduction. A flourishing clam fishery is centered around Mornac and Marennes in France, from introductions started in 1910. In Brittany, Marteil (1956) found large hard clams in several places, from introductions which began about 1936. They breed successfully there, and may have been the source of hard clams around Southampton Water from drifting of larvae, although Mitchell (1974a,b) said that these colonies were introduced deliberately.

LANDINGS ALONG THE COAST

Considerable quantities of hard clams have been harvested in the middle Atlantic region, where greatest abundance occurs, since at least as far back as 1880 when records of fishery landings were first kept by the federal government. New England was second in abundance, then the Chesapeake Bay states and finally the south Atlantic coast from North Carolina to the east coast of Florida, inclusive.

Production fell off after the turn of the century and apparently reached a low point during the 1910s and 1920s. The exact time of the low is not known because records were kept for only a few scattered years prior to 1929 (Fig. 7.1). This drop in landings was said to have been caused by overfishing and by preemption of clam bottom by the growing oyster industry (Kellogg 1903; Belding 1912). In retrospect, it appears likely that the oyster industry was the principal offender, because oystering was at its peak early in the twentieth century and much of the bottom was leased to oyster growers. Thus, the clams there would not be available to clammers, and at any rate, the men were for the most part employed in oystering, and clamming was at best a part-time occupation.

Hard clams obviously were taken in New England and along the middle Atlantic coast earlier than 1880, but not much is known of the history of the fishery before that time. Prices were low, and in New England at least, clams were looked upon, for the most part, as a standby food for hard times — a food not in keeping with American culture and affluence. Many clams were eaten locally and probably not sold at all, and many homes of that time had a store of clams held in wet seaweed.

In 1880 they sold for $2.00 per thousand, or about 70 cents per bushel. They were taken from the time the bays opened in spring until the end of the year, but the season was most active after the oyster season closed, from the middle of June until the middle of September.

Total landings of hard clams along the Atlantic coast of the United States, from Maine to the east coast of Florida inclusive, were about 4000 metric tons of meats prior to the middle 1930s. Landings in the Gulf of Mexico did not add much to this total, and at any rate, were mostly, if not all, the southern species *Mercenaria campechiensis*, which brings a considerably lower price. This species does not have the keeping quality out of water of the northern species and quickly gapes.

After the middle 1930s landings rose rather steadily, and reached a peak during the latter years of the Second World War, lasting until 1951. The peak for the Atlantic coast was in 1950 at about 9000 metric tons. After 1951 landings fell off rather rapidly, remaining at about 6400 metric tons until about 1976, then began to fall off to about 4900 metric tons in 1982.

The price per pound of hard clam meats, adjusted to standard dollars by the consumer price index, has risen steadily, although irregularly, since the first records were kept in 1880 (Fig. 7.2). The price varied with locality, and to some extent was influenced by the relative numbers of littlenecks,

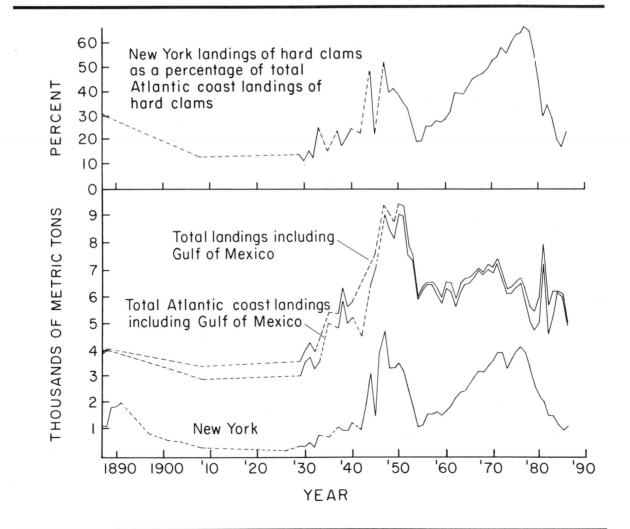

Figure 7.1. Upper panel: weights of hard clams produced in New York as a percentage of total production along the entire Atlantic coast. Lower panel: weights in metric tons of hard clam meats in New York, along the entire Atlantic coast, including the Gulf of Mexico.

cherrystones and chowders in the catch. In general, prices followed a trend, rising to a peak in the late 1920s, dropping off sharply in the 1930s, rising to a peak again in the middle 1940s, dropping off again in the 1950s and early 1960s and finally rising to an all-time high in the 1980s. The adjusted price has risen from about 15 cents per pound of meats in 1880 to about $1.28 per pound in 1986.

In 1898 J.H. Doxsee, Sr., encouraged by the increasing demand for hard clams, went from New York to Okracoke, North Carolina and established a clam cannery. Clams were bought for 40 cents per bushel and were processed as clam juice, clam chowder and whole clams. It has been estimated that as many as 3000 bushels were canned each year during the peak of operations. After about three years of apparent success, the supply diminished and the plant moved to Witt (Sea Level, North Carolina). Still later, some time in the early 1900s, it moved to Marco, Florida to take advantage of the large production in the Ten Thousand Islands region on the west coast of Florida, which lasted about twenty years (Chestnut 1951).

When the federal government first began publishing records of fishery landings, New Jersey produced even more than New York, starting with about 1500 metric tons of meats in 1880, rising to about 2100 metric tons by 1894. By 1926, however, it had dropped to about 300 metric tons. New Jersey landings rose to an all-time peak of about 2300 metric tons by 1950. In 1933 New York exceeded New Jersey in production for the first time, and finally exceeded it almost for good in 1946. Only in 1954 and 1955 did New Jersey lead again. By 1978 production in New Jersey had dropped below 500 metric tons again. The primary causes were water pollution, which led to the closing of some areas, and overfishing.

The other states in which production exceeded 500 metric tons were Rhode Island, peaking at just about 2300 metric tons in 1955; Massachusetts, peaking at about 1400 metric tons in 1931; Virginia, peaking at about 1300 metric tons in 1938; and North Carolina, producing about 700 metric tons in 1979.

HISTORY OF LANDINGS IN NEW YORK

Although it was recognized as inferior to the soft clam *Mya arenaria* at first, the quahog was dug for home consumption for years in New England, and at least as far south as New Jersey. The commercial quahog fishery began on Cape Cod about the beginning of the nineteenth century, growing in extent until about 1860. From 1860 to about 1890 production remained nearly constant. The greatest development of the quahog or hard clam industry, however, was in New York and New Jersey, where by 1880 nearly 2800 metric tons were already being produced commercially. Undoubtedly the existence of large markets in New York City and Philadelphia had a good deal to do with this early development.

Annual production in New York in 1880 was reported to be about 150,000 bushels or about 900 metric tons of meats (Fig. 7.1), but official statistics give a higher figure. About 20,000 bushels of these were packed in cans by a cannery at Islip on Great South Bay (Mather 1887). This cannery belonged to J.H. Doxsee and a man named Low, and it packed vegetables as well as clams. After struggling to perfect the process of canning and to obtain markets, the business grew to such proportions that 400 bushels (10,000 cans) of hard clams were canned daily, and this output continued for years. Three types of clam products were produced: littleneck clams, clam chowder and clam juice.

The baymen lived on profits derived from working the oyster beds and depended for the other three months on clamming and fishing. About 1895

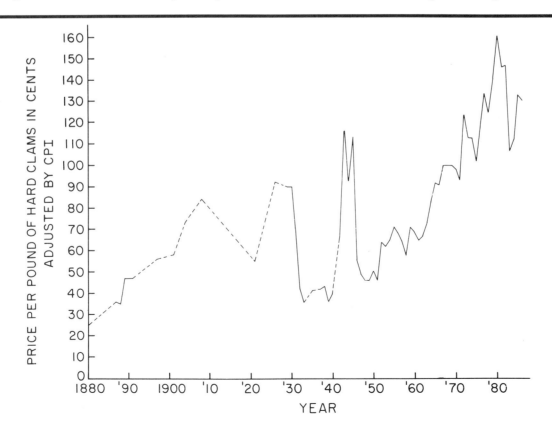

Figure 7.2. Price per pound of hard clam meats in New York, adjusted by the consumer price index (CPI), 1880 to 1984.

the supply of clams began to decrease, and by the turn of the century it became almost impossible to obtain clams. Very few were canned at Islip (Kellogg 1901a,b). Demand had steadily increased, however, and in 1898 J.H. Doxsee, Sr. went to Okracoke, North Carolina and established a clam factory there. Many of the clams canned in North Carolina in those days were labeled as quahogs from Islip, New York (Chestnut 1951).

At that time a good day's work for a man harvesting with tongs or rakes was about 1000 clams, or about three bushels. For that work he would receive about $2.25 in 1880. The dollar changes in value, of course, and that $2.25 would be worth only about 30 cents today — a small amount to receive for a hard day's work.

In 1880, according to official statistics, the total take of hard clams in the state of New York was just about 1500 metric tons of meats, or about 258,000 bushels, worth about $196,000. In 1967 dollars these clams would be worth about three times as much, or about $534,000. In 1986 the total take in New York was about 1200 metric tons of meats, worth about $10.6 million. In 1967 dollars these clams would be worth about $3.2 million. Thus, clams now are worth about six times as much as they were in 1880.

On the other hand, fishes have not increased in price nearly as much. From 1880 to 1986 bluefish have increased, in 1967 dollars, only about 1.33 times, weakfish about 2 times and cod about 2.5 times. Thus, there is no doubt that hard clams have appreciated in price much more than most seafoods.

New York landings reached an early peak of about 1800 metric tons of meats in 1891, then dropped off to a low of about 450 metric tons from about 1908 until about 1926. Landings rose gradually until 1942, then shot up to a peak in 1947 of about 4600 thousand metric tons. They dropped again almost as rapidly to a low of about 910 metric tons in 1954, then rose again to a peak of about 4000 metric tons in 1976. Following that peak they dropped sharply again and by 1984 were about 1300 metric tons.

In percentage of total Atlantic coast landings,

New York was fairly low until the 1940s and reached a peak of just over 50% of Atlantic coast landings in 1947. It dropped sharply thereafter, to a low of just under 20% in 1954, then rose steadily, producing over 50% of total Atlantic coast landings in 1970 and remained above 50% of the total until 1980. In the last three years it has dropped below 50% once again to about 25% in 1984. There is little doubt now that the resource has been overfished in New York.

The price per pound of hard clam meats, adjusted to standard dollars by the consumer price index, has risen, but irregularly, since 1880 (Fig. 7.2). The pre-World War II peak probably was reached at the end of World War I, but there are no data to confirm this. After a drop around 1921, there was a rise again in the period 1926 to 1930, then a sharp drop during the depression, which lasted until at least 1940. There followed a sharp increase during the Second World War, when for the first time the price rose to over $1.00 in 1967 dollars, followed by an equally sharp drop to less than 50 cents by 1947. The sharpness of this drop probably was emphasized by the large production at this time and the general inflation that followed the war. Following the low in the late 1940s and early 1950s, the price rose fairly steadily, reaching an all-time peak of slightly over $1.60 by 1980 (Fig. 7.2), then dropped to about $1.31 by 1986.

By 1870 too many men were working the Great South Bay beds, and too many oysters were being taken from them, threatening the means of livelihood of whole communities. Then began the struggle between the oyster planter and the bayman. The law at that time limited the oyster planter to three acres, but he could avoid this restriction somewhat by taking out leases in the names of his wife and children. He still could not acquire holdings of any considerable size, however. No Bay bottom where natural beds occurred could be leased, but the smart planter could stake out areas temporarily exhausted by excessive dredging because no oysters were there. To counter this the baymen presented a petition to the Town of Brookhaven asking them to cease leasing lots to

private individuals after April 1, 1875, but it was too late and the planters won.

In 1879 Brookhaven modified the law to allow leasing of large areas and the organization of companies to carry on the business. Thus, the period from 1880 to 1890 was characterized by the predominance of the individual planter. In 1891 three large companies made their appearance in Great South Bay. Two thousand acres were leased outright, and in 1894 the first oyster steamer appeared, capable of using six dredges. Its name was "Curiosity," but it was dubbed "Hell's Wagon" by hostile baymen.

In 1891 a rumor developed that a new corporation had obtained options on about 8000 acres of bottom, including some of the best natural beds. This so enraged the baymen that William Underwood of Patchogue trespassed on the land, and he was soon followed by other baymen. After five years of litigation, the New York State Court of Appeals ruled in favor of Underwood, but, although this saved the beds for the future, again it came too late. In 1893 the natural beds gave out, and for three years there was practically no catch. As a result, piracy began to develop in Great South Bay, as baymen tried to scratch out a living by taking clams and a few oysters from private grounds (Taylor 1983).

Great South Bay was far enough away to be comparatively free from the influence of Connecticut at first, but as natural production of oysters declined, Connecticut prevailed, transplanting its abundant seed oysters to the Bay. Thus, the Long Island oyster industry to a large extent became an adjunct to that of Connecticut, and most ground in Great South Bay was taken up with oyster leases. After 1900, and well into the 1930s, clam production fell to an all-time low.

There is no doubt that the drop in hard clam production in New York in the late 1890s, which lasted until the early 1930s, was caused by the growth of the oyster industry. The oyster industry reached its peak in the 1900s and 1910s, and had dropped to less than half the peak amount by 1930. When the oyster industry was at its peak and much of the grounds were in oyster production, the men were employed mostly in oystering, and the few clams that were available brought relatively low prices. There was a slow buildup during the 1930s, but prices were even lower during the depression and demand also was low. It was not until the war that prices began to rise again. The great demand caused by the shortage of red meat toward the end of the war and the increased numbers of clammers caused by demobilization of men from the armed forces resulted in production rising to a maximum in 1947.

The most important change in Great South Bay, from the point of view of the shellfish industry, however, was the breaking through of an inlet at Moriches Bay beach in 1931. In a few years, the increase in salinity in eastern Great South Bay wiped out most of the remaining oyster beds through the increase in abundance and activity of oyster drills. During these same years, however, remarkable and beneficial changes took place in the hard clam stocks, which compensated somewhat for the loss of oysters. After 1931 some very fine clam sets occurred throughout all of the Bay, and hard clam growth also was good. Thus, the history of shellfish in the Bay is to a considerable extent a history of the inlets and their effect upon salinity.

This was not the only factor causing changes in shellfish populations in Great South Bay, however. About 1890 the duck industry began on Long Island. It grew slowly but surely so that by 1924 about 1.5 million ducks were being raised, by 1930 about 2 million, 3 million by 1933, 6 million by 1941 and about the same number in 1950 (Lackey [1951?]).

This growth of the duck population brought increasing amounts of wastes down the streams into the Carmans and Forge rivers, depositing solids on the bottoms of these rivers and carrying liquids into the Bay. Phosphates were unusually high and nitrates were low, and this caused blooms of *Nannochloris spp.*, which colored Bay water a yellow-green, reduced the numbers of other planktonic organisms drastically and clogged the ciliary tracts of shellfishes, thus interfering with feeding. These blooms caused starvation of oysters and clams because small forms were relatively indigestible and in addition had direct toxic effects on shellfishes.

A hurricane reopened Moriches Inlet in 1953[1] and probably saved the hard clam industry, but by 1957 the inlet had begun to refill again, with noticeable effects upon the waters of Great South Bay. In the spring of 1958 Moriches Inlet was again widened and deepened and subsequently was protected by seawalls. This apparently corrected the situation. The duck farms also were forced to treat their wastes, and this, together with a large reduction in the number of ducks, prevented the situation from recurring.

INDUSTRY-RELATED CAUSES OF THE DECLINE IN PRODUCTION

As early as 1860, baymen at the western end of Long Island, from the Rockaways to Coney Island, were harassed by bands of New Jersey and Manhattan pirates, who would lie at anchor outside their inlets for days at a time, waiting for a favorable turn of wind and tide before swooping in to harvest and deplete the enormously fertile hard clam beds in those areas.

Seagoing watchmen were employed to watch for "intruders" with little success, and finally even tried an appeal to Governor Edwin D. Morgan in Albany, but to no avail. Finally, led by a Coney Island clamdigger named Gil Davis, the baymen banded together and began to shoot it out with the intruders. Defying a gubernatorial order to cease these hostilities, the clamdiggers instead organized what soon came to be known as the "Rockaway Republic." Their objective was to have the governor send the National Guard to protect the clam beds from the trespassers, but this was not done.

Following the election of President Lincoln, "Governor" Davis formally announced secession

from the state of New York, saying that "henceforth we are Unionists, not New Yorkers." In reply Governor Morgan dispatched the militia, not to help the Long Islanders, but instead to arrest Davis. Davis, however, was a wily adversary, who managed to be gone clamming so often that the soldiers abandoned pursuit after a week and went back to fighting the Civil War. Davis is reported to have written a letter to the governor, thanking him for having put so many armed militiamen on the bays that the pirates were frightened off the Rockaway coast forever (Bailey 1956; Chekenian 1973).

Maneuvers like this, in which residents of one local area try to block residents of another area from harvesting seafoods in their waters are entirely illegal, for the products of the sea are traditionally open to all. Yet shooting wars between such groups have arisen frequently and are just as bitter now as they were 100 or more years ago.

Disregard for the law has been a problem of the industry from the beginning. Baymen believe that the waters are common property and that anything in them is free for the taking. To a considerable degree they believe that there should be no interference with their right to take whatever is there. Thus, they are apt to regard the laws and regulations lightly and to disregard them whenever possible.

Clammers in Great South Bay are generally in agreement that poaching is the most vexing problem. They say that up to 50% of all clamdiggers work uncertified areas at times, up to 50% work without the necessary permits, and up to 50% take undersized clams in certified areas (Mirchel 1980). These estimates have been generally confirmed by enforcement and management officials. The actual numbers or percentages may be more or less than these estimates (probably more), but there is no doubt that a considerable part of the total harvest is taken illegally.

Kelpin (1981) agreed with these conclusions. She also made the point that most baymen believe that clams from uncertified waters are safe to eat, and therefore, they see no point in closing areas.

---

[1]Moriches Inlet closed spontaneously on May 15, 1951 and reopened on September 18, 1953 during hurrican Edna.

Moreover, there is a general belief that the smaller clams are particularly abundant in uncertified areas along the north shore of Great South Bay, and thus poaching is rationalized by many baymen because it is more profitable. This is especially so in harsh winter weather when the sheltered coves along the north shore of the Bay are relatively protected from the wind.

The shores of New Jersey and Long Island are relatively close to New York City and Philadelphia, which provide large and diverse markets for clams. Therefore, these areas became important for clamming early. Clamming is of prime importance to the bayman system in New Jersey (McCay 1982) and New York. The predictable abundance of clams and the fact that little capital and technology are required to take them make clams an important resource during slack periods in other fisheries.

Clam poaching has been going on in the northern areas of New Jersey for as long as there have been restrictions on fishing activities. Piracy is a custom in New York as well as in New Jersey, and in fact, since the northern bays in New Jersey and the western bays on Long Island have been almost totally closed to clamming by pollution, piracy has become a necessity if clams are to be taken at all.

In Great South Bay the situation is not quite as bad. Considerable areas are still open to clamming, but poaching is still important. As already pointed out, clammers do not have much faith in the need for closing areas. They eat clams from uncertified areas themselves and do not get sick. If they do recognize the need for closing some areas, they believe the requirement that sampling be done under the "worst conditions" is too extreme (Kelpin 1981).

There is the additional incentive that clams are more abundant generally in uncertified areas, and many of these are in coves along the north shore of the Bay where there is protection from the prevailing winter winds. There is also the further incentive of deliberately going into uncertified areas to test enforcement agents. When a patrol boat comes near, clammers scatter in all directions and the patrol boat, being no match for their high speed

motors, seldom catches them. When they are caught, the nominal fine is a small price to pay for the thrill and profits of illegal clamming.

Clammers in New York, as elsewhere, also poach clams in certified areas in the sense that they take significant numbers of undersized clams. The minimum size is one inch across the valves, and culling trays are constructed so that clams smaller than the minimum will pass through and then should be returned to the Bay. The small clams are the most valuable, however; for example, on February 1, 1986 the National Marine Fisheries Service reported from the Fulton Fish Market in New York City that littlenecks were wholesaling there for $135 to $140 per bushel, large littlenecks for $65 to $70, cherrystones for $35 to $38 and chowders, the largest, for $16 to $18. Thus, there is a great temptation to keep those that are undersized.

There is an additional adverse effect from taking undersized clams, which has not been adequately explored. Large clams lay many more eggs than small clams. The difference may be as much as a factor of two to three — large clams laying 6 million eggs per clam on the average, and small clams laying only 2-3 million. The fishery is so intense now that few clams survive much beyond the first year after reaching minimum size (Greene 1978). It therefore seems reasonable to assume, because very few small clams ever reach large size, that a reduction of 50-60% in the number of eggs laid may on the average have an adverse effect on recruitment. Many of us believe that some way must be found to preserve adequate numbers of large adults as a partial spawning stock if adequate recruitment is to be preserved.

POSSIBLE CONTROLS TO MAXIMIZE RECRUITMENT AND REHABILITATE THE RESOURCE

It must first be clearly understood that harvesting levels coinciding with the peaks of 1947 and 1976 cannot be expected again. The peak of 1976 was

clearly attained by overharvesting the resource (Buckner 1984), and thus, the clamming effort expended in 1976 should not be allowed again. There are two principal ways of limiting the catch: either by placing an annual quota on removals, the fishery to be stopped when that quota is reached; or by limiting the numbers of licenses issued, so that each clammer has a chance to make a reasonable income without overharvesting the resource.

Equally important, in fact, essential if any of the measures listed here are to succeed, will be to tighten the laws regarding harvesting, and to improve surveillance in all areas. On uncertified grounds the odds of getting caught must be increased and the penalties for infractions must be set high enough so that once caught, the penalty for further violations will act as a major deterrent. Surveillance must be improved on certified grounds also because of the frequent infractions of the minimum size limit there, with clammers taking more than the allowable quantity of undersized clams. There might even have to be an increase in the legal size of clams to be sure that sufficient eggs are produced and spawned before clams are harvested.

Various remedies have been proposed to ensure that recruitment will rise and be maintained at maximum levels. Perhaps the most appealing from a scientific point of view would be to close from one quarter to one third of the Bay bottom and monitor its rate of recovery to a harvestable state. This would involve measuring recruitment and growth and judging the optimum time to open the ground to harvesting again by watching the size of the first incoming year class.

When most of these clams have reached littleneck size the area would be opened. It is assumed that this would take three or four years, but would depend upon growth rate. This can be determined more accurately as knowledge of the area grows, and the length of time and the number of areas in which to divide the Bay would be determined accordingly. We will assume, for the sake of simplicity, that the period is three years.

The Bay would then be divided into three or a multiple of three parts, depending on the ease of access to all licensed clammers. The principal consideration must be simplicity, so the number of areas should be kept to a minimum. These areas perhaps should be determined so that each has approximately the same number of clams, rather than being of equal area. Then each would be closed in turn, so that two would remain open and one closed, and the closed area would remain closed for three years. All areas must be monitored closely, to watch for changes in clam recruitment, abundance and growth.

This closure probably will reduce the total take of clams for a while and put some hardship temporarily on clammers. In the long run, however, the harvest will be increased. The short-term loss in harvest must be recognized as a penalty for past excesses, one that is needed to improve catches in the future.

The towns of Brookhaven, Babylon and Islip have sizeable harvest management programs in Great South Bay. The Town of Islip, which has the major program, closed an area in town waters in 1983. At the time of closing the density of clams in the area was between three and five bushels per acre. Within a few years after closing, the density rose to about 20 bushels per acre. This area is not completely opened yet because it has not yet reached commercially harvestable densities (S. Buckner, pers. comm.); however, at the request of the baymen, parts have been opened on a scheduled basis in winter. Limitations of weather and the smaller number of full-time clammers available in winter have allowed the town to minimize the impact on the population, thus gradually allowing it to increase, although at a slower rate than if the area were totally closed. This seasonal limited opening, then, has been a compromise between the baymen's needs and the need to reestablish hard clam densities.

The town also has constructed a hatchery, which is already operating. It has a production capacity of about 25-35 million clams per year. After getting some growth in the hatchery, clams will be placed on protected grounds until large enough to plant and begin harvesting. They are mostly *M. m.*

notata, so can be recognized as hatchery-produced individuals. They expect about 50% survival to market size. These are encouraging developments, which promise to begin rehabiliation of the hard clam stocks in Islip waters.

The two alternative ways of limiting the total catch have inequities. A quota system may lead to closing early in the year, making it difficult for clammers who operate only seasonally, and for those who rely upon clamming for their entire income. It will also affect the middleman, who may have customers who wish to have clams at all times of the year, and the consumer, who may also wish to have clams available at any time of year.

There will also be problems associated with the naturally fluctuating supply of clams. The quota may be reached earlier in the year when clams are in good supply because reproduction has been good and later in the year if reproduction has been poor. These are just a few of the problems associated with quotas, which can be corrected partly, although not entirely, by having several open seasons during the year and closing each when the subquota is reached.

Limiting the number of licenses will correct some of these inequities, but will create others. Some of the advantages are that if the number of licenses is calculated correctly, each bayman participating in the harvest will be assured of a reasonable income, provided that he is willing to work hard. On the other hand, those who do not get licenses have no opportunity at all to make money from clamming. How will it be decided which clammers are to get licenses and which are not? And what about problems with clamming in years when reproduction is exceedingly good and the allowable catch is not reached, or in years when reproduction is poor and the allowable catch may be exceeded? Must a quota also be imposed in certain cases, or is overfishing consciously allowed? These are difficult questions that will require considerable thought to resolve equitably.

Another part of the plan must be to continue to improve the present data collection system. This means that measures of recruitment, abundance, growth, fishing and natural mortality must be

continued in all areas. This will permit evaluation of the results of closures and will determine the criteria for opening and closing areas, including a determination that certain areas might have to be closed if abundance of clams drops below a certain point — even if the season is still open. It will lead to improvements in the design of a rotational system for the Bay as a whole and will permit all management options to be evaluated and maximized. A computer program and a data processing system for maximum usefulness will be developed as a part of this phase of the work.

Another part of the management plan would be to establish a brood-stock sanctuary in the area or areas that have been predicted from current studies to be a major source of spawn for the Bay. In some places, for example, Great South Bay, these areas have already been located by dye and numerical modeling studies.

To deter harvesting, materials such as rocks, metal grates or other low cost items that will make harvesting difficult or expensive, yet not interfere in any way with the clams, should be placed on the bottom in these areas. Large quantities of spawner clams such as chowders should be placed here, and the area permanently closed to harvesting. The purpose will be to increase the chances that large quantities of clam larvae will be available for setting. There is no guarantee that this will work all the time, but it must be evaluated, and the cost should be relatively small.

All of these alternatives will produce an optimum yield that will vary considerably from time to time, depending upon environmental factors that affect reproduction and the action of predators. These fluctuations cannot be avoided, even if environmental conditions such as water pollution can be improved. One way to mitigate variations in production would be to adopt some accessory system of mariculture, which would raise young clams in hatcheries, rear them to some size large enough to be relatively resistant to predation, for example, about 20 mm long, and then plant them on the public grounds. This will not eliminate fluctuations completely, but it could help perhaps to alleviate major dips in production and possibly could increase the safe level of yield.

Mariculture is costly, however, and the costs will have to be fully weighed against benefits to determine if anything is really added to the total income. It is not enough to estimate total yields. All the costs of management must be added, then subtracted from the value of the total yield. Otherwise, any management program may turn out to be nothing but a direct subsidy to the baymen who choose to harvest the resource.

A system of limited entry would do much to improve the bayman's source of income, and it would also indirectly improve conservation because the resource would be less likely to be overfished. Because it would prevent some people from entering the hard clam fishery, however, it probably will be strongly opposed in some quarters; thus, the decision to use this method of conservation is likely to be primarily political.

Certain measures can be taken to ease the adverse effects upon present licensees, however. For example, licenses do not need to be reduced in number immediately but may merely be frozen at their present level. Then, by attrition, as men drop out of clamming for one reason or another, licenses can be gradually reduced to a lower level. It may not be feasible to deny entry altogether, but that can be taken care of by allowing, for example, 50% or less of those that are relinquished by attrition to be reissued.

Some method of choosing who will receive the new licenses will have to be employed, since there almost certainly will be more applicants than can be accommodated. A lottery is one way of choosing, or perhaps an allocation among users to determine what proportion should go to full-time clammers, how many to students who clam only part time, how many to teachers, and so on.

Other questions also will have to be resolved, for example, can licenses by transferred, or should they revert to the government when they are no longer wanted? If they revert, should holders be compensated, since the licenses will have value? There will also be opportunities for irregularities,

which must be guarded against; for example, should constraints be placed on efficiency, numbers of men on vessels, size of vessels and so on, since these could conceivably increase catches and earnings and thus weaken the management scheme? On the other hand, they would bring back some of the very kinds of limits that this management alternative was supposed to eliminate.

These difficult decisions would all have to be made. Nevertheless, limited entry, properly conceived, can eliminate many of the problems of an open fishery, improve the well being of fishermen and contribute to conservation. From a purely economic point of view, it avoids the waste of capital and labor.

No matter how high a level of enforcement is achieved, however, it will never be perfect. Some baymen will continue to harvest illegally and escape detection. Penalties will never be great enough to act as a total deterrent. Even on certified grounds some baymen will continue to evade the law. Thus, it is important to provide spawner sanctuaries where large clams are protected from poaching by obstacles placed on the bottom. For the same reasons there is merit in having a maximum legal size as well as a minimum size for harvesting — to protect large spawners that produce large numbers of eggs and that are relatively inexpensive.

A relay program similar to that used in New Jersey also merits consideration, where clams are harvested under state supervision in uncertified waters, transplanted to certified plots assigned to particular baymen and reharvested at stated times by those same baymen. The New York State Department of Environmental Conservation is now transplanting clams from uncertified to certified waters.

Surveillance of two kinds will be essential to success of any scheme of management: (1) to detain and deter violators, which will require understanding and support in the courts; and (2) to gain a full understanding of the population dynamics of hard clams by monitoring the stocks of hard clams and their predators. It will be most important also to attempt to gain the support of

people in the business, to explain the reasons for the steps that are being taken, to show that in the long run they will be to everyone's benefit and to encourage their cooperation.

All of these alternatives, or combinations thereof, are worthy of consideration. All have strengths and weaknesses, but a proper combination of these and other suggestions should improve stocks and yields.

REFERENCES

Abbott, R. T. 1972. Kingdom of the seashell. Crown Publishers, Inc., New York (2nd printing, 1975). 256 pp.

Bailey, P. 1956. Historic Long Island in pictures, prose and poetry. Long Island Forum, Amityville, NY. 168 pp.

Belding, D. L. 1912. A report upon the quahaug and oyster fisheries of Massachusetts, including the life history, growth and cultivation of the quahaug (*Venus mercenaria*), and observations on the set of the oyster spat in Wellfleet Bay. Boston, Wright and Potter Printing Co. 134 pp., 69 figs. (Reissued in 1964 as Mass. Div. Marine Fish., Contr. 12. 134 pp.)

Buckner, S. 1984. Population dynamics of the hard clam, *Mercenaria mercenaria*, in Great South Bay, New York. Ph.D. Thesis, Marine Sciences Research Center, State University of New York at Stony Brook, NY. 217 pp.

Chekenian, J. 1973. All about clams. Long Island, Newsday's Magazine for Long Island, 22 July: 11-16.

Chestnut, A. F. 1951. The oyster and other mollusks in North Carolina. Pages 141-190 *in* Harden F. Taylor et al., eds. Survey of marine fisheries of North Carolina. University of North Carolina Press, Chapel Hill, NC.

_____. 1953. Studies of the North Carolina clam industry. Nat. Shellfish. Assn., Convention Addresses 1951:85-88.

Dow, R.L. 1972. Fluctuations in Gulf of Maine sea temperature and specific molluscan abundance. J. Cons. Cons. Int. Explor. Mer 34(3):532-534.

_____. 1973. Fluctuations in marine species abundance during climatic cycles. Marine Technol. Soc. J. 7(4):38-42.

Ganong, W.F. 1890. Southern invertebrates on the shores of Acadia. Trans. R. Soc. Can. 8(4):167-185.

Gibson, F.A. and C.B. Duggan. 1970. Experiments with the American hard-shelled clam (*Mercenaria mercenaria*) 1969. Irel. Dep. Agr. Fish. Fish. Leafl. 24, 6 pp. + table + fig.

_____. 1973. American hard-shelled clam experiments in Irish waters. Irel. Dep. Agr. Fish. Fish. Leafl. 49, 6 pp.

Greene, G. T. 1978. Population structure, growth and mortality of hard clams at selected locations in Great South Bay, New York. M.S. Thesis, Marine Sciences Research Center, State University of New York at Stony Brook, NY. 199 pp.

Hanna, G. D. 1966. Introduced mollusks of western North America. Occas. Pap. Calif. Acad. Sci. 7(48):1-108.

Heppell, D. 1961. The naturalization in Europe of the quahog, *Mercenaria mercenaria* (L.). J. Conchol. 25(1):21-34.

Ingersoll, E. 1887. The oyster, scallop, clam, mussel and abalone industries. Pages 507-626 *in* G. Brown Goode et al., eds. The fisheries and fishery industries of the United States. Sect. V, Vol. II, Pt. XX, U.S. Commer. Fish Fish.

Kellogg, J. L. 1901a. Clam and scallop industries of New York State. Bull. N.Y. State Museum 8(43):603-631.

_____. 1901b. The clam problem and clam culture. Bull. U.S. Fish Comm. 19:39-44.

_____. 1903. Feeding habits and growth of *Venus mercanaria*. N.Y. State Museum Bull. 71, Zoology 10, University of the State of New York, Bull. 296, 27 pp. + index + 8 figs.

Kelpin, G. M. 1981. Depuration and its implications for Long Island's hard clam industry. M.S. Thesis, Marine Sciences Research Center, State University of New York at Stony Brook, NY. 115 pp.

Lackey, J. B. 1951?. The rehabilitation of Great South Bay. Unpublished. 25 pp.

Loosanoff, V.L. 1946. Commercial clams of the Atlantic coast of the United States. U.S. Dept. Interior, Fish Wildl. Serv., Fish. Leafl. 13, 12 pp.

Mather, F. 1887. New York and its fisheries. Pages 341-377 *in* George Brown Goode et al., eds. The Fisheries and fishery industries of the United States. Sect. II: A geographical review of the fisheries industries and fishing communities for the year 1880. U.S. Government Printing Office, Washington, D.C. 341-377.

McCay, B. J. 1982. The shore fisheries of New Jersey: Centennial reflections. Conf. on Natural Resources in New Jersey History: Three centuries of change. Rutgers University, Center for Coastal and Environmental Studies, and The New Jersey Historical Commission, North Brunswick, N.J., November 6-7. 25 pp.

Merrill, A. S. and J. W. Ropes. 1967. Distribution of southern quahogs off the Middle Atlantic coast. Commer. Fish. Rev. 29(4):62-64.

Mirchel, A. C. F. 1980. Enforcement of hard clam laws on Great South Bay, New York. M.S. Thesis, State University of New York at Stony Brook, NY. 135 pp.

Salchak, A. and J. Haas. 1971. Occurrence of the northern quahog, *Mercenaria mercenaria*, in Colorado Lagoon, Long Beach, California. Calif. Fish Game 57(2):126-128.

Taylor, L. J. 1983. Dutchmen on the bay. The ethnohistory of a contractual community. University of Pennsylvania Press, Philadelphia. xviii + 206 pp.

Tiller, R. E., J. B. Glude and L. D. Stringer. 1952. Hard-clam fishery of the Atlantic coast. Commer. Fish. Rev. 14(10):1-25.

Verrill, A.E. 1873. Report upon the invertebrate animals of Vineyard Sound and the adjacent waters, with an account of the physical characters of the region. Pages 295-522 *in* Spencer F. Baird, ed. Report on the condition of the sea fisheries of the south coast of New England in 1871 and 1872. U.S. Commer. Fish Fish., U.S. Government Printing Office, Washington, D.C.

IAN STUPAKOFF

Size range of hard clams from smallest to largest: seed, little neck, cherrystone and chowder.

Hard clams bagged for market.

CHAPTER 8

THE BAYMEN

Jeffrey Kassner
Town of Brookhaven
Division of Environmental
Protection
3233 Route 112
Medford, NY 11763

Donald Squires
Marine Sciences Institute
University of Connecticut
Storrs, CT 06269

INTRODUCTION

The baymen of Long Island have been the subject of eloquent prose, but seldom words so frank. Baymen are an enigma, for these harvesters of the hard clam are both a part of social and political Long Island and an integral part of the ecology of Great South Bay. It is in the latter, less romantic, seldom considered role that the baymen are treated in this chapter. For, as harvesters of the shellfish of Great South Bay, baymen are among the important predators of the hard clam — certainly the most successful predator on the adult clam — and a powerful instrument stirring and restirring the politics of the Bay.

Great South Bay has been an important influence on human settlement of Long Island. Yet when the first Indians visited the region some 15,000 years ago, Great South Bay didn't exist. It wasn't until after postglacial sea level had nearly risen to its present position, about 5000 years ago, that the Fire Island barrier beach that forms the Bay's south shore could develop and create the Bay. Shell middens dating to 4000 B.C. have been found around New York, attesting to the harvest of shellfish by Indian residents from the Archaic period.

By the time of the first contacts between Europeans and Indians, Indian population densities estimated at as much as 20,000 persons per square mile existed on Long Island (Salwen 1975). Anthropologist Bert Salwen attributed this density, high compared to that of Indians in surrounding regions, to the abundance of shellfish and finfish in the shallow bays surrounding the island. These seafoods provided a plentiful and highly nutritious diet for the Indians.

Wampum — polished, tubular beads made from the shell of the hard clam — was an important medium of exchange as well as personal adornment among Indian tribes (Wilcox 1976). The central role of shellfish to these inhabitants of Long Island is reflected in their names for the island: "Seawanhacky," which has been interpreted as meaning "island of shells" and "Paumanock" as "land of tribute" (Coles 1955).

From the time Europeans settled on the south shore, about 1655, the importance of the Great South Bay as a resource was generally recognized. As townships were being formed, from 1687 onward, inclusion of the Bay within town boundaries was sought, but acquisition was not always simple, or uncontested. In spite of numerous court actions, the Town of Islip didn't gain clear title to its Bay bottom until 1929 when New York State deeded the bottom to the town (Kavenagh 1980).

The Bay also served as a corridor for early commerce with products of local farms carried by schooner to the growing New York City metropolitan area (Dickerson 1975). Manufactured and imported goods were carried out to the island on the return voyage. Beginning in 1844 railroad construction on Long Island spurred development. Resort hotels, country homes and estates for the wealthy sprang up along the south shore of the Bay. Long Island's south shore became a playground for urban society.

At the turn of the century, the population of Long Island was approximately 133,000 (Long Island Regional Planning Board 1982). By 1940 the population had risen to slightly more than half a million people, a relatively modest rate of growth compared to that which followed. It was during this period that the manufacture of aircraft emerged as a significant industry (COSMA 1985).

With the end of the Second World War, gasoline rationing ceased and cheap automobiles made Long Island accessible to all. People flocked from the city to the "Island," and great bedroom communities such as Levittown were spawned. Robert Moses, who later became known as the "power broker" for the enormous impact he had on Long Island, New York City and the State of New York, created a network of highways which linked the city with public beaches and parks throughout Long Island (Caro R.A. 1974). Nassau County's population grew by 93% in the decade of the 1950s, and Suffolk County, awaiting the human tidal wave, saw its population increase 142% between 1960 and 1970 (Long Island Regional Planning Board 1982).

Population growth placed enormous pressures on Long Island's resources and changed forever the character of its coastal waters. A striking example of the effects of these pressures was the loss of wetlands as demand for waterfront property caused salt marshes to be filled to create land for housing. Between 1954 and 1971 Long Island experienced a 47% loss of its wetlands (O'Conner and Terry 1972).

With increasing population, domestic sewage became a problem. Rather than sewers, each home had its own septic tank or cesspool, and the nutrients in the waste water as well as land contaminants seeped into the ground water and from there to the Bay. Runoff from increasingly paved lands carried a host of contaminants into the Bay. The results were pollution and closure of many shellfish beds to harvesting.

Through these exigencies, life in and on Great South Bay went on, slowly changing and evolving. The baymen adapted, but at the same time, resisted change and "progress." For those who are concerned with the fishery and its regulation, the baymen often pose a dilemma, but they must be reckoned with. Little has been written of their heritage, their values and their attitudes (see for example, Taylor 1983). Too often, baymen are visible only when something has gone against them

---

The Island's South Shore...Great South Bay...[is] the haunt of the baymen, a closemouthed, independent breed, some of them descendents of families that had 'followed the bay' since the Revolution, others New England Yankees who, hearing about the Bay's bountiful harvests of oysters and clams, tommycods and smelts, had left the whaling boats and had moved to Long Island, bringing with them their taciturnity and distrust of outsiders.

Less than thirty miles from the borders of New York City, the baymen lived in a world that resembled nothing so much as the remote fog banks of Nova Scotia....

They were fiercely determined to keep their world for themselves. The Bay bottoms...were 'sacred,' their 'priceless natural heritage' and when it came time each year for the townships that bordered on the Great South Bay...to sell leases to mine the Bay's underwater crops of shellfish, the baymen crowded into town halls to listen while the leases were awarded — and no outsider was ever given a lease. No authority could awe them.

(R.A. Caro 1974).

and they are protesting noisily. Baymen are a political force on Long Island, not because of their numbers, now small in comparison to the high tech engineers and businessmen commuting to New York City, but rather because baymen and their lifestyle represent the dream many cherish of a simpler existence when independence was a virtue and "man-against-the-elements" a desired and attainable image.

How do baymen behave? How do they respond to market forces as prices go up and down, as catch fluctuates? How have baymen adapted to deal with the variables of resource and environment? Few if any of these questions can be satisfactorily answered, but we will summarize what is known.

EVOLUTION OF THE FISHERY

Great South Bay and its shellfishery have evolved and changed as a result of a complex interplay of legal, social, economic, physical, chemical and biological factors. During the period of comparatively low human populations and up to about 1850, the Bay supported subsistence fishing. A second phase was entered when Great South Bay oysters became an item of commerce and thus a factor in the island's economy and politics. Following World War I, a combination of social, economic and environmental factors brought a slow end to the oyster fishery but, fortunately for the baymen, a fishery for hard clams emerged, the third phase in the evolution.

At first the hard clam fishery was a booming business, but in the mid-1970s, this resource faltered in part from overexploitation. In response there was a significant increase in governmental attention, management and regulation. It is uncertain when and if a recovery and controlled harvests will begin.

During the days of sparse population, relatively few people harvested large stocks of shellfish. Little change occurred and the Bay became renowned for its plenitude. But as human populations grew on Long Island and in surrounding areas, intense commercial exploitation of the Bay's resources became inevitable.

Great South Bay was well known for its fine oysters. "Blue points," perhaps the Bay's most famous kind of oyster, were marketed from barges on Manhattan's East River and as far north as Albany, New York, 150 miles up the Hudson River. The name "blue points" is still protected from misapplication by New York State law — an oyster must spend at least three months in Great South Bay before it can be so labeled (NY State Environmental Conservation Law {13-0323.1}).

In the early days of shellfishing, oysters were harvested from a single natural bed until it was exhausted; then the baymen moved on to a new bed. But even then the bounty of the Bay could be strained, so in 1847 shellfish "farming" emerged as a practice for enhancing productivity. Several adventuresome baymen harvested and then transplanted several bushels of small, seed oysters from the eastern Bay, where setting was good but survival poor, to the western Bay, where setting was poor but growth good. Upon returning to the site, baymen-cum-oyster farmers found that their yield of market size oysters had been greatly increased (Agassiz 1909).

The economic potential of this discovery was quickly realized, and seed oysters were soon imported from other coastal areas to meet demands. The expenditure required to conduct the transplants, however, was such that participants wanted ownership rights to the adult oysters. In this way the leasing of public Bay bottom to private individuals began. By 1880 the practice of leasing Bay bottom to individuals and companies was well established (Gabriel 1921).

Leasing of Bay bottom rights laid the foundation for the transformation of oystering into a major business enterprise (Taylor 1983). The practice of leasing also gave rise to two types of oystermen: the free bayman who worked the unleased Bay bottom and the oyster farmer who worked his leased grounds. Competition between these two groups for access to Bay bottom became intense, and the oyster business became a focus for local political attention in the 1880s and 1890s (Taylor 1983).

As the area given over to leasing increased, free baymen were being crowded off the Bay. Between 1865 and 1871, 486 hectares of "unproductive bay bottom were turned into oyster farms" (Gabriel 1921). Almost as soon as leasing began, the baymen were asking questions about the appropriateness of leasing. In 1878, for example, baymen were successful in convincing the Brookhaven town trustees to cease leasing, but that action was rescinded only two years later (Town of Brookhaven 1878, 1880). Elected officials then, and later, were ambivalent about the practice. Leasing produced revenues for the town, but an open Bay meant more employment potential for constituents, a political asset.

Leasing of Bay bottom was never extensively practiced in the Town of Babylon. In the Town of Brookhaven, leasing was largely discontinued in 1900, although there were periodic requests to renew the practice. The Town of Islip stopped issuing new leases in 1931; however, existing leases were renewed. In 1982 all leases were terminated when Islip refused to issue renewals.

In the mid-nineteenth century, a significant technological change occurred in the oyster fishery: oyster dredges appeared on the Bay. The dredges were so much more efficient at taking oysters than the hand tongs in use that, while landings of oysters increased dramatically, depletion of the oyster beds occurred just as rapidly. In 1870 it was necessary to prohibit the use of dredges to conserve the shellfish resource (Gabriel 1921). The practice of enforcing technological inefficiency to prevent overfishing remains a principal management tool even today.

Although the hard clam has apparently always been present in the Bay, people were less interested in it as a food than the famous Great South Bay oyster. Harvesting hard clams was something to be done during the summer when oysters were not being harvested. As soon as the oyster season opened, baymen would lay down their clam tongs to work in the oyster business.

It was not until after the First World War that, as the oyster industry began to decline, the hard clam fishery of the Bay began to expand. Oysters

Clamming boat used for tonging.

were no longer setting in large numbers in the Bay, industrial development of the Connecticut shore had decreased the supply of seed oysters for planting, labor was no longer available for the intensive cultivation and the abolition of leasing reduced the inflow of capital required for shellfish farming. Production of oysters fell, and baymen switched to hard clams.

The Bay itself was changing also. On March 4, 1931 the barrier beach at Moriches Bay was breached by a storm, creating Moriches Inlet. The resulting increased inflow of ocean water caused salinities in the eastern Great South Bay to rise (Moriches Bay is connected to the eastern Bay by Narrow Bay). Predators such as the oyster drill, previously excluded by the low salinity, were now able to move in (Glancy 1956). Many oystermen unsuccessfully advocated the immediate closure of the breach to protect their oysters. At the same time, hard clams spread into the eastern third of Great South Bay.

In the 1930s extensive blooms of phytoplankton began appearing in the Bay during the summer months. The prevalent phytoplankter in these blooms was one which oysters and, to a lesser extent, hard clams could not utilize as food — oysters were seen literally starving in the midst of these blooms (Glancy 1956). The consequences of the blooms of "small forms," as they were called, were poor oyster meat quality and little or no oyster recruitment.

It was initially thought that circulation changes from shoaling in Fire Island Inlet were the cause of these dense blooms, but a series of studies conducted by the Woods Hole Oceanographic Institution and funded by the towns of Islip and Brookhaven, suggested otherwise. The blooms were found to be the result of transport of Moriches Bay water, enriched by the discharges of numerous duck farms located on its shores, into the eastern Bay (Ryther et al. 1958).

The closure of Moriches Inlet in 1951 intensified the problem, and the Woods Hole scientists who studied the problem considered it imperative that Moriches Inlet be kept open at the same time that discharges from the duck farms were being reduced (Bumpus et al. 1954). Moriches Inlet was reopened in 1953 and has been dredged repeatedly to prevent the recurrence of blooms of small forms.

The oyster populations never recovered from the trauma of the blooms. Fortunately the hard clam increased in abundance, but baymen who had harvested both oysters and hard clams now only had a single source of income — hard clams. This change meant that the baymen had a greater impact on hard clam abundance, and they became much more sensitive to changes in this abundance.

During its early years, the hard clam fishery was productive and harvesting pressure was low. In the 1960s prices paid for hard clams began to rise and many new baymen entered the fishery; landings rose sharply reaching a peak production of over 700,000 bushels in 1976 (Table 8.1). Since then, the catch has declined by nearly 75%.

"The decline in production is due to a real decline in clam abundance. This has been confirmed by baymen and several surveys (WAPORA, Inc. 1982). There is no clear consensus as to the cause of the decline. Many feel that overharvesting is the prime reason, while others point to the harvest of sublegal size clams, pollution and increasing salinity." (Kassner and Cramer 1983).

Both the magnitude and the rapid rate of the decline exacerbated the debate over hard clam management techniques. A general lack of consensus as to the proper goal of management and how to achieve it has heightened the noise level of the debate. Baymen, by and large, advocate management practices designed to enhance hard clam abundance, while most managers advocate management tools which reduce the fishing pressure on natural poulations, including reduction in numbers of baymen or the harvesting effort of individuals. Responding to the baymen, publicly funded programs of seed clam planting, spawner relays and transplants from closed shellfishing areas to open ones have been undertaken.

BAYMEN AS A COMMUNITY

Baymen form a loose social community linked by common interests and values. Baymen are also a part of the ecological community, or ecosystem, of Great South Bay. There is considerable interplay between these roles and each influences the other.

Table 8.1. Bushels of hard clams landed from the Great South Bay from 1960 to 1986.[a]

Year	Bushels	Year	Bushels	Year	Bushels
1960	147,268	1970	565,600	1980	338,389
1961	130,734	1971	611,553	1981	309,140
1962	137,045	1972	620,817	1982	201,654
1963	154,386	1973	571,324	1983	178,422
1964	251,052	1974	616,431	1984	146,792
1965	343,184	1975	653,058	1985	117,341
1966	385,413	1976	700,465	1986	104,296
1967	413,266	1977	658,443		
1968	461,403	1978	547,773		
1969	523,319	1979	422,946		

[a]New York State Department of Environmental Conservation, unpublished.

First we will examine the baymen as a community.

Because Great South Bay is long and narrow, there is no single location or port in which the baymen have congregated. Rather, the baymen are diffusely settled, and community tradition is often lacking, although the tradition of shellfish harvesting is often passed from father to son. West Sayville is the village most like a "traditional" fishing village. It was settled in 1849 by Dutch immigrants Cornelius Hage and Cornelius DeWall. Their glowing tales of shellfish and fish abundance led to a thriving Dutch enclave focused on the Bay. Even today, baymen from West Sayville are called "Dutchmen" (Taylor 1983).

The shift from an oyster fishery to the hard clam fishery had a significant impact upon the life of a bayman. He would harvest oysters for only nine months of the year and for the other three months either prepare the oyster grounds, fish or clam. Because baymen were not totally dependent upon a single resource, they were better able to cope during times when one declined. Today's bayman, in contrast, relies solely on a single species and, as a consequence, has tied his livelihood to the well-being of that resource.

The cost of becoming a bayman is relatively small and not considered to be a deterrent to entry. Only a New York state and a town shellfishing permit are required. Most baymen, however, use small boats and have several pairs of rakes or tongs, as well as culling racks, boots, gloves and other special clothing and required safety gear. Kelpin (1981) estimated that in 1979 annual equipment and operating costs were in the range of $3,000 to $5,000.

Baymen tend to be very secretive about the areas they work, their landings and their earnings. This is due, in part, to a fear that landings and income will be used against them by the government and to a perceived need to maintain a competitive advantage. Because everyone who is working on the public Bay bottom is restricted to using nonmechanical devices such as hand tongs and rakes, a bayman's catch is dictated by his skill in finding and harvesting hard clams.

Although a wide variety of boats are used by baymen, depending upon financial considerations and needs, the choice of harvesting gear dictates the general form of the vessel. Those who use tongs prefer larger, broader beamed and heavier boats, since tonging requires a stable platform from which to work. Tong boats are usually entirely decked except for a midship's hold and are reminiscent of oyster boats. Those who rake clams favor lighter and narrower, open-decked boats known as *garvies*. The wave-induced rocking motion of the garvie helps with the raking action. Both types of boats are low in the water and usually have a small, one-person cabin aft maximizing working space.

Gear used varies in accordance with the part of the Bay worked: in western Great South Bay, tongers outnumber rakers 3 to 1, while in central and eastern Great South Bay, rakers outnumber tongers by the same ratio (Fox 1980).

A bayman sells to a buyer who represents a wholesaler — there are about 20 such companies currently along Great South Bay. Buying takes place at dockside and is traditionally a cash transaction. Buyers set the prices, and there is little variation among them. When prices drop sharply, it is the baymen who bear the brunt of the loss (C. Brown, National Marine Fisheries Service, personal comm.; see Chapter 7 for a discussion on clam market prices).

Through the years there have been a number of attempts to form cooperatives to free the baymen from dependence on the wholesalers. One, the Great South Bay Farmer's Cooperative formed in 1968, failed through lack of participation, attesting to the independent nature of the baymen.

Permits to harvest shellfish issued by New York State are the only easy, but probably inaccurate, means of approximating the numbers of baymen who work the Great South Bay. In the towns of Babylon, Islip and Brookhaven, a maximum of slightly over 6500 state permits were issued to residents in 1976, with the number declining steadily since then to somewhat less than 1400 in 1987 (Table 8.2). Nearly half the permits are issued to residents of the Town of Islip, with about 30% of the

remainder going to Brookhaven and about 20% to Babylon residents.

In 1979 baymen ranged in age from 16 to 72 with a median age of 24 (Fox 1980). In a 1977 study, Fox (1980) found that only 50% to 67% of baymen considered themselves full-time. In the study by Kelpin (1981), 88% of the baymen surveyed considered themselves full-time (year round) clammers; only 12% were summer workers. Part-timers are resented by full-time baymen who view them as having all the benefits of a land-based job and none of the problems of full-time diggers.

In Fox's study the mean number of days worked reported by full-time clammers was 200; the highest number reported was 280 days. Their work day was a little more than six hours and an average work week was 4.5 days. The average respondent's experience was four years.

The catch of a bayman is difficult to determine and is often given by baymen as "a good day's catch." In 1950 a "good day's catch" was 3 bushels, although some could catch 4, 5, or even 6 bushels (Biles 1950), while in 1979 it was considered to be about 2 bushels of littleneck clams (approximately 1000 clams) (Kelpin 1981). Fox (1980) found the mean catch reported by full-time baymen to be 1.78 bushels of littlenecks, 0.76 bushels of cherrystones and 0.52 bushels of chowders. Using her data, Kelpin (1981) calculated an average gross income for baymen of $20,596. Adjusted for expenses and fringe benefits for the self-employed, a yearly average income of $16,500 was derived — about the regional median income in 1979 (Kelpin 1981).

When asked why they clam, the typical response by baymen is, "because of the satisfaction of being your own boss." That idea of freedom is an integral part of being a bayman. Alternative skills and education are probably not factors. A survey of Rhode Island clammers, which is probably representative of Great South Bay baymen, showed 18% of the respondents having no alternative skills. Fifty-four percent of the Rhode Island baymen had a high school education, while 35% had some college education. Those baymen avowed that

Clammer returning to port.

R. GEORGE ROWLAN

earnings would have to fall 25% before they would drop out (Holmson and Horsley 1981).

BAYMEN AS PREDATORS

The hard clam must sustain its population against the onslaught of a host of predators — only one of which is the bayman. Predation is a major factor in determining the abundance and distribution of the hard clam; abundance of predators may determine whether or not a particular area is a productive shellfishing ground or not (Mackenzie 1977).

Seed clams, those less than about 25 mm in length (about 10 mm in thickness), are the prey of short-lived, voracious (high metabolism) species such as the mud crab and the calico crab (Smith and Chin 1951; Mackenzie 1977). Other predators of the seed hard clam include oyster drills, young whelks, moon snails, starfish, flounder, blowfish, tautog and even diving and dabbling ducks (Carriker 1957; WAPORA, Inc. 1982). Larger hard clams are preyed on by longer-lived, less ravenous (low metabolism) species such as adult whelks (Carriker

1951; Greene 1978) and moonsnails (Franz 1977; Greene 1978).

Just as the hard clam is not distributed evenly throughout Great South Bay, neither are its predators. The salinity of Bay water decreases with increasing distance from tidal inlets, and the distribution of salinity seems to be primarily responsible for limiting numbers and ranges of predators. A major factor in making Great South Bay a productive shellfishery is the fact that predator populations, at least in the past, were not overwhelming.

The most widely distributed hard clam predator in the Bay are the mud crabs *Neopanope texana* and *Panopeus herbsti*. Where they are most abundant, there may be as many as 100 for every square meter of Bay bottom (WAPORA, Inc. 1981). Mud crabs can be voracious consumers of juvenile hard clams. One study suggested that a single crab might eat four hard clams per day (Carriker 1961); a laboratory study suggested a maximum consumption rate as high as 130 clams per crab per day (Gibbons 1984). The oyster drills *Eupleura*

caudata and *Urosalpinx cinerea* can consume up to 19 small hard clams a day (Carriker 1957). They are also widely distributed and can be found in numbers as high as 40 individuals per square meter of Bay bottom (WAPORA, Inc. 1981).

Larger clams are the prey of the whelks (*Busycon caniculatum* and *B. carica*). Because whelks are larger animals, they are found in lesser numbers — a maximum of two to four per square meter (WAPORA, Inc. 1981) and they consume fewer clams — on the order of 40 per year (Greene 1978). But they may, where abundant, kill up to 13% of the hard clam population each year (Greene 1978).

Compared to these "natural" predators, baymen are relatively few in numbers but very effective. Baymen also are not limited by environmental factors such as salinity, but rather hunt the hard clam in most places and at all times.

Just as for other predators, however, the "standing stock" of baymen is determined largely by the relationship between the numbers of clams available and those needed to maintain an individual. That requirement can be translated into catch as follows: for a bayman to earn the median (1983) income, he must harvest 140,000 clams per year ($21,000 = $75/bushel x 280 bushels at 500 clams/bushel). A part-time bayman may only require on the order of 10,000 clams per year.

Our baymen in this model are "consuming" over 583 hard clams per day (140,000 clams per year/240 days per year). Looked at in another way, assuming a clam density of 24 per square meter (e.g. Greene 1978), a bayman must work almost 25 square meters per day (assuming 100% removal efficiency) to meet his income goal. Comparatively then, the 25 square meters needed to support one bayman could support as many as 1000 oyster drills or 2500 mud crabs. Baymen thus rank importantly as predators.

In the case of the bayman, more than nutritional sustenance is needed, since the occupation must provide for the style of life the individual wishes. Most importantly, clamming must also provide the traditional values of freedom and independence. Baymen will forsake high profits if it means

Table 8.2. The number of shellfish harvester permits sold* by the New York State Department of Environmental Conservation to residents of the Towns of Babylon, Islip and Brookhaven.[a]

Year	Permits	Year	Permits
1970	3,863	1979	4,608
1971	4,517	1980	4,275
1972	4,534	1981	3,998
1973	4,796	1982	3,145
1974	5,788	1983	2,355
1975	6,149	1984	1,926
1976	6,517	1985	1,406
1977	6,694	1986	1,282
1978	4,913	1987	1,377

*The number of permits is the only estimate of the number of baymen working on the Great South Bay and includes both full-time and part-time harvesters.

[a]New York State Department of Conservation, unpublished.

compromising their independence and prefer to harvest hard clams, even if income declines due to reduced abundance.

POLLUTION, POACHING AND HUMAN HEALTH

Baymen are not only competing with predators and other baymen for hard clams, they also are working in a bay having external social, political and environmental forces that may deprive them of Bay bottom from which to harvest. The biggest threat to the baymen is the closing of areas of the Bay as a result of contamination by sewage and stormwater runoff. It is just one adverse consequence of the large-scale process of suburbanization of Long Island, a force against which there are few weapons.

Besides placing greater acreage of Bay bottom off limits to harvesting and more harvesting pressure on open areas, pollution of the Great South Bay may pose a threat to the proliferation of the hard clam. Many contaminants are known to be toxic to hard clams, and this may have contributed to the decline in abundance in the 1970s.

Little of Long Island is sewered — most homes are equipped with septic systems or cesspools. However, stormwater runoff is a much more serious problem. Each time it rains, fecal matter deposited by domestic and wild animals is carried to the Bay, and water quality deteriorates. Thus, even after western Suffolk County adjacent to the Bay was sewered, water quality did not improve, and closed areas did not reopen. Controlling stormwater runoff will be a difficult and very expensive undertaking.

Shellfish are indiscriminate filter feeders, obtaining nutrition from whatever is present in overlying waters. If the waters contain human pathogenic bacteria or viruses, then these become concentrated in the shellfish and may be consumed by an unsuspecting human. Hard clams and oysters, therefore, are potential vectors of human disease because they are often eaten raw or only partially cooked.

It was recognized well before the turn of the century that consumption of shellfish taken from waters contaminated by human sewage could have serious public health consequences. The New York State Department of Health began inspecting the sanitary quality of shellfish growing areas shortly after the turn of the century. During the winter of 1924-1925, a severe typhoid epidemic linked to tainted oysters from West Sayville, New York led the U.S. Public Health Service to develop what has evolved into the National Shellfish Sanitation Program. In accordance with this federal-state-industry cooperative activity, New York State commenced inspecting water quality of shellfish growing areas and certifying those approved for harvesting.

The present technique used for determining certification is based on estimating the abundance of fecal or total coliform bacteria. Both naturally occurring coliform bacteria in soil and fecal coliform contribute to total coliform abundance, while fecal coliform abundance is attributable only to feces from warm-blooded animals. Coliform bacteria do not cause illness, but pathogenic bacteria and viruses, also present in feces may cause serious illnesses. The presence of coliforms is used to indicate the degree to which water is contaminated by feces, and thus, possibly by pathogens.

As presently applied, if the median number of total coliform bacteria in a shellfish growing area exceeds a mean probable number (MPN) of 70/100 mL of seawater or if the MPN of fecal coliform exceeds 14/100 mL, shellfishing must be prohibited, and the area is said to be closed. Closure decisions are made by the New York State Department of Environmental Conservation (NYSDEC).

Baymen have long complained that the NYSDEC is unnecessarily stringent, and closures may be undertaken at the whim of some bureaucrat. Baymen are angered when a closure line is taken too literally by officials and see the lines delineating the open and closed areas as being arbitrary. "How different can shellfish on either side of the line be?"

they ask. This has given rise to the practice of "pushing to the line," that is, working 30 to 100 meters into a closed area.

Clammers also say that there is no proof that the shellfish themselves are contaminated, since the tests apply only to the waters in which the shellfish grow. Scientists generally agree with the baymen that the coliform standard is wanting. Neither the test nor the standard distinguishes between fecal matter bacteria derived from humans, which may indicate a serious potential health threat, and those from other warm-blooded animals, which indicate a lesser public health problem. This is important on Long Island where it is believed that many acres of shellfish grounds are closed on the basis of coliform bacteria from cats and dogs whose fecal material gets into the Bay in stormwater runoff.

More importantly, the abundance of coliform bacteria does not correlate very well with the abundance of viruses that are the cause of most disease outbreaks. This means that areas closed because of high coliform bacteria levels may be safe, while open areas may be at risk. Although development of a viral standard is of high research priority, much more research is needed before one will be available.

Despite the baymen's assurances that "no one they know has ever gotten sick from eating shellfish from closed beds," large numbers of people have. Between 1980 and 1986 perhaps as many as 60,000 people became ill with gastroenteritis, hepatitis and other diseases from eating raw shellfish (Rippey and Verber 1986). Not all the shellfish were from New York, but in almost a thousand of the documented cases of illness, New York shellfish were implicated (Guzewich and Morse 1986).

Although numbers of health advisories have been issued by the New York State Department of Health, warning of the hazards of consuming contaminated shellfish, incidents of shellfish-related disease continue. In the view of some public health officials, the frequent occurrence of disease attributed to raw shellfish, sometimes as much as one third of all food-borne disease incidents in New York, is sufficiently serious to warrant an action as stringent as a ban on the sale of raw shellfish in restaurants.

Public enforcement of closed shellfish areas is never likely to be adequate, and baymen seem unable to take effective self-policing actions. They are fearful, therefore, that at any time, adverse publicity from contaminated shellfish-related disease outbreak will weaken the market. While adverse publicity does result in loss of sales — prices may fall dramatically following such publicity — demand rebounds as the matter fades from public consciousness.

Closures compound the public health problem. Because legal harvesting is prohibited, hard clam abundance in those areas increases, quickly becoming very attractive for illegal harvesting. While nearly all baymen occasionally stray into closed areas, there is a special "class" of baymen — the professional poachers who work only in closed areas. They use high speed boats and dredges to work the beds, usually under cover of darkness. Many employ watchmen to warn of police. Their speed and covertness routinely enable them to escape from those enforcing the closure.

It has been suggested that between 25% and 50% of the baymen work uncertified (closed) areas. These figures compare well with estimates by enforcement and management officials (Mirchel 1980). Policing of poaching and other illegal clamming activities is expensive. In 1977 almost $1 million were expended in enforcement activities in Great South Bay, yet enforcement is far from successful.

Closure of shellfish beds is often a rallying point for baymen who seem to join together only when faced by this threat. Closure can also become an important local political issue. For example, in May 1977 the NYSDEC sought to close 1078 hectares of shellfish beds in Great South Bay because the overlying waters did not meet the standard. The towns of Babylon, Islip and Brookhaven, together with the baymen, took the issue into the courts seeking to overturn the closure. After a lengthy and well-publicized hearing, the courts upheld the state, and the area was closed. However, the antagonism between the baymen and the NYSDEC continues.

A number of programs have been undertaken by government to primarily make the closed areas less attractive to poachers and secondarily to recover an economically valuable resource. As early as the 1940s, New York permitted the transplanting of shellfish from closed to open areas where the shellfish could cleanse themselves of pathogens. Since the 1960s the state's goal has been to transplant all the shellfish from the closed areas. However, as the hard clam population in the open Bay declined, the baymen argued that the closed areas were natural breeding areas and, with that in mind, worked to have the program terminated. Recently, baymen have come to view the shellfish in the closed areas as a renewable resource that should be made available on a continuing basis.

BAYMEN AND SHELLFISH MANAGEMENT

Almost since the first oyster was harvested from Great South Bay there has been a realization of the need for a governmental role in assuring the continuity and future of its shellfish industry. It is a goal difficult to achieve. Responsibilities are fractionized among the three towns, Suffolk County, state and federal governments and their numerous agencies.

The towns of Islip, Brookhaven and Babylon have traditionally played the major role in shellfish management. Colonial patents granted ownerships of Bay bottom to the towns, thus, the shellfish have always been considered a property right. Shellfish became a public resource to be managed in the common interest. State government, established after the towns and lacking property rights, became involved in shellfish management primarily through the protection of the public health.

Each of the towns is responsible for the management of resources within its jurisdiction, a tightly held prerogative. Baymen tend to be parochial even though Brookhaven and Islip and Islip and Babylon towns have reciprocal shellfishing privileges. Consequently, town actions are often fragmented, and questions of baywide significance are addressed piecemeal, if at all.

Baymen have traditionally been greatly involved in management. It was the baymen who went before the town trustees to seek funds or legislation. Local officials have, in many instances, sanctioned the representatives of the baymen, concluding that the baymen know what is best. Because other opinions were seldom heard, their requests were generally acceded to, giving baymen a sense of political power.

The baymen's attitudes towards shellfish management are not, however, homogeneous. An example of the diversity of attitudes and of government response may be found in the Town of Islip's "Peanut Clam Debate." In 1931 Islip forbade the taking of small (less than 1 inch in thickness) "peanut" clams. Shortly afterwards another group of baymen argued before the Islip Town Board that the prohibition was unnecessary because, "There will always be peanut clams as long as there is a set" (Suffolk County News 1931). The town board went along, rescinding the then 70 day-old-ordinance. Again, in 1938 the Community Baymen's Association argued for a ban on the taking of peanut clams. Shippers and some baymen argued that the proposal was "unnecessary, unenforceable and unfair" (Suffolk County News 1938). The town board compromised and set a minimum size limit of 3/4 inch (18.4 mm) — a prohibition which remained until New York State established the current 1 inch minimum in 1942. Today, some baymen consider the enforcement of the minimum size limit their most important Bay management concern.

As knowledge of the Bay and its ecosystem becomes more comprehensive, efforts have been made to make management more scientific. The towns, for example, have established separate departments or divisions to implement management programs. But managers and baymen continue to differ on what might be considered conservation — baymen often seeking social legislation that has the unspoken objectives of preserving their livelihood or of increasing their earnings, and managers being more interested in preserving the resource. Baymen are also, at times, skeptical of the studies managers use to justify their actions, feeling that, after all, they work on the Bay and how could an outsider understand what is happening?

Baymen are fatalistic about nature but distrust government. They fear the concept of "management taking away their living" more than loss of employment through declining catch. This distrust possibly arises because most management schemes would require major changes in the fishery, causing loss of valued freedoms. In the end, while management practices are continually improving, progress is made against a gradient of baymen's opinions and mutual distrust.

One issue that has caused considerable disagreement between baymen and managers is the possible leasing of portions of the Bay for private mariculture. It has been shown that leased areas such as those that would be used by mariculturists are more economically productive than common property (Agnello and Donnelley 1975). While managers view mariculture as a means of diversifying and enhancing economic return in coexistence with a "free Bay," baymen see it as a beginning of corporate domination, a continuation of the old conflict between oyster farmers and independent baymen. Baymen have successfully used their political muscle to block leasing. As they see it, as long as there is a free Bay, they will always be able to make a living.

The traditional hard clam fishery is at a critical juncture. With the decline in hard clam abundance, many baymen have had to seek alternative work. Those remaining on the Bay have had increasing difficulty in sustaining their income. Competition from other traditional suppliers in the northeastern states and increasing production from southern states has lessened the dominance of the Great South Bay hard clam fishery.

The market uncertainties caused by shellfish-related disease outbreaks has made both demand and prices subject to extreme disruption from only slight perturbations. Can both the bayman and the hard clam be preserved in Great South Bay?

A number of difficult questions must be resolved:

1) Should the hard clam fishery be regulated in such a way that only those it will financially support are permitted to participate?
2) Alternatively, should the fishery be allowed to further degenerate, even if it forces more baymen to leave?
3) Should actions be taken to improve the situation without interfering with the evolution of the fishery? In particular, should management be neutral, further a social process or seek a particular result?
4) Should government concentrate solely on enhancement and let the balance between size of stock and number of baymen seek its own level?

A sustained hard clam fishery in Great South Bay contributes significantly to the region, the state and the nation. But, as J.L. McHugh has stated, "We depend upon nature to keep the industry self replenished. With greater demands on the industry in the future, we will need better science and management to maintain and increase production." (McHugh 1972).

SUMMARY

The Great South Bay, its shellfish resources and the baymen who harvest hard clams have had a long, dynamic and fairly complex relationship. Each has been influenced by physical, chemical and biological processes and changes, and the Bay and its shellfishery has been further modified in response the the interplay of legal, social and economic factors.

The present commercial hard clam shellfishery has evolved from a subsistence shellfishery that began with the settlement of Long Island and continued up until the 1850s, to a commercial hard clam and oyster shellfishery through the early years of this century and, finally, to a hard clam dependent shellfishery beginning in the 1940s. The hard clam shellfishery has since then gone from a period of rising harvests to declining catches and now awaits recovery and controlled harvest.

The baymen have shaped the shellfishery through their social, economic and political involvement and have, in turn, been influenced by the shellfishery. The baymen are also an integral part of the ecology of the Bay as they are, in effect, a major predator on hard clams. A mud crab can consume between four and 130 hard clams per day, while a baymen, if he is to earn a median income, must "consume" at least 583 hard clams per workday.

The baymen, though, are more than just another hard clam predator. Harvesting hard clams is a skill with its own unique tools. The work and baymen's environment have resulted in a characteristic set of attitudes and personal goals. One consequence is that baymen have a perspective on issues that is oftentimes at odds with fishery managers and government. The baymen must also contend with threats to their livlihood, most notably the loss of shellfishing areas due to the pollution that has accompanied the suburbanization of Long Island.

The future of the shellfish industry is far from certain. How to best preserve both the baymen and the hard clam is a difficult and complex question. Should the number of baymen be limited to what the resource can financially support? Should the fishery be left alone? Should the size of the resource be increased with no limit on the number of baymen? Should management be allowed to alter the evolution of the fishery?

ACKNOWLEDGEMENTS

The support of Henrietta Acampora, Supervisor of the Town of Brookhaven, New York and members of the Brookhaven Town Board is gratefully acknowledged.

REFERENCES

Agnello, R.J. and L.P. Donnelley. 1975. Property rights and efficiency in the oyster industry. J. Law Econ.18(2):521-533.

Agassiz, C. 1909. The romance of the oyster Part IV. The Blue Point Oyster Industry. National Magazine, January.

Biles, H. 1950. It's a tough life, but they like it: Hardy individuals man local clam fleet. Patchogue Advance. 14 September, p.1.

Buckner, S. 1984. Population dynamics of the hard clam, *Mercenaria mercenaria*, in Great South Bay, New York. Ph.D. Thesis, Marine Sciences Research Center, State University of New York at Stony Brook, NY. 217 pp.

Bumpus, P.F., J.H. Ryther, F.A. Richards, and R.F. Vaccaro. 1954. Report on a survey of the hydrography of Great South Bay and Moriches Bay made in July 1954 for the Towns of Islip and Brookhaven, N.Y. Woods Hole Oceanographic Institution Ref. No. 54-85. 9 pp.

Caro, R.A. 1974. The power broker: Robert Moses and the fall of New York. Alfred A. Knopf, Inc., New York. 1,246 pp.

Carriker, M.R. 1951. Observations on the penetration of tightly closing bivalves by *Busycon* and other predators. Ecology 32(1):73-83.

_____. 1957. Preliminary study of newly hatched oyster drills, *Urosalpinx cinerea*. J. Elisha Mitchell Sci. Soc. 73:328-351.

_____. 1961. Interrelation of functional morphology, behavior, and autecology in early stages of the bivalve *Mercenaria mercenaria*. J. Elisha Mitchell Sci. Soc. 77(2):168-241.

Coles, R.R. 1955. Wampum was more than money. L.I. Forum 18(7):27-29.

COSMA, 1985. Suffolk County's hard clam fishery: An overview and an analysis of management alternatives. Report of the Coastal Ocean Science and Management Alternatives (COSMA) Program of the Marine Sciences Research Center, State University of New York at Stony Brook, NY.

Dickerson, C.P. 1975. A history of the Sayville community. The Suffolk County News, Sayville, NY, unpaged.

Fox, R.E. 1980. Investigation of the hard clam resources of Great South Bay, N.Y., New York State Department of Environmental Conservation Project No. 3-263-R. Completion Report, Commercial Fisheries Research and Development Act. 50 pp.

Franz, D. 1977. Size and age-specific predation by *Lunatia heros* (Say, 1822) on the surf clam *Spisula solidissima* (Dillwyn, 1817) off western Long Island, New York. Veliger 20(2):144-150.

Gabriel, R.H. 1921. The evolution of Long Island, A story of land and sea. Yale University Press, New Haven, 194 pp.

Gibbons, M. 1984. Aspects of predation by the crabs *Neopanope sayi, Ovalipes ocellatus*, and *Pagurus longicarpus* on juvenile hard clams *Mercenaria mercenaria*. Ph.D. Thesis, Marine Sciences Research Center, State University of New York at Stony Brook, NY, 96 pp.

Glancy, J.B. 1956. Biological benefits of Moriches and Shinnecock Inlets with particular reference to pollution and shellfisheries. Report to the New York Army Corps of Engineers, 8 pp.

Greene, G.T. 1978. Population structure, growth and mortality of hard clams at selected locations in Great South Bay, New York. M.S. Thesis. Marine Sciences Research Center, State University of New York at Stony Brook, NY. 199 pp.

Guzewich, J.J. and D.L. Morse. 1986. Sources of shellfish in outbreaks of probable viral gastroenteritis: Implications for control. J. Food Prot. 49(5):389-394.

Holmsen, A. and S. Horsley. 1981. Characteristics of the labor force in quahog handraking.

Contribution No. 5, University of Rhode Island Cooperative Extension Service. 7 pp.

Kassner, J. and T.W. Cramer. 1983. The evolution of the Great South Bay, New York shellfish industry. Contribution DEP. 83-01 Town of Brookhaven. p 15.

Kavenagh, W.K. 1980. Vanishing tidelands: Land use and the law in Suffolk County, N.Y. 1650-1979. New York Sea Grant Institute, NYSG-RS-80-28, 265 pp.

Kelpin, G.M. 1981. Depuration and its implications for Long Island's hard clam industry. M.S. Thesis. Marine Sciences Research Center, State University of New York at Stony Brook, NY. 115 pp.

Long Island Regional Planning Board. 1982. Historical population of Long Island communities 1790-1980: Decennial Census Data. Hauppauge, NY.

MacKenzie, C.L. Jr. 1977. Predation on hard clam (*Mercenaria mercenaria*) populations. Trans. Am. Fish. Soc. 106(6):530-537.

McHugh, J.L. 1972. Marine fisheries of New York State. Fish. Bull. 70:585-610.

Mirchel, A.C.F. 1980. Enforcement of hard clam laws on Great South Bay, N.Y. M.S. Thesis. Marine Sciences Research Center, State University of New York at Stony Brook, NY. 79 pp.

O'Connor, J. S., and O. Terry. 1972. The marine wetlands of Nassau and Suffolk Counties, New York. Marine Sciences Research Center, State University of New York at Stony Brook, NY. Prepared for the Nassau-Suffolk Regional Planning Board, Hauppauge, NY. 99 pp.

Rippey, S.R. and J. L. Verber. 1986. Shellfish borne disease outbreaks. U.S. Department of Health and Human Services, Public Health Service,

Food and Drug Administration, Shellfish Sanitation Branch, Northeast Technical Services Unit, Davisville, Rhode Island. 39 pp.

Ryther, J.H., R.F. Vaccaro, E.M. Hulburt, C.S. Yentsch and R.R.L. Guillard. 1958. Report on a survey of the chemistry, biology and hydrography of Great South Bay and Moriches Bay conducted during June and September, 1958, for the Townships of Islip and Brookhaven, Long Island, New York. Woods Hole Oceanographic Institution Ref. No. 58-57. 18 pp.

Salwen, B. 1975. Post-glacial environments and cultural change in the Hudson River basin. Man in the Northwest 10 (Fall):43-70.

Smith, O.R. and E. Chin. 1951. The effects of predation on soft clams, *Mya arenaria*. Proc. Nat. Shellfish. Assoc. Conv. Add. pp. 37-44.

Squires, D.F. 1981. The bight of the big apple. N.Y. Sea Grant Institute. NYSG-RS-81-00, 84 pp.

Suffolk County News. 1931. Town Board rescinds peanut clam ordinance. August 14, 1931. p. 1.

Suffolk County News. 1938. Shellfish code after parleys. October 14, 1938. p.1.

Taylor, L.J. 1983. Dutchmen on the bay; The ethnohistory of a contractual community. University of Pennsylvania Press. Philadelphia, 206 pp.

Town of Brookhaven. 1878. Minutes of the Meetings of the Town Trustees, May 7.

Town of Brookhaven. 1880. Minutes of the Meetings of the Town Trustees, February 10.

WAPORA, Inc. 1981. Estuarine impact assessment (Shellfish Resources) for the Nassau-Suffolk streamflow augmentation alternatives, draft report on existing conditions. U.S. Environ. Prot. Agency, New York 114 pp.

_____. 1982. Impact assessment on shellfish resources of Great South Bay, South Oyster Bay and Hempstead Bay, N.Y. (draft report). U. S. Environ. Prot. Agency, New York. pp. 1-6.

Wilcox, U.V. 1976. The manufacture and use of wampum in the northeast. Bead J. 3(1):10-19.

Open garvie used for raking clams.

R. GEORGE ROWLAND

CHAPTER 9

JURISDICTION

Lee E. Koppelman
Center for Regional Policy Studies
State University of New York
Stony Brook, NY 11794

INTRODUCTION

The 75-mile-long south shore bay system stretches from East Rockaway Inlet at Hempstead Bay in western Nassau County to Shinnecock Inlet in Shinnecock Bay in eastern Suffolk County. This bay system constitutes one overall bay, separated from the Atlantic Ocean by a barrier beach. This beach is punctuated by five inlets: East Rockaway, Jones, Fire Island, Moriches and Shinnecock and is commonly identified by its segmented portions. The waters in Nassau County are called Hempstead Bay and South Oyster Bay, according to their respective town jurisdictions. The two easterly bay sections in Suffolk County are named Moriches and Shinnecock Bays. The central portion of the bay system starting at the Nassau-Suffolk border, including the Towns of Babylon, Islip and the western half of Brookhaven, is approximately 48 km (30 miles) long and contains the widest portion, 8.7 km (5.4 miles), at the Town of Islip, and is known as Great South Bay (Fig. 1.1).

This Bay and its shorelines are subject to numerous activities: commercial and recreational fishing and shellfishing, commercial and sports boating, swimming, shellfish culturing, dredging, ferry transportation, private and public shoreline recreation, barrier beach protection, home construction and environmental education. Each of these categories is legitimate in itself. Some of these uses may even be harmonious with other uses. However, it is more likely that multiple uses result in conflict. For example, one user's "good" dredging may result in habitat destruction for a shellfish user. Swimmers may be imperiled by boaters. Home development may limit shoreline access. In fact, development of all types may contribute to the pollution of the Bay. Even

individual uses, when not confronted with competition from other uses, may pose a serious concern if carried out too intensively.

Along with use, there is often the problem of misuse or abuse. For example, the harvesting of undersize or seed hard clams is certainly a misuse of the resource. Poaching of shellfish from closed areas constitutes an abuse that is criminal and also detrimental to the public image of shellfish as a healthy food.

As a result of the myriad uses of the Bay and concerns for the protection of its various resources and public health and safety, a plethora of regulations, enforcement actions, advisory coalitions, permit requirements and jurisdictional participants have developed to control and manage the activities in the Bay. At least 34 departments, agencies, commissions, administrations and legislative bodies exercise, to one degree or another, jurisdiction over Great South Bay. This chapter is an attempt to concisely and clearly identify these various controlling bodies according to their functional interests and degrees of control. Each level of government, i.e., federal, state, regional, county and municipal is categorized separately. The conclusion of the chapter contains an amalgam of all levels with cross-references to jurisdictional overlaps.

FEDERAL PARTICIPANTS

Eight separate federal agencies exercise fairly continuous interest in and control over Great South Bay and its surrounds. The Fish and Wildlife Service (FWS) and the National Park Service (NPS) are two divisions of the Department of the Interior that exercise regulatory and management responsibilities. All federal dredge or fill permits, particularly those submitted to the United States Army Corps of Engineers (COE), must be reviewed by the Ecological Services Branch of FWS to ensure that impacts of biological importance are considered. The COE permits are issued pursuant to Section 10 of the Rivers and Harbors Act. Section 404 of the Federal Water Pollution Control

Act must also be complied with.

In addition, the FWS manages all national wildlife refuges in accordance with 50 CFR Subchapter C, which refers to the National Wildlife Refuge System. This includes the 200 acre Seatuck National Wildlife Refuge located on Champlain Creek in the Town of Islip, which is operated as an urban refuge primarily for forest and wading birds. The 2600 acre Wertheim National Wildlife Refuge located on the Carmans River at Shirley in the Town of Brookhaven is designated primarily for migratory bird habitat use, with particular emphasis on the provision of winter habitats for black ducks.

The NPS manages the Fire Island National Seashore, a part of the barrier beach. This includes development control within the boundaries of the seashore and police control over users and uses within the park. The COE carries out beach erosion control projects for navigation improvement and hurricane protection. Table 9.1 identifies three recent or current authorized projects that lie wholly or in part in Great South Bay.

A more recent entrant in the list of participants is the Federal Emergency Management Agency (FEMA). Created according to Reorganization Plan No. 3 of 1978 (43 CFR 41943), FEMA is responsible for the administration of the National Flood Insurance Program. This program was established by Title XIII of the Housing and Urban Development Act of 1968 and subsequently amended twice by the Flood Disaster Protection Act of 1973 and the Disaster Relief Act of 1974. The amendments require the purchase of flood insurance as a condition of receiving any form of federal or federally-related financial assistance for acquisition or construction of insurable buildings within a designated special flood hazard area.

Qualification for federally subsidized flood insurance is predicated on the adoption of flood plain management regulations by the local community. The criteria to be met are contained in 44 CFR Part 60, which generally applies to the elevation of structures above the 100-year base flood elevation and structural flood proofing requirements. All communities surrounding the

Great South Bay have adopted flood plain management regulations. FEMA has completed mapping the coastal high hazard area and the 100-year and 500-year flood plains.

FEMA also provides funding for special disaster-related studies. The Long Island Regional Planning Board prepared a comprehensive hurricane damage mitigation plan, sponsored by the Region II office of FEMA, with funding provided under 44 CFR Part 300.6 Earthquake Plans and Preparedness (Koppelman and Davies 1984).

The United States Coast Guard (USCG), a branch of the Treasury Department, carries out regulatory and service operations affecting the Bay. In conjunction with the United States Environmental Protection Agency (USEPA), the USCG is responsible for supervision of cleanup activities when petroleum products are spilled in any of the navigable waters of the nation. The spiller is responsible for the actual removal of these pollutants from marine waters. If the on-scene coordinator for the USCG determines that the spiller is incapable of timely cleanup operations, an outside contractor can be retained and paid out of the pollution fund, established under Section 311(A) of the Federal Water Pollution Control Act (FWPCA) (86 Stat. 816). The spiller is liable to reimburse the fund for all expenses associated with the cleanup.

The USCG is also responsible for certification of marine devices pursuant to 86 Stat. 871 and also enforces vessel discharge standards set forth in the act. Setting standards and regulations for boats and associated equipment is another duty called for in Section 12 of the Federal Boat Safety Act of 1971.

Of indirect, but nevertheless, great concern to the environmental well-being of the Bay is the potential threat to the entire south shore of Long Island by off-shore drilling activities. In fact, the county of Suffolk engaged in lengthy legal actions against the United States Department of Interior, whose division for Outer Continental Shelf (OCS) operations oversees the award of leaseholds on the shelf. One issue raised by the county was the potential conflict of interest, and in fact, the possible malfeasance of the Secretary of the Interior. The Secretary's sworn duties include the protection of national parks and resources under the jurisdiction of FWS, while at the same time promoting OCS, which as Santa Barbara, California demonstrated, is at variance with these objectives. Although Suffolk County ultimately lost in the higher courts after winning in the Federal District Court, the case did generate Congressional action to amend the OCS Act to provide greater support to local governments in the case of a spill (Koppelman and Robbins 1980).

Thus, the role of the USCG in carrying out its statutory responsibilities for the safe operation and maintenance of OCS facilities and vessels pursuant to the Outer Continental Shelf Awards Act (43 USC 1331), as amended by the 1978 amendments (P.L. 95-372), is important. Each OCS facility is subject to an annual on-site inspection, which includes checking all Coast Guard approved or required equipment and procedures designed to prevent or mitigate fires, spillages and other major accidents on OCS facilities.

In addition to USEPA's role with the USCG,

Table 9.1. U.S. Army Corps of Engineers Authorized Projects.

Project	Description	Area Covered	Percent Complete	Latest Cost Estimates
Fire Island Inlet to Jones Inlet—beach erosion control and navigation improvement (authorized in 1958).	Dredge Fire Island Inlet shoal to relieve pressure of tidal currents against Oak Beach, provide deposition area for littoral drift, obtain fill for a feeder beach, nourish Oak Beach and construct sand dike across gorge channel.	15 miles of ocean shoreline.	100%	$4,919,600 total first cost.
(Authorization modified in 1962.)	Excavate littoral reservoir and navigation channel at Fire Island Inlet and periodically transfer sand to a feeder beach. Construct dike and jetty extension when need is indiciated by actual operating experience.		100% Jetty and dike extension not included.	$43,620,000 estimated first cost.
Fire Island Inlet to Montauk Point—beach erosion control and hurricane protection (authorized in 1960).	Widen beaches along developed area; raise dune elevations along most of project area; plant grass on dunes; construct three interior drainage structures and, as needed, not more than 50 groins; participate in cost of beach nourishment for up to 10 years.	83 miles of ocean shoreline.	5%; 17 of 50 groins completed; about 2 million cubic meters of fill in place.	$137,864,000 estimated cost. $846,000 estimated annual cost for nourishment.
Fire Island Inlet-channel improvement (authorized in 1937; modified in 1950).	Construct a jetty (5000 ft. long) at Democrat Point and excavate a channel from ocean to deep water within inlet.		100%	$684,545 total cost.

Sources: U. S. Army Corps of Engineers, North Atlantic Division. 1981. Water resources development in New York. 115 pp.

U. S. Army Corps of Engineers, New York District. 1983. General design memorandum. Moriches Inlet project, reformulation study and environmental impact statement.

they also play a major role in water pollution control as set forth in the Federal Water Pollution Control Act (P.L. 92-500), as amended by the Clean Water Act (P.L. 95-217). The USEPA provides regulatory controls for most of the state and local environmental regulatory programs with jurisdiction over the Bay. They also provided the catalytic spur that was the basis for state and local governments instituting these programs. For example, Section 201 provides grants to localities for the construction of publically-owned treatment works. Although administered by the State of New York, no money can be released unless the proposed work conforms to a USEPA site-specific waste treatment plan that details how the waste discharges will be abated. Section 208 provided funds for the development of area-wide waste treatment management plans.

Another important element of the USEPA water pollution regulation is Section 301, which calls for standards and enforcement procedures for effluent limitations, water quality standards, national performance standards and toxic and pretreatment effluent standards. Finally, Section 402 created the National Pollution Discharge Elimination System (NPDES), which served as the model for New York State's program: the State Pollution Discharge Elimination System (SPDES).

Two additional federal participants, whose influence is felt in the management of Great South Bay are the Food and Drug Administration (FDA) in the Public Health Service and the Office of Coastal Zone Management (OCZM) in the Department of Commerce. Their jurisdiction is advisory in nature with implementation powers exercised by state and local governments.

The National Shellfish Sanitation Program (NSSP) was established in 1924 in response to an outbreak of typhoid attributed to shellfish. The FDA, in cooperative collaboration with shellfish producing states and by drawing members from the commercial shellfish industry, produced guidelines and techniques to help ensure the healthy quality of shellfish consumed by the public. Even though the program is voluntary and the guidelines are not enforceable by the NSSP or the FDA, compliance is achieved by requiring the members to strictly follow the guidelines and programs.

New York State is a member and meets the requirement by enforcement of the State Environmental Conservation Laws (ECL), as well as the regulations of the Department of Environmental Conservation Rules and Regulations (NYCRR), which are based directly on the guidelines. Thus, the shellfish activities of Great South Bay are regulated as to the certification of harvest areas, the identification of harvesters and processors and the inspection of harvesting and processing sectors. A further protective measure provided by the FDA is an annual review of shellfish sanitation practices in participating states. If any problems are noticed, the appropriate state agencies are requested to remedy them. The key elements of the guidelines address the prevention of harvesting from closed areas and the arrest of violators.

The Coastal Zone Management Act of 1972 (P.L. 92-53) was an attempt to encourage the 34 coastal states and territories of the nation to preserve, protect and wisely develop their coastal resources. The administrative responsibilities were assigned to a newly created OCZM in the National Oceanic and Atmospheric Administration (NOAA) of the Department of Commerce. Funds were made available to the states to assist in the development of a Coastal Management Program (CMP) which, upon adoption by the state and approved by the Secretary of Commerce, would trigger two federal responses: (1) each approved state and its localities would become eligible for a variety of technical and financial aids to be used to strike a balance between economic development and resource preservation; and (2) a federal consistency clause would fall into place.

This unique aspect of law represents a most interesting departure in the practice of intergovernmental relations over the past half century. Namely, it provides that no federal action can be taken that would contradict the policies set forth in the State CMP, except for the actions of the Department of Defense and the operation of OCS activities by the Department of the Interior. The import to the management of Great South Bay and its surrounding communities is significant— the prime jurisdiction over this area is in state and local control. Other than the two noted exemptions to the consistency requirements, no federal agency can expend funds or initiate programs unless the action would be in furtherance of the CMP.

Table 9.2 contains a summary of the eight federal agencies and their respective juridictional interests in the Bay. Perhaps a ninth intermittant federal entity should at least be acknowledged. The Congress both indirectly and directly takes actions that indicate its exercise of jurisdiction. Its most obvious role is in the enactment of general legislation in the national interest that also includes the activities of the Bay. For example, the FWPCA and the CZM Acts of 1972 and the various

Table 9.2. Federal agency roles in the Great South Bay.

Agency	Funding	Zoning	Permit	Enforcement	Operations	Review	Advice
NPS	x	x		x	x		
FWS			x	x	x	x	
COE	x		x		x	x	x
EPA	x		x	x		x	x
USCG			x	x		x	
FEMA	x				x	x	x
OCZM	x					x	x
FDA						x	x

amendments to the Rivers and Harbors Act have such relevance. Periodically, special congressional action is taken to address a specific problem in the Bay, whether it be for navigation, shellfish enhancement or creation of the Fire Island Seashore Park or hurricane remediation.

STATE PARTICIPANTS

New York State exercises numerous controls over Great South Bay, which can be grouped into nine broad categories ranging from environmental review procedures to wetlands protection and preservation. Most functions and responsibilities are carried out by the New York State Department of Environmental Conservation (NYSDEC). The Health Department and the Office of the Secretary of State periodically become involved whenever public health or coastal planning issues arise. Although most health matters are handled by the Suffolk County Department of Health Services on behalf of the state, the commissioner occasionally invokes state control directly. For example, during the concern over shellfish quality in 1986, edicts were evoked from Albany prohibiting the sale and use of raw clams.

After passage of the Coastal Zone Management Act of 1972, the Governor assigned state responsibility for administering the act to the Secretary of State. Although most of the actual planning was performed by regional agencies, the state coordinated the assembly of the individual plans into an overall state package of recommended plans and programs. The Secretary of State was also responsible for securing from the state legislature the necessary laws required by the Secretary of Commerce to achieve certification of the state-wide plan. Subsequent to federal approval, the Secretary of State administers the consistency clause provisions to ensure compliance with the state's CMP.

The Waterfront Revitalization and Coastal Resources Act, which resulted from the original plan, is also administered by the Office of the Secretary of State. This program provides funds to local governments to enable them to carry out waterfront revitalization plans and programs. Such work has already been carried out by the Towns of Islip and Brookhaven, covering their respective portions of the Great South Bay.

The continual presence of state involvement over the Bay is, however, carried out by NYDEC. Whether it be the administration of the New York State Environmental Quality Review Act (SEQRA), issuance of boat permits, management of tidal wetlands, management and regulation of the waters to control pollution, promotion and regulation of shellfish, control over fisheries and wildlife or administration of several programs concerned with flood control and damage mitigation, it is fair to observe that NYSDEC has one of the major jurisdictions in the Bay. In fact, NYSDEC is the only one of the three agencies discussed that has established a regional office in Suffolk County owing to its range of activities over environmental concerns on Long Island.

A preponderance of time and resources is expended daily on shellfish management in the Bay. NYSDEC is responsible for certification of shellfish grounds in accordance with Part 41 of the Environmental Conservation Law (ECL) and inspection of these grounds relative to standards established by them as provided in Part 47 of the ECL. They also regulate digging permits, maintain records of harvesting and sales of shellfish and monitor the diggers' recordkeeping. These powers are provided for in Part 42 of the ECL. Part 48 of the ECL gives the NYDEC the right to issue permits for shellfish hatcheries and off-bottom culture within the Bay. They also are the designated state participant for the administration of the NSSP pursuant to Article 13 of the ECL. In particular, Title 3 refers to marine fisheries.

The protection, enhancement and safe consumption of the Bay's living resources is directly related to the quality of the waters in the Bay. Thus, it is entirely consistent that another major responsibility of NYSDEC concerns water pollution (see Chapter 4 on the status of water quality in the Bay). In this regard they classify the Bay waters according to state standards and they administer control over discharges into the Bay.

WATER QUALITY STANDARDS

Under Article 17, Title 3 of the ECL, quality standards are established in the Bay for the following constituents: coliform bacteria; dissolved oxygen; toxic wastes and deleterious substances; garbage, cinders, ashes, oils, sludge or other refuse; pH; turbidity; color; suspended, colloidal or precipitable solids; oil and floating substances; and thermal discharges. The tributaries that empty into the Bay have numerous classifications including I, D, C, B, SC, SB and SA. Table 9.3 summarizes the general description of these classifications. NYSDEC has classified the open water portions of the Great South Bay as SA.

The NYSDEC publishes periodic bulletins called "Notice to All Shellfish Harvesters," in which they indicate those shellfish grounds that do not comply with sanitary conditions and therefore cannot be harvested. Figure 9.1 is an example of an announcement by NYSDEC, establishing a conditional clamming area. Each year NYSDEC receives requests from the towns to consider specific town waters eligible for designation as conditional clamming areas. NYSDEC staff then test the waters in question, review the historical data for the area and make a determination whether or not the area is eligible for the program. These areas vary from year to year.

STATE POLLUTION DISCHARGE ELIMINATION SYSTEM (SPDES)

Under Article 17, Title 8 of the ECL and consistent with Sec. 402 of the FWPCA Amendments of 1972 which created the NPDES, NYSDEC issues permits for any discharge of sewage and industrial or other wastes into the Bay. The NPDES established the criteria and standards for imposition of treatment requirements and any

Table 9.3. Water quality standards.

Class	Usage
SA	Shellfishing for market and primary and secondary recreation.
SB	No shellfishing for market; suitable for primary and secondary recreation.
SC	Suitable for fishing and fish propagation; suitable for primary and secondary recreation.
B	Primary contact recreation - not water supply.
C	Fishing and fish propagation; primary and secondary recreation.
D	Suitable for fishing; no fish propagation; suitable for primary and secondary recreation.
I	Secondary recreation, not primary; no shellfishing.

waste discharge by means of a permit system for point source discharges. The SPDES program carries out these requirements. In practice it means that any facility that discharges more than 1000 gallons per day must have a permit.

Discharge permits for the Bay are administered by NYSDEC and the Suffolk County Department of Health Services (SCDHS). Permits must be renewed every five years and are categorized by the following groupings: industrial wastes, industrial discharges, sewage treatment plant discharges and subsurface disposal systems. Discharges are classified as industrial (more specifically as significant, nonsignificant, toxic or nontoxic); municipal discharges (waste water); and private/commercial/institutional discharges.

Since the inception of the program in January 1970, NYSDEC has issued six NPDES and SPDES permits for surface water discharges into the Bay. However, there are hundreds of stormwater discharge locations that are not regulated by any level of government. This is a point of serious contention, and these locations should be monitored and regulated by state or county agencies.

WETLANDS PROTECTIONS

The Tidal Wetlands Act of 1972 (ECL Article 25) provided $30 million for acquisition of important tidal wetlands by NYSDEC. It also provided for a regulation program requiring issuance of permits by NYSDEC for any alteration or perturbation of all tidal wetlands and the surrounding uplands to an elevation of 10 feet.

Three other areas of jurisdiction exercized by NYSDEC include environmental review for compliance with the SEQRA, control of dredging or disposal of fill in or around the Bay by means of a permit process and administration of several programs geared to flood control or mitigation.

STATE ENVIRONMENTAL QUALITY REVIEW ACT

This law requires that all state and local governments or private developers undertaking, funding or approving any projects that may have a significant effect on the environment prepare or request the preparation of an environmental impact

statement (EIS). The EIS must be comprehensive in scope, detailing the effects likely to result from the project, the ways in which negative effects can be minimized or eliminated and the identification of alternatives that may be available.

Table 9.4 contains a summary of the three state agencies and their respective jurisdictional interests in the Bay.

REGIONAL AGENCIES

There are two regional agencies that fall between the three (federal, state and local) levels of government. The first is the Interstate Sanitation Commission (ISC), which exists as a three-state compact covering portions of New York, New Jersey and Connecticut. Its main environmental mandates cover surface water quality and air quality. The second is the Long Island Regional Planning Board (LIRPB), which in effect is the only regional entity for both Nassau and Suffolk Counties with prime concern for comprehensive planning on the island.

The ISC, created in 1936, was the first and only governmental body that promulgated and applied water quality standards for all waters within the ISC's jurisdiction. The eastern extremity runs from New Haven, Connecticut on a straight line southwesterly to include the Suffolk County Sewer District No. 1, serving the State University of New York at Stony Brook, and terminating slightly east of Fire Island Inlet, thus including the western half of Great South Bay.

Suffolk County's Sewer District No. 3 (Southwest) is under ISC jurisdiction. All of the waters in the Bay and the contiguous offshore vicinity are classified by them as Class A waters. This is the highest designation and means that the area is suitable for all forms of recreation and fish propagation. The waters are also suitable for shellfish harvesting in designated areas.

The ISC carries out effluent and ambient water quality monitoring programs and also inspects and takes samples at wastewater treatment facilities that discharge into the receiving waters. They work in cooperation with EPA and NYSDEC to determine compliance with federal and state SPDES permits.

Table 9.4. State agency roles in the Great South Bay.

Agency	Funding	Permit	Enforcement	Operations	Review	Advice
NYSDEC		x	x	x	x	x
Secretary of State	x				x	
Dept. of Health			x		x	x

The creation of the LIRPB in 1965 was a response to the explosive growth that the communities throughout the island were experiencing and a recognition that the problems of uncontrolled growth related to land use, transportation, housing, economic development and environmental protection were not amenable to solution by the 13 towns, two cities and 92 villages taking independent action.

Although the agency is advisory in nature, it nevertheless plays a role in making decisions affecting Great South Bay. With the very creation of the LIRPB, the members recognized that the marine environment was an integral and vital feature of the island. They designated an ad hoc group of leading experts from industry, academia and the various coastal businesses to undertake a

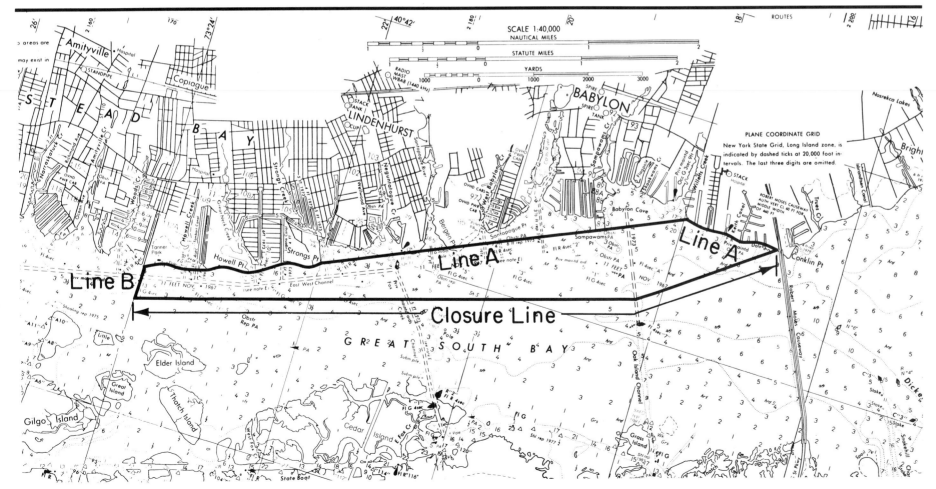

Figure 9.1. New York State Department of Environmental Conservation designated conditional area under the Conditional Clamming Program initiated in 1986.[1]

[1] Under the program, the area south of line A, north of the closure line and east of line B is open for clamming on the eighth day following seven successive days of low rainfall (not to exceed 0.15 inches for each day) and remains open until more than 0.15 inches of rain is recorded in 24 hours.

study of the marine environment and to report their findings to the LIRPB. By the end of 1965 the ad hoc committee produced a report entitled "The Status and Potential of the Marine Environment of Long Island" (Koppelman 1965).

An important segment dealt with the issues of dredging, protection of wetlands and enhancement of the shellfish industry, particularly in Great South Bay. The report also identified the need for research into problems affecting these activities. In response, the LIRPB institutionalized the group into the Regional Marine Resources Council and launched major studies covering these activities. Much of the current policy recommendations covering the management of the Bay grew from this initial work.

Subsequent to the passage of the Ocean Coastal Zone Management Act of 1972, which was patterned in part on the work of the LIRPB, a comprehensive coastal zone plan was developed by the board, setting forth broad guidelines for the planned development of Great South Bay as part of the overall coastal environment. The LIRPB, with strong support from the Secretary of State, encouraged the towns to undertake coastal zone planning, particularly waterfront revitalization planning.

Three Suffolk County departments, Planning, Health Services and Police, also exercise limited functions related to the Bay. The Suffolk County Planning Commission (SCPC) reviews proposed zoning and subdivision actions throughout the county, and more specifically, all those within 152 meters of the coastal edge of the county. Since most of the land adjacent to the Bay is almost totally developed, the commission's actions are infrequent. The Suffolk County Department of Health Services (SCDHS) plays a more continuous role in its certification of swimming areas within the Great South Bay system. The Suffolk County Department of Police (SCDP) maintains a Marine Bureau and serves as the primary law enforcement entity for control of marine traffic and policing of shellfishing areas to enforce the laws against poaching in areas closed to harvesting.

LOCAL GOVERNMENTS

The Towns of Babylon, Islip and Brookhaven exercise the most direct controls over the Bay and perhaps are the most responsible for the problems that plague this body of water. Although each town has specific departments or agencies exercising jurisdiction that ranges from planning, permitting powers, policing and limited operations such as dredging or shellfish seeding programs, the actual jurisdiction is primarily controlled by the respective town boards. This is in contrast to federal, state and regional participation where the departments and agencies make the decisions in accord with their statutory responsibilities. At the local level the elected town boards play a far more direct and day-to-day control than the Congress, New York State Legislature or the Suffolk County Legislature.

Perhaps the single most important impact on the entire Bay system is the pattern of urbanization that has occurred over the past 30 years. Virtually all of the land use and zoning decisions have been taken by the town boards, sometimes in concert with their own planning boards, but quite often in opposition to staff recommendations. Fortunately, the towns have striven in recent years to improve their management over the Bay.

Table 9.5 contains a summary of the regional and local agencies and their respective jurisdictional interests in the Bay.

REFERENCES

Koppleman, L.E. 1965. The status and potential of the marine environment of Long Island. Nassau-Suffolk Regional Planning Board, Hauppauge, NY. 92 pp.

Koppelman, L.E. and S. Robbins. 1980. The Long Island response to the risks of outer continental shelf oil production. Pages 163-184 *in* Coastal zone management journal. Vol. 7, No. 2, 3, 4. Crane, Russak & Company, New York.

Koppelman, L.E. and D. Davies. 1984. Hurricane damage mitigation plan for the south shore of Nassau and Suffolk Counties, New York. Long Island Regional Planning Board, Hauppauge, NY. 196 pp.

Table 9.5. Regional and local agency roles in Great South Bay.

Agency	Planning	Zoning	Funding	Permit	Enforcement	Operations	Review	Advice
ISC				x			x	
LIRPB	x		x				x	x
SCPC	x	x					x	x
SCDHS				x	x	x	x	
SCDP					x			
Towns	x	x	x	x	x	x	x	

Water traffic near Robert Moses Causeway.

IAN STUPAKOFF

CHAPTER 10

USES, MISUSES AND ABUSES OF THE BAY

Lee E. Koppelman

Center for Regional Policy Studies
State University of New York
Stony Brook, NY 11794

INTRODUCTION

From the time of the Poospatuck, Shinnecock and Wyandanch Indians to the present, the human history of Long Island indicates a continued but varying dependency on the marine environment. The Great South Bay offered the Indians an ample protein diet to be had literally for the taking in the form of fish and shellfish. Fish and hard clams were important staples in the Indian diet, and as discussed in Chapters 7 and 8, the hard clam has been a major commercial fishery since at least the 1800s, when records were first kept, to the present and was a major subsistence fishery before then.

Despite a commercial decline in the value of commercial fisheries and maritime commerce, the Great South Bay still plays an important role for those living on or near its shores. Recreational boating and fishing are significant activities—an estimated 25,000 pleasure boats are used on the Bay annually. About 140 yachting clubs and marinas service this flotilla. Multitudes of people seek recreation at beaches and by fishing and operating boats. All these activities leave their mark on the Bay. It is constantly and increasingly subjected to the influences of growing suburbs, sewage and pollution from surface runoff (nonpoint sources).

The dramatic changes that have occurred in the Bay as the result of man's presence have been instantaneous compared with the natural geological processes that created the Bay and its surrounding land areas. The south shore bays of Long Island were among the first of the nation's waterways to be impacted by urbanization and the environmental problems caused by densely populated shoreline areas. The Great South Bay is now ringed by suburban development along its entire north shore. Approximately one-half million people, most of

IAN STUPAKOFF

whom have arrived during the past three decades, live along the Bay's margin.

Tracing the growth of these communities is an easy task; describing the effects of this growth on the waters and marine life of the Bay, however, is not so easy. The complex relationships between human settlement and natural systems have only recently begun to be studied scientifically (see Chapter 5, for example). The real drama is in the day-to-day interactions that occur on, in and around this marine environment as the result of burgeoning urbanization. The changes wrought by humans profoundly affect the Bay's sediments, salinity, chemistry, beach profiles and living organisms. Ever increasing demands on the Bay affect, and are affected by, the condition of the Bay.

Change, and perhaps deterioration, is inevitable as the shoreline and waters of the Bay are used, misused and abused for many competing and incompatible purposes such as waste disposal, fisheries, recreation, transportation, dredging and real estate development. Competition for uses of the Bay is not a recent phenomenon, but has recently intensified.

Today's suburbanite is likely to find the manifestations of the effects of development—unplanned, unregulated and uncontrolled waste disposal. During summer, for example, the Bay frequently has an unusual color along with unpleasant odors accompanied by intermittent fish and shellfish kills. These are the symptoms of algae blooms fed by excess nutrients from septic tank seepage and fertilizer-laden land surface runoff. That such changes are taking place in the Bay and that they are in large part cumulative human-induced changes is clearly evident.

Future uses of this marine system for fishing, swimming and tourism are threatened. The greater the population, the greater will be its recreation demand and the greater the impact on the Bay and its capacity to fulfill the demand. Present trends that degrade the natural environment can be offset, however. The first step is to increase our knowledge of the system itself. Other chapters in this volume

have attempted to identify and describe what is currently known about Great South Bay—its geology, chemistry, biology and hydrography, as well as to identify its problems and the additional knowledge needed to provide the basis for intelligent management of the Bay (see Chapter 11). A second step is to adopt sound conservation practices, the key to maintaining and enhancing the Bay.

When examining without preconceived bias how the Bay's margin is used, two conclusions quickly become evident. First, certain conflicts are inherent between one use of the water or the shore and another use. Competition among uses is inescapable because there is a finite quantity of shore and water. Second, pollution has a direct damaging impact on shellfish and recreation industries and an indirect damaging impact on most marine activities. A sound marine economy, therefore, rests on a properly conserved marine environment.

Conservation of this natural environment is important, and therefore, one might reasonably ask, What is the problem? Why aren't good practices adopted?'' Each use by itself can be justified (aside from illegal uses such as shellfish poaching); however, conflicts arise when one legitimate use impinges on another. For example, the desire to maintain wetlands is in conflict with the desire to extract sand or to utilize the shoreline for residential or marina development.

It is axiomatic that use of the Bay requires access. The type and location of access depends on the particular use, and uses range from developed harbors and marinas to natural, undisturbed shorelines. Uses of the Bay can be neutral in their effects on the ecosystem, such as transportation or recreation uses. On the other hand, uses can actively impact the ecosystem, such as resource removal (fishing and aggregate mining) or introduction of anthropogenic materials (sewage and solid waste disposal).

Hundreds of point sources introduce storm water into the Bay, and non-point sources of surface runoff carry a host of nutrients and contaminants from communities surrounding the Bay. The flow pattern of each of these five major use categories—transportation, recreation, housing, resource removal and introduction of foreign materials—is depicted in Figure 10.1.

Following is a discussion of each of these broad categories of use: water transportation, including ferry operations, freight shipments and port facilities; recreation, including swimming, boating and sport fishing; vacation and year-round housing; resource removal, including minerals and food; and introduction of anthropogenic materials, including sewage and solid waste input and agricultural contaminants.

WATER TRANSPORTATION

FERRIES

Until the development of railroads, water transportation was the only economical method for moving heavy goods over great distances. To move goods over land required a tremendous effort of road building. The only construction involved for water transportation is the building of ports at either end of the route to permit the transfer of people and goods from the land to the ship.

Regular ferry service exists between the mainland and the various communities on Fire Island, including the National Seashore. In 1986 there was a total of 52,380 ferry trips across the Bay, carrying almost three million passengers in addition to the dry cargo. Figure 10.2 summarizes the existing routes and terminals.

FREIGHT

According to the U.S. Army Corps of Engineers' "Waterborne Commerce Statistics - Year 1986" more than 8000 tons of commodities and building cement were transported in the Great South Bay.

RECREATION

SWIMMING

It is important to note that there is a certain amount of conflict or competition even within one use category. Within recreational use, for example, swimmers must stay in areas separate from those used by power boats for their own safety; fishing is incompatible with water skiing. Different uses have different maximum densities for safe enjoyment. From a safety standpoint—from beach and nearshore water users such as sunbathers, swimmers and windsurfers to fishermen in slowly-moving boats to fast moving boats such as ferries and water ski boats—the density of users has to be given consideration. Figure 10.3 depicts the bathing beaches throughout the bay area.

BOATING

The space required for boating is much greater than that needed for swimming. Docking or launching facilities must be provided on the shoreline, as well as parking spaces for cars and boat trailers. The number of boats that can safely use nearshore water is limited; as more people become affluent enough to buy boats, the demand for boating space will rapidly exceed the available space. For mooring space, a waiting list of four to five years is common in most marinas. There is great danger that the proliferation of boats will choke the marine byways as the automobile has choked the roads in many parts of Long Island. The management and planning problem is how to

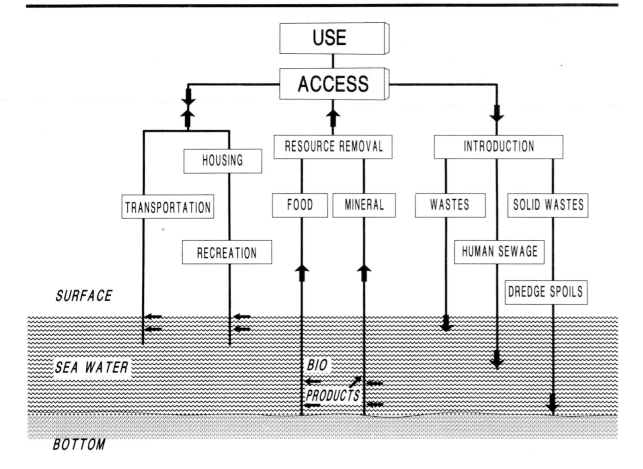

Figure 10.1. Flow pattern of use categories.

IAN STUPAKOFF

Runoff water enters Great South Bay directly through storm drains.

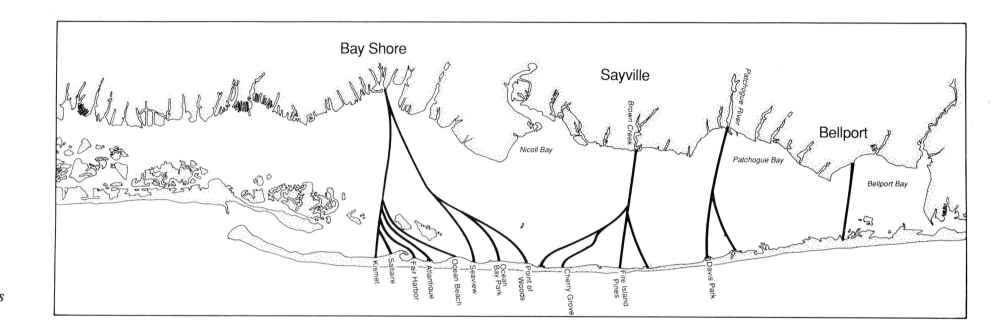

Figure 10.2. Great South Bay ferry routes and terminals.

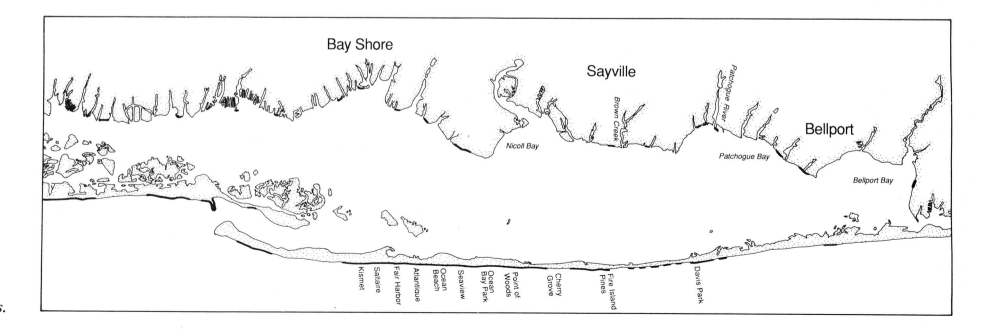

Figure 10.3. Great South Bay bathing beaches.

allocate limited boating resources equitably among a growing population of boat owners. Shore facilities should be limited to the capacity of the offshore area. Figure 10.4 depicts the public and private marinas.

SPORT FISHING

Sport fishing is closely tied to the boating industry. Continuation of this sport depends largely upon water quality in the Bay and upon navigable channels. However, many occasional and serious anglers, who do not have the means or desire to fish from boats, rely on facilities such as fishing piers to provide access to water. Although most sport fishing is from private boats, a sizable fleet operates out of the Captree Boat Basin, catering to day fishermen on an open charter basis.

HOUSING

The marine environment has an important, though indirect, bearing on the real estate industry. People build and rent houses near the shore partly because the water is there, near enough for recreation and visual enjoyment. In fact, access to the harbors and bays increases property values substantially. Any kind of waterfront land is a valuable asset for the owner, developer and the people who live nearby. Water frontage creates low-maintenance open space, provides many kinds of recreation facilities, and is so popular that it increases surrounding land values. The tremendous and growing demand for available waterfront land complicates the choice between development of new home sites and protection of the shoreline in its natural state. In the past, prior to the New York State Tidal Wetlands Act of 1972, development often meant the filling in of irreplaceable wetlands.

The development of the shores of Great South Bay, the lands of the barrier beach and the mainland south of the Montauk Highway illustrate the problems of environmental conflicts resulting from intensive suburbanization. Present adverse environmental factors include water pollution in the Bay from overflow of domestic sewage and general contamination from a variety of non-point sources that emanate from the paving over of once undeveloped land. Added to this are the multitude of human activities that occur in urbanizing communities such as lawn fertilizing, use of pesticides and petroleum residues resulting from the use of automobiles and motor boats.

RESOURCE REMOVAL

MINERALS

Sand and gravel are among the most important mineral resources taken from the marine environments of Long Island. The glacial formation of Long Island left a valuable heritage of high quality aggregate material. The large demand for marine deposits exists for two reasons. First, as land deposits of aggregate materials are becoming exhausted, mining operators attempt to exploit nearshore deposits in sheltered waters. Second, many zoning controls now prevent opening up new terrestrial sand and gravel pits because of the unsightly land scars they leave behind. Consequently, navigation channel deepening, yielding aggregate as a by-product, may offer one compatible means of resource removal. Mining in areas that should be used for other purposes, however, does create conflict and negative

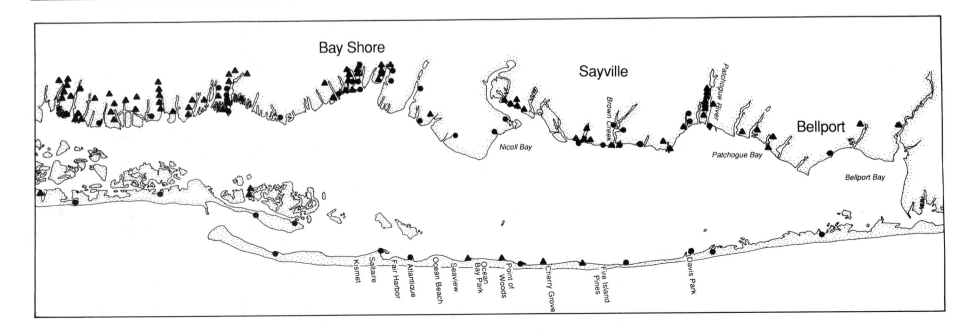

Figure 10.4. Public (●) and Private (▲) Marinas on Great South Bay.

environmental conditions.

Although the quality of the aggregate in Great South Bay is too sandy, or fine, for many construction uses (i.e., is does not contain enough gravel), it is suitable for beach nourishment. Since the Bay bottom is in the public domain, dredging operations are usually part of town or county public improvement projects. Towns may dig new channels, maintain existing channels, improve a beach or modify the circulation in the Bay or one of the inlets. Sand mining is a by-product of these other activities.

Controversy over dredging focuses once again on the crux of the problem of uses and misuses: competition among different uses of the marine environment. Much of the heat in the current debate comes from lack of information on such issues as bottom rehabilitation through dredging, the effect of dredging on saltwater intrusion, how the dredging of inlets affects their stabilization and where dredge materials should be dumped. Although controversial, it has been argued that because wetlands are important in the life-cycles of marine organisms, offshore dredging that does not directly affect wetlands will result in minimal ecological loss. Furthermore, mining operations may clean up an ecologically useless "mucky" bottom, leaving behind a bed more suitable for bottom growth. Finally, it is claimed that to the extent dredging improves water circulation, particularly in polluted portions of the Bay, ecological conditions may in the long run be enhanced rather than damaged.

The counter arguments focus on two adverse consequences of dredging. First, mining operations disturb the communities of bottom-dwelling organisms in the dredged area, and sometimes leave a silt blanket rather than a clean bottom, making it unfit for many desirable organisms like oysters, which grow better on a sandy bottom. Increased turbidity resulting from the dredging operations reduces the penetration of light into impacted waters, temporarily reducing photosynthesis by phytoplankton and rooted aquatic plants.

IAN STUPAKOFF

Another objection is that controls on dredging operations have often been lax or non-existent. Contractors are accused of having dredged deeper channels than permitted.

Dredging can be beneficial, but must be planned and properly supervised for compatible use. Inlets and channels in the Bay do fill with silt, thus requiring maintenance dredging. It is also necessary to rebuild beach profiles to rectify erosion conditions in order to protect private and public properties.

FOOD FROM THE BAY

The removal of living resources for food has a long history in the Bay and is the subject of much folklore and nostalgia (see Chapter 8). Lately, however, the decline in both fishing and shellfishing industries caused by overfishing, brown tide blooms and closures because of pollution have caused great concern.

The United States' per capita consumption of fish for food remained remarkably constant for many years at approximately 11 pounds per year. The rising concerns relating to consumption of red meat and its effect on the cardiovascular system because of cholesterol and the fact that fish is high in protein and low in harmful cholesterol, has recently boosted the consumption of fish. Given the increased desire for seafood and its nutritional value, it is all the more desirable to enhance the productive capabilities of the Bay. The prior chapters on the shellfish industry identify the major options and problems.

Up to the present, fishing is and has been a form of hunting and gathering. Thus, the sustenance and sports fisherman has had very little affect on the stock. Intense fishing, however, can affect the stock in a negative way. A conflict exists between commercial and sport fisheries in that each claims the other is overfishing. Although each alone has a legitimate use, between them both, they may be fishing beyond the maximum sustainable yield.

Fish species are subject to natural and human-induced changes in abundance. Their population dynamics produce a certain age distribution for each species so that, on the long-term average, the population may be maintained in a steady state. If fish are removed at a constant rate below the maximum sustainable yield, a new steady state is established with a population of more, but younger, harvestable fish. This is tolerable, but if the rate of fishing is high, beyond the maximum sustainable yield, the standing stock will eventually drop and commercial fishing may become unprofitable.

Various types of pollution and the destruction of part of the wetlands in the Bay have also contributed to the reduction of available stock. The vitality of many fish stocks is intimately tied to the health of the wetlands because they are spawning and nursery areas for fish and shellfish. Many of the offshore fish caught by local anglers mature in these Bay wetlands. Unfortunately, much wetland production has been poisoned by waste discharges from homes, boats, industries, farms, and municipal sewers and lost to development. Furthermore, past county dredging and ditching operations and DDT spraying to eliminate mosquitos have damaged or destroyed wetland production of planktonic and benthic food chain organisms. Hence, the existing wetlands often show marked reductions in productivity.

INTRODUCTION OF ANTHROPOGENIC MATERIALS

WASTES

Wastes have to be disposed of somewhere and in some form. Both sewage wastes and solid wastes such as rubbish, construction debris, and dredge spoils have undergone some transformation before being dumped into the water. They are compressed, separated mechanically or treated biologically or chemically. We still have to learn exactly how much impact these transformed wastes really have on the water chemistry and how that might affect growth of plants and animals.

HUMAN SEWAGE

Overflow from cesspools, seepage of polluted

ground water, and direct discharge of sewage from boats are problems that must be addressed. Boats directly discharging sewage into the water need to be stopped by enforcement of regulations, a good education program and convenient dockside evacuation facilities.

DREDGED MATERIALS

The problems posed by these wastes depend on their composition and quantity. At the very least, such wastes, when dumped, cover bottom-dwelling organisms. After dumping ceases, organisms adapted to the new substrate can become established, but a more serious consequence may arise from waste deposits that have a large oxygen demand, or from toxic components that leach into overlying waters. Wastes may remain within disposal sites or may be spread by bottom currents. Wastes from dredging are extremely variable in composition and may range from useful and reusable clean sand to materials contaminated by petroleum products, duck sludge, agricultural chemicals and the products of an urban society.

SUMMARY

Conflicts among competing demands for use made of the waters and shores of the Great South Bay are the crux of the present situation. What this tidal Bay will be like in the future—economically and aesthetically—hangs precariously on how well the environment is protected now, at a time when intense competition has been created by recent urbanization and development. An intractable and direct conflict exists over wetlands: the need for preservation to sustain fish and shellfish life cycles versus the need for housing with its often deleterious impacts on these wetlands.

More is involved than just competition for space or use, however. Actual misuse is evident; that is, a use which is unacceptable and undesirable. Land-based practices, particularly in the past but still active such as agricultural fertilization, pesticide use and the disposal of human and animal sewage have been and continue polluting Bay waters.

Some of the conflicts may be resolved by increased public awareness and financial support for conservation programs. Some of the conflicts can be ameliorated by stringent enforcement of existing rules and regulations. Some of the conflicts will yield only to energetic coastal planning and management. A great deal is already known about the marine environment. A number of intelligent laws exist. Putting this knowledge and laws to work more effectively now depends on active and concerned citizens.

The next and final chapter sets forth an array of management procedures, policies and administrative recommendations that, if implemented, offer a promise for the continuance and enhancement of the Great South Bay as one of the nation's finest marine resources.

R. GEORGE ROWLAND

CHAPTER 11

A MANAGEMENT APPROACH

Lee E. Koppelman
Center for Regional Policy Studies
State University of New York
Stony Brook, NY 11794

INTRODUCTION

The previous chapters portray a current summary of the jurisdictions, users, resources, chemistry, biology, and water quality of the Great South Bay. Such a knowledge base is an essential beginning to the process of developing a rational management program. Yet it is only a first step. Added to this array of diverse uses and users and natural characteristics is the variety of management responses exercised by the various jurisdictions.

Lord Bryce observed more than a century ago that one of the great strengths of the American political system is the fact that each jurisdiction, in effect, is a separate laboratory for the development and testing of new approaches, thereby maximizing flexibility. A confusing array of splintered efforts to manage the Bay sometimes complement, but more often conflict with each other in the continuing attempt to properly manage this complex natural system.

The fact that different approaches may be taken for the same set of problems, e.g., shellfish management, is not necessarily wrong. What is wrong, however, is the absence of an assessment of the many programs to manage the Bay and the development of an overall comprehensive plan and codified management scheme to implement the plan. This criticism is not a new one. In 1970 the Fish and Wildlife Service observed:

All levels of government have had a hand in managing the region, but there has not been a well rounded, integrated, and long range program conceived which could bring together all factions in the interest of preserving this great national estuarine heritage....If Great South Bay is to survive the onslaught of the progress of civilization it is imperative that all levels of government work together to develop, without delay, a comprehensive management plan that meets the needs of the people while preserving the quality of the estuarine environment.

U.S. Department of the Interior 1970.

Five years later, in a special reprint on the Bay published on June 9, 1974, *Newsday* concluded:

The biggest problem of Great South Bay, according to varied experts, is not its deteriorating water quality, dwindling wetlands or unmanaged shellfish industry. Serious as they are, such troubles can be controlled with unified action. The problem of the bay in terms of managing its threatened resources is that nobody is in charge. About 35 agencies and municipalities from the Fire Island Pines Fire Department to the U.S. government have jurisdiction of some kind, with the result that everyone's responsibility has become no one's.

Allegiance to home-rule practice; current laws; and a plethora of federal, state, county and municipal agencies with mandated powers and interests in the activities taking place in the Great South Bay account for this fragmentation of management.

The quest for managing the Bay started more than two decades ago. Quite often public policy formulation follows from crisis, rather than from planning. Instead of looking to the future to forestall or at least to ameliorate potential problems, governments at all levels tend to respond after a problem becomes so noticeable as to be unavoidable.

These 'real politik' issues pose a most serious problem for the planner-managers. If one must wait for a crisis to happen to be responsive, the range of options may be unduly limited. A preferable course is either to identify a potential or to exploit a perceived crisis. A problem that is perceived or imagined by the public is no less a problem to them than one deemed by planner-managers to be real. The identification of potential crises and preventing their occurrence is the most challenging job facing managers and scientists, but it usually is difficult to interest the public in potential problems.

Unfortunately, in the case of Great South Bay, serious problems already exist, and a variety of responses have come forth. However, the management attempts have been and continue to be piecemeal, fractionated according to jurisdiction and often mutually competitive.

Although the Coastal Zone Management Act of 1972 required that participating states include a description of the management structure to administer the program and the methods to be used for controlling land and water uses within the defined coastal zone, nothing has been achieved for the Great South Bay since the adoption of the overall Nassau-Suffolk Comprehensive Coastal Zone Management Plan (Koppelman 1974). One major attempt was made to secure state legislative support for the creation of a Great South Bay Commission to serve as the umbrella management entity, but it failed to win support.

Favorable action will not occur until the solution recommended is considered to also be technically competent and politically acceptable. Legislators have to weigh the political consequences and trade-offs that result from each course of action as judged by the interaction of the multiple interests vying for use and control of the Bay.

The observation that politics has to be considered is not directly stated in the Act and may offend the administrative purists who still cling to a vestige of the reform politics-administration argument. Nevertheless, any administrative or control proposal that cannot meet the challenge of successful testing in the crucible of political heat is almost assured of defeat, decline or impotency. This is mentioned in the 1972 Stockholm Conference on the Human Environment:

Finally, any act of management of the environment, any intervention in the relationship between man and his surrounding milieu implies decisions of a political nature.... Environmental decisions are, hence, ineluctably political...and, thus, whoever wishes to pursue the achievement of a sound environment must be prepared to deal with the relevant political factors.

U.S. Secretary of State Advisory
Committee on Education 1972

The delineation of a political agenda for the Great South Bay is not, however, integral to the scope of this book. The intent and focus have been to serve as an exposition of the Bay in its various social, economic and scientific contexts, in order to serve as input—and we hope valuable input—into the public discussion and debate that will lead to a more successful management program for the entire Bay system and its uses. The intent of this chapter is to draw conclusions and recommendations from the preceding chapters.

Following a brief mention of growth implications resulting from anticipated population and land use trends is a major segment dealing with two major components of activity and conditions within the bay: the management of the hard clam industry and the management of dredging activities.

GROWTH IMPLICATIONS

DEMOGRAPHIC AND LAND USE TRENDS

Population growth has been dramatic in the towns of Babylon, Islip and Brookhaven, the land areas of which constitute the watershed of Great South Bay. In 1950 the three towns had a combined population of 161,500; by 1988, the population had increased 577% to 932,748 (Long Island Lighting Company 1988).

Saturation populations have been calculated for the three towns according to 1984 zoning regulations and review of the data indicates that the populations of the towns of Babylon and Islip on Great South Bay are nearly at saturation levels. The Town of Brookhaven, however, has the capacity for an increase in population of approximately 200,000. The saturation population for the three towns is 1,140,000. By 2020 the projected population of Babylon, Islip and Brookhaven is estimated at 1,010,000, an increase of 77,252 over the 1988

population. It is important to note that the Town of Brookhaven, which has the greatest potential for increased population of any of Suffolk County's 10 townships over the next 35 years, borders on Long Island Sound as well as Great South Bay.

The total land area of Babylon, Islip and Brookhaven is about 240,000 acres, or approximately 375 square miles. In 1981 about 50% of the land was undeveloped, i.e., used for recreation, open space and agriculture, or was vacant; 29% was used for residential purposes; and the remaining 21% was divided among commercial, industrial, transportation and institutional uses.

Between 1966 and 1981 the three towns lost over 63,000 acres of vacant and agricultural land. It has been projected that vacant and agricultural land in Babylon, Brookhaven and Islip will decline from 71,000 acres in 1981 to 39,000 acres in 2020.

IMPLICATIONS FOR MARINE RESOURCES

The commitment of roughly 32,000 acres of vacant and agricultural land in Babylon, Islip and Brookhaven to uses requiring development over the next 35 years and the projected increase in population of 77,000 people by the year 2020 will impact Great South Bay's marine resources—affecting spawning, survival and growth of finfish and shellfish and availability of resources to a potentially greater number of recreational and commercial harvesters.

Population and land use changes should be considered in the analysis of alternatives for management of marine resources and habitats. These changes will have long-term effects, not only on the resource, but in selection of management alternatives that are eventually implemented. While forecasting the nature of the impacts in any sort of quantitative way is impossible now, the following important questions should be considered:

1) How will environmental modifications caused by land use and activity changes affect marine habitats?

2) How will pollutant loadings to Great South Bay be modified, and how will these

modifications influence important fisheries and wildlife populations?

3) How will population growth and land use changes modify the acreage of underwater lands certified for taking of shellfish and for bathing?

4) Can coliform control measures be implemented that will reduce the acreage of closed waters?

Coastal modifications, such as construction of bulkheads, marinas, berms and other man-made structures reduce the amount of natural shoreline along a given bay. Transformation of coastal wetlands, beaches and other habitats such as the change from natural to developed shores, has implications for adjacent marine ecosystems. Thus, the percentage of natural shoreline adjacent to a bay may be an important indicator of the condition of that ecosystem—the edge effect. Unfortunately, no criteria exist which can be used to evaluate when the cumulative effects of shoreline change reach a critical threshold as far as the ecosystem function is concerned. It is generally agreed that the edge effect associated with marine wetlands is of vital importance to local fisheries.

During the period 1950 to 1970, when Suffolk County experienced a growth of 400% in its population, dramatic changes were apparent in coastal land use and modification. In 1954 there were approximately 20,600 acres of tidal wetlands in Suffolk County; by 1971 only about 12,700 acres remained—a 38% loss in 17 years (Green 1972). The rate of wetland loss was curtailed by an increased environmental awareness, the subsequent passage of the Tidal Wetlands Act of 1972 and implementation of other regulatory programs at the town level. No data are available to document either the rate of wetlands loss or the absolute loss of wetland acreage along the shore of Great South Bay at the present time. However, an issue of almost equal importance to the elimination of wetlands is the diminution in their productive capabilities as the result of pollution. Therefore, stringent upland controls on development must be practiced to

IAN STUPAKOFF

protect the wetlands from point and non-point pollution sources.

Population and land use changes will have a definite impact upon the distribution of waters that are certified for the taking of shellfish. Using population changes as an indicator of development, Maiolo and Tschetter (1981) found a statistically significant positive correlation between intensity of development and acreage closed to shellfishing during a 27-year period for two coastal counties in North Carolina. They found that as the resident population of coastal counties increased, a resultant decline in water quality necessitated closure of additional shellfish harvesting areas. In Carteret County, North Carolina, an increase of 1000 permanent residents in shoreline communities was found to be correlated with the closure of 200 acres of underwater lands to shellfishing. In New Hanover County, North Carolina there was a closure of 320 acres per increase of 1000 residents.

An analysis of the causes of the change in areas uncertified for shellfishing in Suffolk County has

not been undertaken. There is probably a positive correlation between suburban residential and commercial development and marine water quality deterioration, but detailed studies would be needed to identify the relationships between population growth with concomitant land use changes and deterioration of marine water quality in Suffolk County.

While quantitative correlations relating various aspects of the development process to water quality degradation at local areas are not available, regional data do suggest the gross nature of the problem. In 1965 there were approximately 5660 acres of uncertified shellfish grounds in Great South Bay and the total population of Babylon, Brookhaven and Islip was estimated at 571,000 (COSMA 1985). By 1986 the population had increased to 904,500, and 10,160 acres were closed to shellfishing. During this 21-year period, one additional acre of shellfish grounds was closed for every increase of 75 people in the resident population near the Bay. Since the hard clam industry has historically been the major commercial activity in the Bay, in terms of the

Residential development along the Bay's margins.

IAN STUPAKOFF

number of baymen supported by the resource, the management issues relating to this industry has to be the linchpin of any management program and agenda for the Bay.

KEY MANAGEMENT ISSUES
MANAGEMENT OF THE HARD CLAM INDUSTRY

The speculation as to the causes for the low harvests of hard clams in recent years includes overfishing, illegal harvesting, deterioration of water quality and reduced hard clam reproductive success. Recent occurrences of the algal bloom, or brown tide, in Great South Bay (see Chapter 4 for discussion) have exacerbated the concern about water quality, giving rise to ominous predictions that unless positive changes in management practice are made, the hard clam fishery in Great South Bay will not recover and stabilize. Decreased harvests are but a manifestation of a more basic problem— the failure of society and its institutions to effectively manage hard clam resources. Although it is not possible at present to specify the best mix of strategies to achieve this goal, management optimization will only be possible by field testing various options.

Since available information is limited, it could be argued that an ideal plan would be to gather more information in order to have answers available to all of the important questions before proceeding with a management plan. Unfortunately, short-term management inaction while gathering more information may cause further decline. Even though some of the recommendations will undoubtedly be controversial, it is preferable to test and take risks than to allow further diminution of the hard clam industry. The recommendations which follow should lead to the recovery of the industry. At the very least, there can be agreement on the three general goals that underlie a set of management strategies (Koppelman and Davies 1987).

1) Actions should be identified that can be taken to assure the survival of a viable commercial hard clam industry capable of supporting a significant number of baymen harvesting clams on a full-time basis.

2) Actions should be identified that can be taken to preserve a hard clam industry that provides baymen with a source of income and provides others with the opportunity to enjoy clam harvesting on a recreational basis.

3) Actions should be identified that can be taken to maintain environmental conditions in local marine waters that are conducive to the reproduction, growth and survival of hard clams and to maintain the certification of these waters for the harvest of shellfish resources.

The translation of goals into hard clam management strategies requires a move from the general to the specific. Fifteen topics are included for discussion of the various strategy scenarios. These are: spawner sanctuaries, transplants, seed clam planting, stock assessments, control of entry into the commercial fishery, catch per unit effort, alternative openings and closings of harvest grounds, hydrographic suitability of the Bay for establishment of spawning sanctuaries, protection of spawning stocks, limitations imposed by natural physical factors and predation on hard clam resources, public and private hard clam mariculture activities, ownership rights to underwater lands, enforcement of hard clam management and environmental protection laws, marine water quality and sewage treatment plant monitoring and mitigation of coastal construction impacts on water quality and biota. It should be noted that it is likely only a few of the strategies will be implemented and evaluated at any one time. It will require a concerted, long-term effort and a substantial allocation of funds to specify, test and select the best combination of strategies.

One further limitation is the presence of technical constraints, including information and data gaps, and the outcome of various feasibility studies. In some cases, research is needed to help establish a better understanding of fundamental concepts. In other instances, the application of a strategy is limited because of the need to obtain more site-specific data such as water circulation and shellfish or predator population size. Feasibility studies incorporating cost-effectiveness and benefit to cost ratios may need to be performed to determine whether or not a given strategy is appropriate. The outcome and, hence, suitability of the strategy is highly dependent upon such factors as scale, existing conditions and site characteristics.

Other non-technical constraints, including the availability of funds, interest group attitudes and enforcement, pose serious obstacles as well. It should also be noted that actual implementation may be constrained by the need for additional research or feasibility testing. In the following discussion, the 15 management strategies have been grouped into three broad categories: hard clam stock enhancement, fishery management information and enforcement and marine water quality monitoring and fishery habitat protection. The various recommendations are identified as to which level of government, i.e., state, county or town, should implement the actions.

HARD CLAM STOCK ENHANCEMENT

Barring efforts to control the diminution of hard clam stocks resulting from disease or predation, four programs can be carried out that would enhance hard clam production and availability. This would include the establishment and protection of spawner sanctuaries, the transplantation of clams from uncertified waters, the periodic planting of seed clams, and the establishment of mariculture areas in the Bay.

The Coastal Ocean Science and Management Alternatives (COSMA) program developed at the Marine Sciences Research Center defined a spawner sanctuary as a site that is stocked with large, fecund adult clams and located so as to maximize the setting of larvae from the site in specially selected areas that are well suited for clam development (COSMA 1985). The use of spawner sanctuaries has gained increasing support in recent years. A factor in favor of sanctuaries is that hard clam recruitment is unpredictable and does not always occur on an annual cycle. Hard clams in a sanctuary environment can spawn over several years, thereby increasing the probability of obtaining successful

sets. In addition, sanctuaries do not have to be created each year since the spawner clams carry over for a period of years.

Placement of a large number of spawner clams in a dense concentration and the ensuing protection of the progeny from harvest certainly enhances the overall stock. Several techniques can be applied to protect these sanctuaries including the selection of sites in uncertified waters, the placement of obstructions on the bottom to inhibit harvesting, the use of low market clams for spawning stock, and the establishment of information and education programs for baymen in order to secure their cooperation.

The current efforts of the towns of Babylon, Islip and Brookhaven to establish, monitor and evaluate spawner sanctuaries should be continued. New sites should be established where feasible, and all levels of government should provide funding support for evaluation studies of ongoing sanctuary programs.

Another approach to enhance the stock would include the transplanting of clams from uncertified waters, either to sanctuary sites or certified waters. This strategy has been conducted in one form or another for the past half century. From a resource management perspective, a transplant can be viewed as having either long or short-term benefits. Long-term benefits could occur if the transplant is used as stock in spawner sanctuaries. Short-term benefits are associated with transplants used to supplement shellfish harvests. Of course, the harvest must only take place after the 21-day closure period required by the state to ensure the purity of the clam. If the source of the clams is from polluted areas that may contain pathogens and toxic pollutants, it is likely that the 21-day period is not sufficient.

Transplanting will continue in practice when the opportunities arise; that is, when an ample supply is located in uncertified waters and public funds are made available for the program. It is recommended that long-term benefits be stressed. If the transplants are meant for short-term harvesting, they should be scheduled to include a period of closure that would enable the clams to spawn at least once before the area is opened. This not only

would enhance the production of larvae, but also would insure the healthful depuration of the clam. This practice would require better coordination among groups and better planning of the projects.

State and county health and environmental regulatory agencies should determine the degree of toxic pollutants that exist in the source areas of the clams to be transplanted. If the pollutant standards are exceeded, the transplants should not be used for short-term harvest purposes. Evaluations should be made to determine if problem organisms associated with hard clams are present in the source areas and, when necessary, transplants from those areas should not be allowed.

The practice, extent and limitations of seed clam planting conducted by several of the towns, were reviewed as part of the COSMA program (1985). It was found that although seeding projects are popular with baymen and public officials, they nevertheless did not contribute a large number of clams available for harvest in comparison with the yields in non-seeded areas. This infers that ongoing evaluation, in terms of costs and objectives of the program, should be integral to seeding projects to measure survival rates of seed that contribute to harvestable stocks.

While it is unrealistic to sustain a large scale commercial fishery with seed clam planting, the technique could produce positive smaller scale benefits when applied to areas where the stocks are below harvestable densities, or where dispersion of spawner larvae from sanctuaries is limited by circulation characteristics. This leads to the fourth strategy, the use of mariculture to produce larvae under nursery conditions.

Since it has been difficult in the past to obtain seed clams of the desired size and quantity when needed, either from Long Island or New England hatcheries, it seems reasonable to conclude that a regional hatchery and nursery should be established on Long Island to meet these needs, despite the fact that the towns of Islip and East Hampton, with state support, have recently built such facilities. Cost effectiveness should be the major consideration for such an effort. Thus, additional research to evaluate large scale seeding programs should be undertaken to assess the survival rate of planted seed clams and their overall contribution to recruitment and standing stock before new hatcheries are undertaken.

FISHERY MANAGEMENT INFORMATION AND ENFORCEMENT

Assuming there will be a stock sufficient to warrant a management program, several components should be ongoing elements of the program. Stock assessments throughout the Bay should be conducted to obtain reliable information on the population dynamics of the resource. A program must also be designed, implemented and evaluated to control entry into the commercial hard clam fishery.

The ultimate quality of any environmental management plan is directly related to the caliber of information used in arriving at conclusions and recommendations. Issues of coastal concern, in particular, must be informed by rigorous coastal science. It is the integration of such science into the planning-management process that serves as the foundation of the process. This is as true for hard clam management as it is for all coastal processes and activities.

The stock assessment surveys should provide the base on which research can be undertaken to yield estimates of the quantity of harvest or catch per unit of effort. Existing information on landings and number of permits is not adequate to develop a reliable index. This management objective is undoubtedly the most difficult to achieve due to the reluctance of baymen to divulge their activities for a variety of reasons. At the very least, questionnaires must be anonymous.

A more reliable data collection effort would shift gathering information from the baymen to the customer. The towns and New York State Department of Environmental Conservation (NYSDEC) should increase their data collection efforts, perhaps by encouraging or requiring buyers to collect data on the number of bushels harvested (which is a record of their purchases). These data

would reflect the effort expended by the baymen in fishing time and equipment used as the transactions occur. The data could be centrally stored by NYSDEC, or any other central administrative agency that may be created to exercise regional oversight of the Bay. The resulting catch to effort index would provide a means of tracking the condition of the fishery on an annual basis.

Recreational catches may also have to be recorded if the catch is considered significant in relation to the commercial catch. The easiest method to accomplish this task would be to require recreational harvesters to indicate their previous year's catch when new licenses are applied for. Inherent in this last recommendation is the need for universal licensing in the towns of Babylon, Islip and Brookhaven.

Control of entry into harvesting areas is another potentially effective means of stock enhancement and provision of a research opportunity to quantify recovery rates to harvestable rates. The criteria used to open or close particular areas include the size of the harvestable stock, yield, seasonal considerations and changes in water quality. The following options were identified in the COSMA program:

1) Closing an area where there is a high concentration of seed clams, until the clams reach legal size.

2) Closing areas to harvesting of a fishery on a rotational basis after a minimum threshold population level has been reached; the area is opened to harvesting after stocks rebuild from natural recruitment, which could be supplemented by seed clam planting.

3) Establishing winter grounds in protected near-shore areas; such areas are closed during the summer to reduce harvest pressure and maintain stocks that are subject to fishing during adverse winter weather conditions.

Thus far, none of the towns has implemented the first option. Islip has initiated evaluation work on option two, and Brookhaven has utilized the winter grounds option. Sporadic and voluntary closings have taken place in various Bay locations, but not

in any systematic or properly monitored fashion. The use and evaluation of access control should be encouraged and funds should be provided by the state, county and towns to prepare plans, schedules and monitoring programs to test the efficacy of openings and closings of harvestable areas.

Another aspect of control involves the strict enforcement of existing hard clam management laws by increasing patrol capability and efficiency and by intensifying the prosecution of major offenders. All levels of government currently have enforcement powers and responsibilities. In fact, law enforcement activities have increased since the outbreak of shellfish-related illnesses several years ago, yet current enforcement manpower is insufficient to provide adequate patrols of the Bay.

The problem was further exacerbated by the rich harvest available in the 1960s and 1970s, which attracted many new people into the industry. Unfortunately, some of these baymen had no concern for the long-term health of the fishery and overharvested it, poaching clams from uncertified waters and illegally harvesting undersized clams. Enforcement agencies were understaffed, and the judicial system was ineffective in prosecuting cases, thereby giving encouragement to illegal practices.

The following recommendations were advocated by these enforcement agencies to bring the situation under control:

1) New York State should continue to urge neighboring states, particularly the state of Pennsylvania, to ban the sale of hard clams less than 1 inch in thickness. This would eliminate a market for the sale of seed clams poached in Suffolk County.

2) More funds should be allocated to provide for additional state and county enforcement personnel to patrol the Bay.

3) Coordinated patrols and activities among the various federal, state, county and local enforcement agencies should be expanded and strengthened.

4) Heavier fines and confiscation of equipment should be imposed on repeat offenders

caught poaching in uncertified waters or taking seed clams.

5) License fees for commercial clammers should be increased, and the additional revenue should be earmarked for hard clam research, enhancement programs and law enforcement.

It was noted in the introduction to this section on fishery management that research is the linchpin to any management program that attempts to be comprehensive, rational and verifiable. A research program designed to enhance the knowledge base of the hard clam industry involves studies to determine where and under what circumstance hard clam populations are limited by either natural physical factors such as inlet configuration and flushing rates or ecological factors such as predator populations. Alteration of inlet dimensions and approach channels, for example, may change Bay environmental conditions, which in turn could impact successful sets of hard clams in the Bay.

MARINE WATER QUALITY MONITORING AND FISHERY HABITAT PROTECTION

State and county water quality monitoring in the Bay and related investigations of water pollution problems need to be improved. It is currently difficult, if not impossible, to determine how water quality changes over time, since a comprehensive data base for defining trends is lacking. Enhanced monitoring capability will help provide information to answer questions on the pollutant loads that various sources contribute to local waters and will help to determine whether or not uncertified shellfish grounds can be opened for harvesting that would fully comply with health standards to protect the consuming public.

A strong monitoring program should also enable the regulatory agencies to achieve greater detection of existing and potential illegal discharges. The recent increase of personnel in the Marine Resources Bureau of the Suffolk County Department of Health Services Division of Environmental Quality should improve monitoring efforts. However, the ambitious action program recently developed by

that agency may require an even greater staff commitment to adequately accomplish the collection and analysis of their suggested four-part effort:

1) Synoptic monitoring of marine surface waters and tributary streams conducted on an annual basis.

2) Increased monitoring of sewage treatment plant outfall locations and, if required, effluent discharges.

3) Monitoring the onset and development of algal blooms, including the potential occurrence of toxic red tides.

4) Analysis of trace contaminants in bottom sediments, finfish and shellfish.

The extent to which salinity levels have changed in the Bay is a major concern. Additional data on salinity are needed to detect and quantitatively describe potential impacts adequately. Two processes impacting salinity, for example, are the discharging by Southwest Sewer District directly into the ocean, which reduces the amount of fresh water flow into the Bay, and the navigation projects at Fire Island Inlet, which tend to increase salinity levels in the Bay. The COSMA Program indicated that the considerable variation in salinity levels would necessitate collecting up to a decade of daily observations at several station locations during the summer months to detect trends (COSMA 1985).

Surface water quality modeling performed a decade ago as part of the Long Island Regional Planning Board's comprehensive waste water management plan predicted that stormwater runoff was the most significant contributor of coliform loadings to the Bay with stream base flow being an order of magnitude lower and point sources of pollution three orders of magnitude lower (Koppelman et al. 1978). The obvious way to control coliform levels in near-shore areas is by controlling non-point sources, especially stormwater runoff. Therefore, better control of development at the coastal edge is needed to conserve the natural state of the marine shoreline and to minimize marine water quality deterioration. It cannot be overem-

phasized that all development proposals that may affect the Bay should receive the most rigorous review by all town and county agencies responsible for zoning, subdivision and construction projects to protect marine habitats and water quality.

In the past, stormwater runoff systems were designed to transport storm water off paved surfaces and into drainage systems which discharged the storm water and associated contaminants directly into the Bay and into streams feeding the Bay without any treatment (Koppelman et al. 1982). A more comprehensive approach to stormwater runoff management, in which performance standards and site development techniques are used to protect the natural resources of the site to be developed, the downstream watershed area and adjacent marine surface waters, is receiving more attention and support by the towns. Recommendations contained in the storm water chapter of the Nonpoint Source Management Handbook (Koppelman et al. 1984), if implemented by local municipalities, could serve as preventive measures to minimize stormwater contaminants entering the Bay.

Regional concerns should also be integrated into the land use control process. More emphasis is needed on understanding the cumulative effects of incremental development on ecosystem function and the formulation of policies and regulatory responses that will protect the Bay's environment and the fisheries supported by the Bay. It must also be understood that the availability of knowledge and techniques to overcome the negative impacts of development on shellfish resources is not sufficient alone. Marine resource protection must be given a higher priority by all levels of government in the design, review and approval of private and public projects.

DREDGING

In Chapter 10, it was noted that most uses of the Bay can be legitimated when examined in the context of their economic and social benefits to various users. It is when one use or activity impinges negatively on other uses and users that conflict arises. Conflicts between fishery people and advocates of dredging projects, for example, can be minimized when there is a common objective. All the users need navigable channels, yet when the benefits of dredging result in the destruction or even diminution of the Bay's fisheries, then difficult policy choices have to be made. Priority must be given to the enhancement of the fisheries, albeit at the expense of other users, except where vital transportation requirements must be met.

It has been clearly established (Suffolk County Planning Department 1985) that dredging creates physical effects on estuarine environments such as increased turbidity at both the dredging location and the dredge material disposal site, changed topography bottom and changed mechanical properties of sediments at the dredging and spoil disposal locations. These perturbations generate related chemical and biological effects as well.

Topographic changes such as increasing the cross section of an inlet can produce changes in tidal range, currents, shoaling and scouring patterns and salinity levels in back bay areas. The most critical yet least understood chemical effect of dredging is the potential remobilization of contaminants that are sorbed onto the surfaces of fine-grained particles that typically settle to the bottom. Dredged material disposal can, at least temporarily, depress dissolved oxygen levels in the water column and increase the concentration of nutrients.

Biological effects include the obvious destruction of habitats such as wetlands, spawning grounds and grassbeds; and the direct burial of benthic, sessile organisms such as oysters. More subtle biological effects include the chronic impacts of suspended sediments on filter feeders and the potential uptake and concentration of released contaminants through the food chain.

Although dredging might be considered a necessary evil, mention should be made of its positive attributes. The elimination of shoaled inlets by dredging can improve boating safety and thus save lives. Dredging can also improve flushing action, thereby contributing to improvements in water quality. In the case of Great South Bay, the

IAN STUPAKOFF

fine sand from dredging is eminently suitable for beach nourishment. Dredging can also be used for pollutant removal and to improve the quality of the Bay bottom. An obvious example is the accumulation of duck sludge in Mud Creek and Carmans River that feed into the Bay, and the similar situation in Forge River, Terrell River, Tuthill Cove, Hart Cove and Little Seatuck Creek in Moriches Bay. These duck sludge deposits are sources of bacteria and excess nutrients to the water column. Duck waste is a concentrated source of nitrogen, phosphorus and potassium and ultimately causes a reduction in oxygen in the water column.

Nutrient release from sludge in the form of ammonium (NH_4) has been measured in the Carmans River. When disturbed by clam raking, the sediment released ammonium and increased the concentration in the overlying water by two orders of magnitude (100 times). This indicates the importance of physical disturbance in increasing the release of nutrients from sediments in the water column. The issue of duck sludge removal, therefore, is a most serious one, and additional research should be initiated before any broad-based duck sludge removal program is undertaken. If organic-rich sediments are encountered during navigation channel operations or if sludge removal is deemed necessary, precautions should be taken to minimize removal and disposal operations. Siltation curtains should be employed, or the project area should be isolated with temporary dikes or cofferdams to prevent contamination of the surrounding waterway with undesirable material. Such operations should generally be performed during the fall and winter months to prevent interference with biological reproduction and growth. Disposal strategies for duck sludge could include confined disposal with subsequent dewatering and planting for habitat creation or use in a composting operation.

The construction of marshes and islands with dredged material placed in diked areas and along the shoreline is a promising alternative for disposal of dredged material. Research indicates that such wetlands creation is feasible (Woodhouse 1979).

This innovative use of dredged material was demonstrated by the U.S. Army Corps of Engineers in creating a new tidal wetlands area of 16 acres through seeding and transplanting, in conjunction with new ponds and tidal flats, adjacent to Barren Island in the Chesapeake Bay (Earhart and Garbisch 1983).

Several management opportunities could enable necessary dredging projects to be more compatible with other formerly competing uses. The first item should be a clear statutory policy that limits all county dredging projects to ones that clearly are in the public interest. Future construction and maintenance of navigation channels should occur only when the general public has access from the land and the water to the improved location. Privately owned residential channels or privately owned marinas should not receive dredging support paid for from public funds. This policy alone would greatly curtail the past tendency to dredge every creek, stream, channel and shallow shoreline in the Great South Bay.

The projects that could be defined as "public interest" projects have been part of Suffolk County's dredging plan for almost three decades. This plan sets forth the permit application procedure, design criteria, volumes to be excavated and method of disposal. One additional element that could be included in the plan would be a long-range disposal plan that would call for the creation of a large-scale wetland habitat demonstration project. The project should be designed to determine the feasibility in dollar and environmental costs and benefits and its effectiveness as a method of spoil disposal in contrast to beach nourishment or upland landfilling.

COMPREHENSIVE PLANNING

THE PLANNING PROCESS

A common thread woven through the various recommendations discussed in this chapter is the need for a plan to guide future actions. The diverse aspects, needs, activities, constraints, users and jurisdictions mandate that comprehensive management is essential if a rational and enhanced future for the Bay is to occur. The prime input in the development of a comprehensive management planning package is the incorporation of general community planning, coastal zone planning, coastal revitalization planning and water quality planning.

Many comprehensive land use plans have been developed that focus on the aesthetic, efficient and compatible distribution of land uses and that address the needs of a population (Branch 1988). These plans typically consider environmental resources as constraints on the development process. There is relatively little planning for water use from the point of view of specifying the mix of land uses and activities that will not exceed the carrying capacity of marine systems, that is, the ability of a natural or man-made system to absorb population growth or physical development without significant degradation or breakdown (Schneider et al. 1979).

The crux of the problem is to determine what the limitations of the marine environment are, even in a general sense, in terms of such parameters as water and sediment quality and fish and wildlife populations. The limitations must be described by the scientific community and should be in a form that can be used to determine the controls needed to be placed on land and water use and associated activities. The planner must then assess the extent to which alternative plans with different mixes of land and water use are compatible with these limitations.

The planning process can be applied in five steps to the Great South Bay area:

1) Identify goals to achieve Bay use priorities.
2) Inventory and analyze existing Bay conditions.
3) Project user demands and impacts on Bay resources.
4) Analyze land use and management alternatives.
5) Select comprehensive plan recommendations and implementation mechanisms.

The identification of goals and priority uses in step 1 can occur simultaneously with the inventory and analysis of existing conditions. A determination would have to be made of Great South Bay resource problems from the perspective of different users such as commercial and recreational fishermen, boaters, shoreline residents, swimmers, hunters, bird watchers and various commercial interests pertaining to tourism, product transfer and the like. The views of specialists involved with each of these user groups—the regulatory agencies involved with resource protection, real estate interests, environmental groups and marina operators—must also be ascertained. In this way, concise statements of problems can be developed.

Once the resource problems have been defined as precisely and quantitatively as possible, the planning team would provide sets of goal statements for review. This is often difficult to accomplish, given the desire to obtain constituency support by including only those aspects that are backed by as broad a group of interests as possible.

The inventory and analysis of existing conditions in step 2 is primarily technical in nature and involves the summarization, interpretation and portrayal of information from a variety of sources and in a format that is understandable by the public and elected officials. The topics that are typically included in preparation of a local watershed analysis plan by the Long Island Regional Planning Board are shown on Table 11.1.

This list of topics would have to be amended depending upon the level of effort and scale of a Great South Bay investigation. For example, it would be useful to include an inventory of underwater land habitats, if the information could be obtained to map them, but Bay resource characteristics change temporarily and spatially, making it difficult to portray such information on maps. The limited availability of data is also a serious constraint.

Given projections of population size and land use, it would be necessary to project user demands by type and location that will be placed on Bay resources in the future (step 3). This stage of the process should also address use conflicts involving such resources as space, habitat quality, fish and shellfish availability and whether or not carrying capacities are being exceeded by certain levels of use.

The next process (step 4, analysis of land use and management alternatives) recognizes the limitations of Bay resources to accommodate user demands. The spectrum of acceptable alternatives can be widened by inclusion of actions that mitigate adverse impacts.

The fifth, and last, step in the process identifies the best set of plan alternatives to achieve the desired ends and also includes an implementation package that describes how, where and when management actions should be taken. Actions can include land use changes, support activity modifications or restrictions on resource use.

Integrating Science with Coastal Zone Management

Deciding optimal planning solutions for marine resource allocation problems requires the integration of various disciplines into an overall management framework and the use of marine science information to improve coastal decision making. While perhaps simple to state, the integration process is often hard to grasp and apply to specific coastal situations. The difficulty of integrating scientific information into coastal zone management decision making has been well documented (Koppelman 1974). Many natural scientists, either because of training or personal philosophy, have traditionally presented their findings in technical jargon and have not discussed the normative and policy implications of their work. Schubel (1982) noted the following aspects that contribute to this problem:

a. disagreement among scientists as to the impacts of man's use of the marine environment;

b. the failure of coastal managers to realize the benefits of conducting rigorous, comprehensive evaluations of coastal decisions and policies; and

Table 11.1. Inventory and Analysis of Existing Conditions. Historical perspective - shoreline modifications and changes in usage.

Existing Land Use
   Residential
     - low density (1 Dwelling Unit [D.U.] and
      less/acre)
     - medium density (2 - 4 D.U./acre)
     - intermediate density (5 - 10 D.U./acre)
   Commercial
   Open space and recreational
   Agricultural
   Vacant
   Institutional
   Utility

Zoning
   Residential
   Commercial
   Industrial
   Other

Land Available for Development
   Vacant individual lots
   Vacant subdividable lots
   Reusable lots
   Vacant commercial lots

Population Analysis
   Year-round population (census)
   Seasonal population
   Occupied housing units
   Average household size
   Seasonal estimated average household size
   Potential housing units
   Saturation population

Natural Resources
   Environmental resources inventory
   - dune
   - beach
   - bluff
   - dredged materials site
   - channel
   - surface waters
   - tidal wetlands
   - intertidal

- high
- formerly connected
- freshwater wetlands
- maritime shrubland
- landscaped/open areas
- old field
- forest
- nursery grounds/agriculture
- developed areas
- endangered and threatened flora and fauna

Marine Water Quality
- surface water classification
- shellfish certification status
- marine water quality indicators
- circulation
- pollution susceptibility

Fisheries
- commercial fisheries
- recreational fisheries

Soils
- soil categories
- depth to seasonal high water table
- profile
- permeability
- pH value
- limitations on development

Groundwater Quality
- sampling locations
- depth of well
- ground water quality standards (chemical and
  organic)
- wells contravening drinking water standards
- public water supply well locations
- water main locations
- areas served by public sewers

Watershed Analysis
- swales and major depressions
- depth to seasonal high water less than 4 feet

- gentle slopes (10%)
- moderate slopes (10-20%)
- steep slopes (less than 20%)
- 100-year flood plain
- "V" zone
- "A" zone
- direction of surface water flow
- direction of ground water flow
- critical aquifer recharge areas/special ground
  water protection districts
- public water supply wells
- water main
- contaminated wells
- culverts and storm drains

Cultural and Recreational Resources
   Archaeologic and historic sites
   Cemeteries
   Trails
   Parks
   Boat ramps

Development Constraints
   Beach and dune
   Bluff with 150 foot buffer
   Major swales and depressions
   Depth to seasonal high water less than 4 feet
   Moderate slopes (10-20%)
   Steep slopes (less than 20%)
   Flood hazard areas—100 year flood zone
   Tidal wetlands
   Freshwater wetlands
   Surface waters
   Endangered and threatened species of flora
   and fauna
   Critical aquifer recharge areas/special ground
   water protection districts
   Public water supply wells
   Water main
   Contaminated wells
   Archaeologic and historic sites
   Cemeteries
   Trails

c. the fragmentation of management responsibility among agencies at all levels of government, where day-to-day decisions are based on a plethora of often conflicting legal mandates.

Coastal decision making is also hindered by the lack of basic environmental data, the difficulty of transferring the results of research and management experience from one locale to another because of differences in site conditions and situations and the lack of methodologies geared to estimate the varied impacts of incremental coastal development. As a result, most shoreline management plans do not specifically take into consideration the special properties or potentials of different marine systems. Hence, ad hoc marine resource decisions are often made using the process of extrapolation, which can be quite risky, or even worse, on the basis of general impressions.

Two seminal studies that addressed the integration of scientific data with the planning process were both funded by the United States Department of Housing and Urban Development's Office for Policy Development and Research and were carried out in the early 1970s (U.S. Department of the Interior 1971). One project was undertaken by the Menlo Park, California Office of the United States Geodetic Survey in conjunction with the San Francisco Bay Commission in which a comprehensive set of earth science maps with interpretive reports were developed for the San Francisco Bay area. The subjects included coastal geomorphology, erosion studies, seismicity in the coastal zone, offshore geology, dune identification, sand supply data, ground water and waste water management and general mapping. This material was meant to test the application of natural science information as an input into the planning process and to enable the planners and land use managers to develop guidelines and standards in a more rigorous fashion. The other project was specifically to translate such data into useful and usable information that will be understandable to planners and policy makers and not to develop scientific data.

The reluctance of research personnel to mix scientific inquiry with policy issues places the burden on the managers to determine the relevance and applicability of the scientists' contributions. Therefore, the essential tasks are to combine the diverse elements of coastal land use planning and environmental knowledge to yield the following policy-oriented objectives:

1) To determine the probable environmental impact of proposed plans on marine resources and conversely to determine the influence of the marine environment on land uses and functional components of development plans.
2) To identify and recommend modifications to development plans that can minimize any adverse effects on marine resources.
3) To prepare a set of guidelines for the integration of comprehensive planning and coastal zone management, that can assist decision-makers in the project area.

Much has been written about the need for the maximum input of scientific findings into the comprehensive planning process (Koppelman 1974). Although the development of a specific research agenda for the Great South Bay, which would go beyond the findings already expressed in previous chapters, is not within the scope of this chapter, the reader can find the outline of a comprehensive research program developed for the Chesapeake Bay Program (Appendix 1). The research needs for the Great South Bay are not synonymous with those for the Chesapeake, yet the outlines could serve as an excellent guide for Long Island.

Finally, among management concerns is the development and application of an implementation program. The finest comprehensive plan based on the maximum input of science, planning data, analyses, citizen support and political feasibility will languish without the administrative mechanisms in place to carry out the implementation of the plan.

IMPLEMENTATION
ADMINISTRATIVE MODELS

The Coastal Zone Management Act of 1972 (Public Law 92-583) required that participating states include a segment of their plan, which would define the governmental structure to administer the coastal zone management plan and the methods by which land and water uses within the zone would be controlled. Each state had the option of choosing a form of control within three broad categories that were specified in the act: direct regulation by the state, local regulation consistent with state-established standards and local regulation subject to state review.

The major constraints to any coordinated program are home rule practice; current laws; a plethora of state, county, and municipal agencies with mandated powers and interests in the activities taking place in the Bay; and a variety of planning groups that currently exercise advisory and regulatory land use controls in and adjacent to the Great South Bay. This would appear to eliminate from serious consideration a management plan that provides for direct regulation by the state, except where such control is functionally limited, e.g., wetlands, state parks and preserves. Despite 'Dillon's Rule' which observed that municipalities are but "creatures of the state," any attempt to seriously curtail or abrogate local zoning and planning prerogatives would face vigorous and perhaps overwhelming opposition.

It is not so clear as to which of the remaining two options will provide the most effective management device. If past experience on Long Island is any guide, it would seem that maximum initiative and control will have to be local. It is not even realistic to expect the agencies of the State of New York to set all the standards, guidelines and criteria since there is a larger planning and scientific base on the local scene than exists in Albany. Acceptance of the status quo is not a viable solution either, as indicated by Suffolk County's response to the need to protect the Pine Barrens that are found mainly in the towns of Brookhaven, Riverhead,

Southampton and East Hampton. The towns exercise final authority over zoning and subdivision actions within their jurisdictions, but county proponents felt that more stringent and more uniform review was needed.

A Suffolk County Pine Barrens Commission was created, whose major task is to examine all proposals that may occur within the Pine Barrens and to report their findings and recommendations to the Suffolk County Planning Commission. If the two planners do not concur with the Pine Barrens Commission, they have to exercise a 75% majority vote to overturn the resolution.

One method to achieve greater coordination and oversight for the Great South Bay would be to establish a Suffolk County Great South Bay Commission. This would differ from the ill-fated attempt several years ago to pass such legislation at the state level in that all members would be appointed by the county and the three towns, and the powers and functions of the commission would also be set by the county and towns. The commisison could set the specific standards, guidelines and criteria that should be followed by all users of the Bay, public and private. It could also review all local plans and either recommend or require modifications, and serve as an appeals board. The municipalities would continue to exercise their normal functions. Table 11.2 lists the organization of the proposed Commission and its functional responsibilities, as well as the functions exercised by the municipalities. Table 11.3 lists the interactions between the Commission and the municipalities.

Conclusion

Great South Bay is one of the nation's important estuarine areas. It serves the needs of millions of people and is of national significance by virtue of the Fire Island National Seashore and the Wertheim Sanctuary; of state significance by virtue of the Robert Moses State Park and bridges; of county significance by virtue of the several major county holdings; and of local economic significance by virtue of having been the nation's leading producer of hard clams. The obvious key to its future is the development of a coordinated and integrated management mechanism to insure the implementation of comprehensive plans for the Bay in order to protect, preserve and enhance this important resource.

REFERENCES

Branch, Melville C. 1988. Regional planning: Introduction and explanation. Praeger, New York. 205 pp.

COSMA. 1985. Suffolk County's Hard Clam Industry: An overview and an analysis of managerial alternatives. Special Report No. 63. (+ Addendum: History of uncertified waters in Suffolk County and their impact on the hard clam industry.) Marine Sciences Research Center, State University of New York, Stony Brook, NY. 282 pp.

Earhart, Glenn H. and E.W. Garbisch, Jr. 1983. Habitat development utilizing dredged material at Barren Island, Durchester County, Md. Paper

Table 11.2. Function of Commission and municipalities.

GREAT SOUTH BAY PLANNING AND CONSERVATION COMMISSION 13 Member Body	Functions	MUNICIPALITIES Functions
Each Town	Set standards, guidelines and criteria	Preparation of development plans
County Planning Health Services		
	Provides appellate functions	Control over local actions
NYSDEC Fire Island Seashore Baymen	Reviews and can require modifications to local plans	
Fishing industry	Can establish moratorium during plan development	
General member		

Table 11.3. Interactions between Commission and municipalities.

COMMISSION	MUNICIPALITIES
Delegates powers to the Municipalities	Appeals cases to the Commission
Reviews plans and participates in planning	Prepares local plans and actions for the Commission
	Reviews plans and participates in planning

presented at 4th Annual Meeting of the Society of Wetlands Scientists, June 5-8. St. Paul, MN.

Green, Ralph F. 1972. Wetlands on Long Island. The Center for the Environment of Man. Hartford, CT. 80 pp.

Koppelman, L. E. 1974. A methodology to achieve the integration of coastal zone science and regional planning. Praeger Publishers, New York. 116 pp.

Koppelman, L. E., et al. 1978. The Long Island comprehensive waste treatment management plan. Nassau-Suffolk Regional Planning Board. Hauppauge, NY. Vol. I and II, July. 611 pp.

Koppelman, L. E., and D.S. Davies. 1987. Strategies and recommendations for revitalizing the hard clam fisheries in Suffolk County. Suffolk County Planning Department. Hauppauge, NY. 58 pp.

Koppelman, L.E., E. Tanenbaum and C. Swick 1982. The Long Island segment of the nationwide urban runoff program. Long Island Regional Planning Board, Hauppauge, NY. 248 pp.

Koppelman, L.E., E. Tanenbaum, and C. Swick. 1984. Nonpoint source management handbook. Long Island Regional Planning Board, Hauppauge, NY. 466 pp.

Long Island Lighting Company. 1988. Population survey: Current population estimates for Nassau and Suffolk Counties. Hicksville, NY. 38 pp.

Maiolo, J. R., and P. Tschetter. 1981. Relating population growth to shellfish bed closures: A case study from North Carolina. Coastal Zone Management Journal, 9(1):1-18.

Newsday. 1974. "The Great South Bay," Special Reprint, June 9. p. 14.

Public Law 92-583. The Coastal Zone Management Act of 1972.

Schneider, D.M., Godschalk, D.R., and N. Axler. 1979. The carrying capacity concept as a planning tol. Planning Advisory Servide Report No. 338. American Planning Association, Chicago, IL.

Schubel, J.R. 1982. Background statement for research grant application on the New York Harbor information system, program for coastal science and management alternatives (COSMA). Ref. No. 822DA1. Marine Sciences Research Center, State University of New York at Stony Brook, NY.

Suffolk County Planning Department. 1985. Analysis of dredging and spoil disposal activity conducted by Suffolk County: Historical perspective and a look to the future. Hauppauge, NY. 85 pp.

U.S. Department of the Interior, Geological Survey and U.S. Department of Housing and Urban Development, Research and Technology. 1971. Program design for San Francisco Bay region environment and resources planning study. October. Menlo Park, CA. 123 pp.

U.S. Department of the Interior, Fish and Wildlife Service. 1970. National Estuary Study, Vol. 3, pp. 59, 60, 63.

U.S. Secretary of State Advisory Committee on Education. 1972. Social and cultural aspects of environmental problems. Staff Issue Paper, February 18, Stockholm Conference on the Human Environment.

Woodhouse, W. W. 1979. Building salt marshes along the coasts of the continental United States. S.R.-4. U.S. Coastal Engineering Research Center, Fort Belvoir, VA.

Adductor muscle. A muscle that pulls together or closes the valves or shells of an organism; as the adductor muscles of barnacles or bivalve mollusks.

Algae. Marine or fresh water one-celled or multicellular plants that have no root, stem or leaf systems; simple plants.

Algal bloom. *See* phytoplankton bloom.

Anthropogenic. Manmade or caused.

Aquaculture. Cultivation or propagation of water-dwelling organisms.

Barrier island. A long, generally narrow island or peninsula parallel to the coast but separated from it by a lagoon or marsh.

Bathymetry. The measurement of the depth of a body of water.

Benthic. That portion of the marine environment inhabited by marine organisms that live permanently in or on the bottom.

Benthic organisms. Bottom-dwelling marine organisms.

Berm. Low, nearly horizontal portion of a beach (backshore), having an abrupt fall and formed by the deposit of material by wave action. It marks the limit of ordinary high tides and waves.

Biota. Biotic community. All the organisms that live within some definable area.

Biomass. Amount (weight) of living matter per unit of water surface or volume.

Bloom. *See* plankton bloom.

Breakwater. Structure, usually rock or concrete, protecting a shore area, harbor, anchorage, or basin from waves.

Byssus. A series of hairlike threads that attach a mussel to the substrate.

Chlorophyll. A group of green pigments found in plants that are essential for photosynthesis.

Cilia. Short hairlike structures common on lower animals. Beating in unison, they may be used for locomotion or to create water currents that carry food towards the mouth of the animal.

Coliform bacteria. Bacteria usually found in the intestine of humans or animals.

Colonial animals. Animals that live in groups of attached or separate individuals. Groups of individuals may serve special functions.

Contaminants. Any substance or material that causes contamination.

Continental shelf. The shallow part of the sea floor immediately adjacent to the continent.

Convergence. Area or zone where flow regimes come together or converge, usually resulting in sinking of surface waters.

Crenulate. Having a series of small indentations along an edge, giving a scalloped appearance.

Crystalline style. In bivalve molluscs and a few other filter-feeding molluscs, a rod-like gelatinous structure in the first part of the intestine which functions to stir the stomach contents and slowly release digestive enzymes.

Ctenophore. Any of the phylum (Ctenophora) of marine invertebrate animals resembling jellyfishes, having biradial symmetry, and swimming by means of eight rows of ciliated comblike plates.

DDT. A water insoluble organic substance used as an insecticide.

Depuration. The action of getting rid of impurities or polluting matter. Molluscs contaminated with coliform bacteria cleanse themselves when transplanted to clean water.

Desiccation. The drying out or the removal of moisture of an object of organism.

Detritus. Loose material produced by rock disintegration. Organic detritus consists of decomposition or disintegration products of dead organisms, including fecal material.

Diatoms. Microscopic phytoplankton organisms, possessing walls of overlapping halves (valves) impregnated with silica.

Dinoflagellates. Single-celled microscopic organisms that may possess chlorophyll and belong to the plant phylum Pyrrophyta or may ingest food and belong to the class Mastigophora of the animal phylum Protozoa.

Diurnal. Occurring daily. Referring to tides, one low and one high tide within one lunar day (about 24 h, 50 min).

Divergence. Horizontal flow of water in different directions from a common center or zone; upwelling results from divergence.

Dorsal. Pertaining to the back or upper surface of most animals.

Drift. Sand moved by wave and current action.

Ebb current. Tidal current directed away from shore or down a tidal stream.

Ecosystem. Ecological unit including organisms and the non-living environment, each influencing the properties of the other and both necessary for the maintenance of life.

Eelgrass. Seed-bearing, grasslike marine plant that grows chiefly in sand or mud-sand bottoms; most abundant in temperate water less than 10 m depth.

Ekman transport. The net transport of surface water set in motion by wind. Due to the Ekman spiral phenomenon, it is theoretically in the direction 90° to the right of the wind direction in the northern hemisphere and 90° to the left of the wind direction in the southern hemisphere.

Environment. The sum of all physical, chemical, and biological factors to which an organism or community is subjected.

Estuarine circulation. Circulation characteristic of an estuary and other semi-enclosed bodies of water. Circulation resulting from differences in salt concentration from an excess of runoff and precipitation. Surface flow is toward the ocean with a subsurface counterflow.

Estuary. A semi-enclosed coastal body of water having a free connection with the open sea and within which seawater is diluted by freshwater derived from land drainage.

Eutrophic. A condition characterized by an abundance of nutrients which promotes the growth of algae.

Fauna. The animal life of any particular area or of any particular time.

Fecundity. The number of eggs produced per female per unit time (often per spawning season).

Filament. A threadlike structure.

Filter feeders. Animals that filter and trap edible particles from seawater, a feeding mode typical of many zooplankton and other marine organisms of limited mobility.

Flagellum. A whiplike tail or part that is an organ of locomotion in certain cells, bacteria, protozoa.

Flood current. Tidal current associated with the increase in the height of a tide. Flood currents generally set toward the shore or in the direction of the tide progression.

Flora. The plant life of any particular area or of any particular time.

Food chain. The passage of energy materials from producers (mainly green plants and algae) through a sequence of herbivores and carnivores.

Gamete. One of the germ cells, a sperm or an egg.

Gill. A thin-walled protection from some part of the external body or the digestive tract used for respiration in a water environment.

Gradient. Rate of decrease (or increase) of one quantity with respect to another; for example, the rate of decrease of temperature with depth in the ocean.

Grazing. The feeding by zooplankton upon phytoplankton.

Ground water. The water beneath the surface of the ground, consisting largely of surface water that has seeped down.

Habitat. A place where a particular plant or animal lives. Generally refers to a smaller area than environment.

Hydrocarbon. An organic compound consisting solely of hydrogen and carbon. Petroleum is a mixture of many hydrocarbon compounds.

Inlet. A narrow passageway connecting the ocean and lagoon, estuary, bay, or other semi-enclosed body of water.

Lagoon. Shallow sound, pond, or lake, generally separated from the open ocean by a barrier island.

Laminar flow. Flow in which a fluid moves in parallel layers or sheets. The direction of flow at any point does not change with time; nonturbulent flow.

Larva. An immature form of certain animals which has different structural characteristics than that of the adult species.

Lunar tide. The part of the tide caused solely by the tide-producing force of the moon.

Macroalgae. Algae that is multicellular and clearly visible to the unaided eye; often called "seaweed".

Mantle. In mollusks, the dorsal body wall which secretes the shell in shelled forms.

Maximum sustainable yield. In fisheries biology, the maximum catch obtainable per unit time under the appropriate fishing rate.

Microalgae. Phytoplankton not easily seen by the unaided eye, but easily recovered from the ocean with the aid of a fine-mesh plankton net.

Nitrogen fixation. Conversion of atmospheric nitrogen (N_2) to nitrogen oxides usable in primary food production.

Nutrients. Any number of organic or inorganic compounds used by plants in primary production. Nitrogen and phosphorous compounds are important examples.

Patchiness. Used in marine biology to describe the nonrandom or clumpy distribution of organisms.

Pathogenic microorganism (bacteria and viruses). Microorganism that produces diseases once inside the body of humans or animals.

Pelecypoda. A class of molluscs characterized by two fairly symmetrical lateral valves with a dorsal hinge. Many posses a hatchet-shaped foot used for burrowing. Includes clams, oysters, mussels and scallops.

Pesticides. A chemical preparation for destroying pests such as flies or mosquitoes.

pH. A measure of the alkalinity or salinity of a solution. pH is the logarithm of the reciprocal of the hydrogen ion concentration.

Photosynthesis. The production of organic matter by plants using water and carbon dioxide in the presence of chlorophyll and light; oxygen is released in the reaction.

Photosynthetic pigments. Colored organic compounds capable of absorbing light and transferring the energy to chlorophyll *a* during photosynthesis.

Phytoplankter. Any of the organisms that constitute phytoplankton.

Phytoplankton. The small algae which float or drift near the water surface; the most important

community of primary producers in the ocean.

Phytoplankton bloom. (Also called algae bloom) A very high concentration of phytoplankton, resulting from rapid rate of reproduction as conditions become optimum during the spring in high latitude areas. Less obvious causes produce blooms that may be destructive in other areas and other times of the year.

Plankton. Passive-drifting or weakly swimming organisms that are dependent on currents, includes most microscopic algae, protozoa, and larval forms of higher animals.

Planktotrophic larva. Planktonic-dispersed larva that derives its nourishment by feeding in the plankton.

Poach. To take fish, shellfish or other organisms illegally or out of season.

Primary productivity. Amount of organic matter synthesized by organisms from inorganic substances per unit time in a unit volume of water or in a column of water of unit area extending from the surface to the bottom; also called gross primary production.

Pseudofeces. Potential food material that is rejected by suspension or deposit feeders before entering the gut.

Recruitment. The production, successful survival and colonization by newborn organisms.

Salinity. Measure of the quantity of dissolved salts in seawater. Formally defined as the total amount of dissolved solids in seawater in parts per thousand (ppt) by weight when all the carbonate has been converted to oxide, all of the bromide and iodide to chloride and all organic matter is completely oxidized.

Salt marsh. A relatively flat area of the shore where fine sediment is deposited and salt-tolerant grasses grow. One of the most biologically productive regions on the earth's surface.

Sand. Particles that lie between silt and granules on the wentworth scale of grain size, ranging from 1/16 to 2 mm.

Sediment. Particulate organic and inorganic matter that accumulates in a loose, unconsolidated form. It may be chemically precipitated from solution, secreted by organisms, or transported from land by air, ice, wind or water and deposited on the bottom of water bodies.

Sedimentation. Process of transportation and deposition of particles onto the bottom of a body of water.

Sessile. Permanently attached by the base of a stalk; not free to move.

Silt. Intermediate size particels between sand and clay, ranging from 1/128 to 1/16 mm.

Spatial distribution. The arrangement of individuals in a space.

Standing stock. The biomass or weight of plankton or nekton per unit volume or area of water (mg/l, g/m^2).

Stock. A population of a fishery species which is relatively independent of other populations.

Substrate. The base on which an organism lives and grows.

Suspension feeder. An organism that feeds by capturing particles suspended in the water column.

Synoptic monitoring. Numerous measurements taken simultaneously over a large area.

Tidal current. Horizontal movement of water associated with the rise and fall of the tide caused by the tide-producing forces.

Tidal cycle. Elapsed time between successive high or low waters.

Tidal flat. Marshy or muddy areas which are covered and uncovered by the rise and fall of the tide; also called tidal marshes. Usually covered by plants.

Tidal range. The difference between successive high and low waters. The period of comparison can be different, such as the range over a week, month, or year.

Tide. Periodic rise and fall of the ocean surface and connected bodies of water resulting from the unequal gravitational attraction of the moon and sun on different parts of the earth.

Turbidity. A state of reduced clarity in a fluid caused by the presence of suspended matter.

Veliger. A planktonic larval stage of many gastropods with two ciliated lobes.

Ventral. Pertaining to the lower or under surface.

Virus. A submicroscopic noncellular particle, composed of a nucleic acid core and a protein shell, which is parasitic and reproduces only within a host cell.

Wetland marsh. An area of soft, wet land. Low land periodically covered by low water, common in portions of lagoons.

Zooplankton. Those plankton that are of the animal kingdom.